Your
Marriage
Can Survive
Mid-Life
Crisis

Your
Marriage
Can Survive
Mid-Life
Crisis

Jim & Sally Conway

THOMAS NELSON PUBLISHERS
Nashville

Published in Nashville, Tennessee, by Thomas Nelson, Inc., and distributed in Canada by Lawson Falle, Ltd., Cambridge, Ontario.

Printed in the United States of America.

Scripture quotations, unless otherwise noted, are from THE NEW KING JAMES VERSION of the Bible. Copyright © 1979, 1980, 1982, Thomas Nelson, Inc.

The Bible verses marked TLB are taken from *The Living Bible* (Wheaton, Illinois: Tyndale House Publishers, 1971) and are used by permission.

Library of Congress Cataloging-in-Publication Data

Conway, Jim.
   Your marriage can survive mid-life crisis.

   1.   Marriage—Religious aspects—Christianity.
2.   Middle age.   I. Conway, Sally.   II. Title.
BV835.C64   1987   248.8′4   87-22123
ISBN 0-8407-7616-0

3 4 5 6 7 8 — 92 91 90 89 88

TO OUR PARENTS

Carl Henry Christon
and
Altha Larson Christon
who were married 56½ years
until Carl left for heaven August 15, 1985
and
Floyd Frank Conway
and
Margaret Strodtbeck Conway
who have been married 57 years

THEY TAUGHT US TO BE

Caring
Honest
Innovative
Adventurous
Committed

THEY HAVE LOVED US
AND PRAYED FOR US
THROUGH ALL OUR SEASONS

Contents

PART ONE

▼

The Way We Are: The Marriage Situation by Mid-Life

1

A
Familiar
Pattern

It was love at first sight. Steve and Norene* met one warm fall day when the church's college and career group had a picnic to begin the school year.

As a college freshman, Norene was excited to be included in this group which contrasted so sharply with her friends and activities during the last two years of high school. Her high-school friends had seemed so immature, the classes were boring, and her personal life was without direction.

Steve stood out as a natural leader in this group. People were attracted to him. His smile was warm as he said hello to Norene. She was impressed by his tall, muscular body and his legs which were sinewy from years of competitive track.

Steve remembered that picnic as well. He recalled that when he first saw Norene, he was overcome with an urge to stare. He kept glancing at her, hoping she wouldn't catch him looking. Every look excited him. He had to force himself to look other directions. She was magnificent. Her light brown hair was

---

*In this story and throughout the book, we have changed names and disguised circumstances to protect the privacy of the people involved.

golden in the sunlight, her skin looked so smooth, and her face radiated an enthusiasm for life.

During dinner Steve made sure he was part of the small group with which Norene was eating. He was aware that she was noticing him, and an easy friendship began to develop. After dinner the group sat around the campfire, singing and enjoying the evening. Norene's heart raced and her body felt flushed as Steve asked if he could sit next to her. Yes, they were in a group of people, but she felt it was just the two of them in front of the crackling fire.

Norene remembered the warmth of his arm as he adjusted his body so that their upper arms touched each other's. She wished that he would put his arm around her to keep her warm in the evening chill, but she realized that was expecting too much since they barely knew each other. The two of them sat side by side, singing and enjoying the evening, and wishing for more.

As the group broke up, Steve asked Norene if he could take her back to her dorm. Her eager response encouraged him so that when they arrived, he reached across the car seat, took her hand, and asked to see her again. She said yes as she got out of the car.

Steve kept pushing the persistent thought of her out of his mind, but repeatedly it crowded back in. He had only known Norene for a few hours, yet he longed to hold her close, to be with her, to know her. He kept saying to himself it wasn't possible, but he was in love with this woman whom he had just met.

Cloud Nine

Steve called Norene the next morning, and their date that evening was the beginning of a fast-moving romance filled with fun, sharing, and passion.

They were engaged the next spring, just eight months after they had met. Norene had finished her first year of college and Steve his third.

Their engagement year was a difficult one. Both sets of parents were in agreement with the couple's decision to marry, but they encouraged Steve to finish school before marriage. To

Steve and Norene it seemed like a meaningless year. Why couldn't they be together?

Their physical attraction for each other was strong. They both were deeply committed to Christ, yet the hunger to touch and fondle each other often overwhelmed them. The resulting guilt seemed to damage their spiritual relationship. They frequently talked of eloping, but the societal pressures always kept their actions in check.

Finally, Steve graduated from college. Norene finished her second year. Their wedding was exhilarating with the affirmation of both families and their college friends. Everyone agreed that they were the perfect couple, so much in love and so much going for them.

FUTURE GLITCHES

Some might call Steve and Norene a storybook couple. Yet twenty years later, after the nitty-gritty experience of living together and raising a family, their marriage relationship had not only become dull—it was all but over.

Nearly every couple starts their marriage with high expectations but then runs into snags, which have caused almost half of recent marriages to break apart. In addition, many of the couples who haven't divorced are very unhappy.

David and Vera Mace, who have written extensively on marriage and the family, say, "Only a small portion of marriages come anywhere near to being really good. . . . The proportion of 'stable-satisfactory' marriages in the United States today does not exceed five to ten percent."[1]

We are concerned about marriage—yours, ours, and others. Some people do have strong, healthy marriages. They've had hard times, but they've come through together. The snags didn't tear them apart. What made these couples different from the ones who divorced?

We want to share with you the success traits of the marriages that held together. But first, let's continue the account of Steve and Norene. Their story will give you insight into the stages of life. You might even see yourself or a friend in their lives.

Delayed Dreams

After marriage Norene dropped out of college and both she and Steve went to work full-time—Steve for an electronics firm and Norene as a secretary. Their plan was to work in these positions about four years and save money. Steve would be gaining work experience, and then he would buy into the electronics firm as a junior partner.

However, their first child, Todd, came in a year and a half. They agreed that Norene should quit her job. They decided to stay in the apartment where they were, still trying to save some money and just pushing their dreams back a few years. After all, they had plenty of time and the new baby was a joy.

About two-and-a-half years later, Meg was born. By rearranging their small apartment, they were able to make room for this baby too. Life seemed richer and fuller. Norene was totally absorbed in the raising of these two children, homemaking, and being a supportive wife to Steve.

Steve was learning the electronics business. He was glad he hadn't tried to get into the company as a partner on his projected time schedule. Yet "some day" he would own his own firm. "Some day" they would have their own house. "Some day" there would be time and money to do everything they couldn't do now.

Out of Sync

When Steve had his twenty-ninth birthday, Steve and Norene were still living in their cramped, two-bedroom apartment. They had very little cash in the bank. He was growing restless with his slow progress in the electronics business, and now Norene was pregnant again. A growing sense of urgency and anxiety gnawed inside Steve. He had easily adjusted to the first changes in his life's time schedule, but now he felt he was making no headway.

Norene had wanted this third baby at this time, because she felt it was important for the children to be close in age. She also wanted a third child while she was young enough to have one safely, with adequate energy to raise him or her. She had argued that money was not the important thing; family was. "In the long run," she said, "we'll be happier with more children than with more financial success." Steve had agreed, but he really wanted to be farther along with his career goals before increasing their financial and parental responsibilities.

Foreshadows

The year following Steve's twenty-ninth birthday was one of deep turmoil. Joanna was born. They moved to a three-bedroom home with a high mortgage, and Steve placed his business plans on hold again.

At times Steve felt like running away. He saw his dreams repeatedly being set aside. Norene seemed totally preoccupied with the children, with little time or energy left for him. His mind frequently flashed back to the days before they were married when he could hardly restrain himself from touching her and holding her tightly; now there was coldness and distance.

Sometimes Steve felt as if he were a servant, providing everything that Norene and the children needed. Oh, it wasn't that he didn't love them, but what about those dreams of owning his own company?

For the next two years Steve battled silently with a feeling that life was slipping by. His goals were not being met. He kept pushing the feeling aside, telling himself not to be selfish, there was still time ahead. But many days he thought of starting over. For the first time, the thought of divorce crossed his mind. If he were single again, he could pursue his own dreams without the limitations and restraints of being a husband and father. These thoughts frightened Steve. He was afraid to tell Norene or any of his friends because they might not understand. If the ideas frightened him, they would terrify Norene.

Daylight in the Tunnel

When Steve was thirty-two, one of the senior partners of the electronics firm formed a new company and asked Steve to come with him, the break he and Norene had been praying for. Steve's doubts and fears of the last few years faded away. He had more energy again. He enjoyed living.

Their marriage relationship seemed to improve. Norene was busy with the kids, but now that two of them were in grade school, she also had more time for Steve. Steve was really coming into his own as a good husband and father. He felt that life was finally on track.

The new job provided more money and prestige, but it also demanded more time away from home and more days on the road. Steve wanted to show the boss that it was a wise decision to ask him to join the new firm. He also knew that good progress now would open the door for future success and ultimately his own company.

The next five years were peaceful and fulfilling for Steve and Norene. Yes, there were struggles but they were the good kind: keeping clothes on happy, growing children; litters of puppies, new bicycles, piano lessons, summer camps, family vacations, and even broken bones.

"MIDOLESCENCE" AND ADOLESCENCE

When Steve was thirty-seven, Norene was thirty-five and their oldest child, Todd, was thirteen-and-a-half. These three family members would experience major changes over the next years. Steve and Norene would soon be facing mid-life crisis and acting almost like teenagers (midolescence), while Todd would be responding to his own adolescent development of establishing his independence and identity.

The late thirties and early forties are dangerous years, filled with stress for both men and women. Our studies show that about 75 percent of men and women will experience a moderate to severe mid-life crisis. The crisis affects a cross section of people of all educational, economic, and religious backgrounds.

Mid-life crisis will disrupt the normal daily flow of life and can spell disaster for the marriage. (Our previous books in the mid-life series talk in depth about the problems of both men and women at this time in life. These books—*Men in Mid-Life Crisis, You and Your Husband's Mid-Life Crisis,* and *Women in Mid-Life Crisis*—share how the individual can work through mid-life crisis and how the mate can understand and help.[2])

Steve and Norene were entering those dangerous mid-life years. Steve felt he had accomplished about all he could in his current job and wanted to throw off the leadership of other men and launch his own company. Steve and Norene had saved some money, but they still went deeply in debt to start Steve's electronics firm.

Norene felt as if she were the glue holding everything together. She tried to be an understanding wife to her husband as he started his own business and a patient mother to her teenage son and the two daughters in grade school. Sometimes she felt as if she were expected to be everything to everyone, a task she knew was impossible.

New Worlds

Then Steve asked even more of her. Would she go back to work for just a couple of years until his new company got on its feet?

Norene took a job as a secretary again. But now, almost fourteen years later, she entered a strange world of electronic typewriters and computers, with symbols, memories, word processors, floppy discs, and printers. She felt like an old woman next to the young secretaries who seemed to know what was happening. Norene, an intelligent woman, however, soon caught on and was able to carry her end of the workload.

In many ways this family was achieving what they wanted, yet without realizing it, they were being pulled apart. Steve was totally preoccupied with his career. Todd many times seemed embarrassed that Steve and Norene were his parents. He was moving away from the family toward his own peer group. Norene was overbusy as a full-time secretary and a full-time homemaker. Steve, Norene, and Todd each were deeply involved in what they felt they needed to do, yet their busy preoccupations were moving them into separate worlds with little or no contact with each other.

Two years later, when Steve was thirty-nine, his company had grown significantly. Yet that wasn't enough for Steve. His goal was to make his company the major electronics firm in the city. He felt he only had a few prime years left. His energy and creativity were at their peak now. He poured himself into his work with long hours, extensive traveling, and very little emotional reserve for his marriage and family.

Unanswered Questions

Norene experienced new anxieties. She felt as if she had been replaced by a mistress—Steve's business. It was all-consuming. There was never any time or emotion for the two of them. With both of them working long hours, they were always just too tired for intimacy.

Norene began to ask herself, *Why is life like this? I'm working at a job I don't like for a business that's taking my husband away and for children who are separating themselves from the family.*

Norene was delighted to see her children growing, but she was also afraid. Meg, their middle child, was now a teenager of thirteen-and-a-half, but looked as if she were nineteen. Norene asked herself, *Who am I and what will I be when they're gone? What will be left?*

At times when she would see Meg's young, firm body, Norene was all too aware of the changes she could see in her own body. *Maybe I'm not attractive to Steve any more. Maybe his tiredness is not the business but another woman. Who really loves me? Who really needs me?*

These were hard years for Norene as she wrestled with these questions and still tried to be the support that held the family together. She was haunted by the question, *Who am I without these people?*

Steve's business had prospered so that Norene's income was nice but unnecessary. This reality reinforced the fact of her expendability. Some days she got into the car and drove far out into the country to think. She asked the same questions a thousand times. *Who am I? What is life all about? What will I do with the years I have left? Where is God in all of this?*

Out of this questioning, Norene decided it was time for her to become a person in her own right. As a high school girl, she had had a flickering dream of becoming a lawyer. Now was the time to pursue that dream.

School Days

Norene quit her job and enrolled in the nearby university part-time. At first, the family ignored Mom's return to school to finish her college education and go on to law school, but soon they noticed that their built-in housemaid was not serving them as they were accustomed. Finally, when a major blowup occurred, the family was forced to rethink the homemaking responsibilities. Norene still carried the major load, but the children and Steve took on some of the tasks. Expectations were scaled down so that meals and housekeeping were not so elaborate.

During the first year of university classes, Norene continued to ask herself the same old questions. She was still troubled by Steve's and her dull marriage and felt overwhelmed by her teenagers' rapid development. She had been a confident woman all her life, so sure of herself, her relationship to God, and her love commitment to her husband. Now she spent a couple of afternoons a week drinking coffee in a quiet restaurant with Tom, a fellow student.

It wasn't an affair. It was a friendship. He was interested in her dreams to be a lawyer. He didn't put her down as Steve often subtly did. He was older than Steve and seemed so much more settled and less tense about life.

Norene became frightened when she realized she was looking forward to seeing Tom each time she went to class. It became a spiritual battle, and she was glad when the semester ended so she wouldn't easily see him again.

This experience caused her to realize how vulnerable she was to a man's caring and affection. She craved love. She wanted it from Steve, but he was so preoccupied and exhausted.

During this shaky point in their marriage, Norene recommitted her life to God and determined not to get involved in any affair. At the same time, she firmly committed herself to finish college.

Cloud Nine Again?

It was a big year. Steve was forty-two, Norene forty. Todd was graduating from high school and Norene was graduating from college. In the fall Norene would enter law school and Todd would start college. The business was successful, and from all the external appearances, the family was really succeeding. Steve and Norene had come to accept the fact that they were very busy and had little time for each other. They both decided that marital love cooled off in the middle years, and they were willing to allow their marriage fires to slowly die. After all, they had other glowing successes that compensated for their cold, boring marriage.

Everything went along successfully in this "All-

American" family until Steve was forty-six. His firm was the most successful in the city. Steve and his family had moved to a larger house, which demonstrated the achievement of his goals. Norene had finished law school, had passed the bar examination, and was practicing in a small law firm. She was immersed in her new-found career. Todd had finished college and was entering graduate school. Meg was starting her junior year in college, and Joanna was a high-school senior.

Dark Clouds Gather

Now Steve began to ask the questions. *All right, I've made it big. My company is successful. I have a big house with a three-car garage, two nice cars, a boat, and a cottage on the lake. I'm respected by people in town and in my church. But what's the purpose of it all? I'm too busy with my job to enjoy any of it. Norene is busy with her work, and the kids are all leaving. What is life all about? I feel empty inside. I don't want to live the next thirty to thirty-five years with this emptiness.*

Steve had a special relationship with his two daughters, who reminded him so much of Norene when she was younger, when she was carefree and not endlessly involved in school or career. But now he was seeing the end of those close relationships with his daughters. Meg was engaged. Joanna would be at home only one more year before college, and then he would be left with a big, empty house, a wife who was always gone pleading other people's cases, and a successful business that no longer held any challenge for him.

Steve found himself reflecting on his earlier life, wishing he had made some changes. Sometimes he wished he had never started the business. The business had put them in debt, it had sent Norene back to work, and everyone had become consumed with surviving. What for? For this big hollow house?

Many people flattered him and congratulated him on his success. Yes, it was fun to hear their appreciation, but most of the time they wanted something from him. Very few people could just accept him as he was.

Love the Real Me

Maybe that's why he enjoyed extra moments around the office talking to Marianne. She was never overawed by his success. She always seemed to be able to tease him out of his depression. When she found him crying in the office one time, she didn't make him feel less of a man. She told him it was O.K. to cry.

Marianne was ten years younger than Steve. She was struggling with her own marriage and her own questions about life. She was reaching out for a man who could give meaning to her life, and Steve was reaching out for a woman who could provide warmth.

Their relationship was under control until Steve's youngest daughter left for college. As he and Norene drove home from taking Joanna to school in a nearby town, he realized how empty their marriage really was. He didn't want to be with this woman. She was a stranger. He longed to be with Marianne, but he was obligated to live in the same house with Norene.

The next Monday Steve went into Joanna's room after Norene had gone to work. He remembered the times he would wake Joanna for school. She'd pull the covers over her head and scream, but it was a game they both enjoyed. Now the shrieks of "Oh, Dad!" were gone. The bed was perfectly made, no clothes lay scattered on the floor.

Steve got into his Cadillac and thought, *Even this thirty-thousand-dollar car doesn't really satisfy me.* He drove to work and parked in the space marked President, walked into his office, sat down behind his huge walnut desk, and began to cry.

Deceptive Joy

Marianne sensed something was wrong and came into his office. He got up from his chair, and for the first time he put his arms around her and sobbed as he held her close. He shared with her the emptiness he felt with his children gone and the dryness of his marriage. He told her of the coolness he felt as he lay in bed beside Norene, who had become a stranger.

Then Steve told Marianne that he loved her, wanted her, was going to divorce Norene, and would marry her. Their restraint was broken. Steve felt a passion that he had not known for many years. The affair, at first secret, became obvious around the office. Soon people around town and the church heard about their relationship.

Finally, Norene confronted Steve about the long hours at

the office, the long weekends out of town, and the gossip being bantered around the community and church. They had a nasty confrontation with many accusations, each one blaming the other. Each was crying out for intimacy yet claiming the other one wasn't interested. Steve packed a suitcase and left the house.

The next day Norene talked to Marianne. It was a friendly yet firm confrontation. In the process, Marianne began to realize that she could not live a fantasy life with Steve. At the same time, Norene knew she was the one who was Steve's wife. She wanted to be, and she was willing to fight for him.

Healing Retreat

A few weeks after Steve left home, he went to a·retreat center where he spent a great deal of time in quietness, reflecting on the questions he had been asking himself over the past year and a half. He read a lot from the Bible and from books about men and women at mid-life. The two-week retreat helped him realize he really wanted to be married to Norene, but he wanted her to be like Marianne. He needed intimacy. He needed the love and care they had given each other at the beginning of their married life.

What Steve needed was what Norene really wanted as well. She was also reading, and she had decided to see a counselor. She was determined that she was going to change to meet his needs.

When Steve returned, they each shared their discoveries. They committed themselves to continue talking, reading, and seeing a counselor. Their marriage, they decided, would now take precedence over all else. As the months went by, Steve and Norene found themselves increasingly attracted to each other, and they could sense some of that old spark returning. They had many ups and downs but they were hopeful that their marriage could survive and be better than ever.

WHERE WE ARE GOING

Did you see yourself or someone you know in Steve and Norene's situation? What were your feelings as you watched their marriage come to the brink of failure? Steve and Norene took several important steps to save their marriage, which may give you an example of how to save yours or the marriage of someone you know.

For many years we have been working with people whose marriages are breaking or broken due to mid-life pressures, but we've also seen many successful marriages. In our own marriage we've had some scary tests and almost flunked some of them, but we've learned some important things that have strengthened the bonds between us.

This book is based on a national survey of 186 couples who shared with us their ingredients for a lasting marriage. We have also drawn on our other research and the experiences of the many couples we have counseled, as well as our own marriage.

In the rest of Part One, we will take a quick overview of what mid-life marriages are like today, how they got that way, and the major problems they face. Knowing where we are in our current culture will help us understand how marriages can stay together and show younger couples how they can make their marriages more secure.

The object of this book is to tell you about the glue that can hold your marriage together. We'll share with you the ten common traits that enabled our survey couples not only to survive but also to make their marriages stronger. We feel that these traits are **ten keys to an intimate mid-life marriage.**

Finally, we'll look at how we can make a mid-life marriage effective and satisfying. We'll consider how to face the most troublesome problems and the steps for strengthening a good marriage or reconstructing a troubled one. Valuable insights will be shared by some of our research couples who went through serious problems.

We believe **your marriage can survive mid-life crisis.** Ours did, and we've worked with hundreds of others who have also survived. No matter how bad your marriage relationship has become, there is hope.

Marriage
by
Mid-Life

Steve and Norene experienced a growing chasm of separateness, a pattern that is common for most couples. You may know about it very well—firsthand! Courtship and early married years include the new and novel: getting to know each other, exploring sex together, launching a new career, bringing children into the world and raising them. Then the focus expands to buying a home and getting those extra gadgets—a second car, boat, video cassette recorder, special trips—those things that mean "we have arrived."

Tragically, a subtle shift takes place, which goes unnoticed until the middle years. The couple increasingly focuses on everyday activities and the accumulation of things rather than on each other. This outward direction—facing away from each other—is justified because they are buying a house, raising children, starting a business, getting the luxuries of life.

Suddenly, as when the first snowstorm of the season hits, a chilling realization descends. This couple who were once in love with each other see that they have become boring mid-life people with no common interests except their children, investments, and properties. They have fallen into routines that are necessary but humdrum and lifeless.

Many mid-life couples find themselves trapped into pretending they like what they do, lying to everyone around them. They live out a farce, acting as if all is well in their marriage and their individual lives.

Another blow to your mid-life marriage may be that yours is turning out just like your parents' marriage. You promised that yours would be different, but it probably is following their pattern. On top of that, you have finally realized that you married someone just like your father-in-law or mother-in-law. That isn't exactly what either of you had in mind!

WHY ALL THE PROBLEMS NOW?

Many mid-life couples wonder, *Why all the problems now?* Marriage problems at mid-life tend to be those that are longstanding. To an outsider the break appears to be sudden when a couple separates or divorces, but the insiders know these problems have been there for a long time.

Often these problems are like a brown mole on your face that becomes a skin cancer. Sooner or later it will have to be removed. Longstanding problems that may cause a mid-life marriage to break are 1) excess baggage carried from earlier years, 2) the myth that marriage will bring happiness, 3) the hope of changing the other partner, and 4) denying the reality that you both have changed.

Excess Baggage from the Past

All of us bring problems into marriage, because we bring ourselves. We are a combination of strengths and weaknesses, positive experiences and crushing blows. We are people who have a light, transparent side as well as a dark, secretive side. We carry our total selves into the marriage relationship. Any unresolved problem, inadequacy, or liability from our past may become the seedbed for future marital breakup.

Sometimes mid-life marriage dissatisfaction can be traced directly to something that happened in childhood or teen years. Often these childhood or teenage problems are like floating mines in the sea of matrimony, waiting to explode and cause the marriage to break up.

The way a child related to his or her parents often has a strong influence on what happens in the marriage. If the child was emotionally, physically, or sexually abused, he or she carries those scars into marriage.

The authors of *The Indelible Family* show that our parental family makes an indelible and, in some ways, irrevocable imprint in our lives.[1] The impressions may be both positive and negative, but marriage partners need to acknowledge the impact of these impressions on the relationship.

Frequently we hear a story like that of Ken, age forty, who is quite insecure and married to a strong woman. In the early years he was glad that Carol helped him with many of his decisions, but in his late thirties he began to throw off mentors and helpers and resented having his wife continually mothering him.

In marriage counseling it was apparent that their problems went back to their individual development in parental homes where their mothers were dominant. Ken had not realized he married Carol partly because he admired her leadership abilities. She had learned well from her mother; he had *not* learned from his father. As he grew older, however, he wanted to take more responsibility for personal decisions. Ken and Carol needed to work on a new style of leadership or they would be eaten up by the friction of their old, ill-fitting patterns.

A troubled past can't simply be stifled or blithely forgotten any more than an ugly nose or despised body shape can be forgotten. A person can change some things he doesn't like about his body and accept those things he can't change. The negative events of the past also can be acknowledged and dealt with so that they no longer control present experiences. You can accept who you are, the good **and** the bad, because all the pieces of life that have formed you can be turned into positive strengths for a healthy marriage.

For more help regarding your parental family's influence on you as an adult, we suggest reading *The Blessing* by Gary Smalley and John Trent and chapter 3 of *Tough Marriage* by Paul Mickey.[2]

Marriage Doesn't Mean Happiness

If you are an unhappy person before marriage, you are likely to be unhappy after marriage. Marriage may provide a temporary change in your happiness because of the novelty of the situation, but eventually you will settle back into the level of happiness you had as a single adult.

Courtship or living together is not a true indicator of what future married life will be. The dating couple only has a glimpse of married life.

Married life, after all, is not exclusively made of picnics, dinners out, roses, and little surprise gifts. It's ordinary living, with not enough money, too much work, and too much stress in an uptight world. It's good stuff mixed with bad. If married partners believe their marriage is going to be just like their courtship, they'll find themselves continually frustrated. They will blame themselves or their partner for what appears to be a failed marriage compared to their idealized courtship dream. It's not a failed marriage—it's just life.

Unfortunately, some people keep hopping from one marriage partner to another, ignoring the stark reality that marriage can only be as satisfying as the sum of its participants. Putting two unhappy people together ultimately means there is **double** the unhappiness.

When we counsel people who have been divorced and desire to be remarried, we look at two areas: why they got married the first time and how well-adjusted as individuals they are now. Do they really know who they are and have they come to terms with their unique lives and experiences? Or are they anticipating that marriage will solve all of their problems?

People who have not resolved their problems from a failed first marriage tend to marry someone with a similar personality type as their first mate. They're still unhappy and now they've added the complications of divorce, remarriage, and maybe two sets of children. You can see why the rate of marital success in second marriages is lower than in first marriages.[3]

Remember: Happiness is a choice. You choose to be happy with your mate and situation, or you choose to be miserable. Often the unhappy person is a perfectionist who moves from one event and person to the next, hoping that next time he or she will be happy.

Happiness is an attitude, not a circumstance. The Bible says, "I have **learned** to be content."[4] This idea implies that we are to be active, not passive, in a decision to be happy, whatever the situation.

No Hope of Changing the Other One

Before marriage each one unconsciously said, *Well, this person isn't exactly what I want, but I'll be able to help him or her change.* And there **are** some changes. People do modify and adapt but, basically, only in areas that are inconsequential to them.

When we were first married, Sally wanted me to be neater, to throw my dirty laundry in the washbasket. I wanted her to tolerate a little more messiness. On Sunday afternoons, after a hard morning of preaching and teaching, I wanted us to leave the Sunday dishes and take a nap together—just turn off the world, hold each other, fall off to sleep together, or make love if we cared to. But she would say, "I can't relax when I know there's a pile of dirty dishes in the kitchen."

Now that sounds like one of the more easily solved problems of married life, doesn't it? And we **have** adapted to each other. Both of us have made compromises. (We eventually got a dishwasher! Now we can go to bed. This arrangement is a lot more fun!) But after more than thirty years of being married to each other, those conflicting traits continue to come up. She is basically tidy. I am basically messy.

The other day I asked her, "How do you handle my messiness?" She said, "I just throw your socks in the laundry basket, close the closet door, and forget them."

By mid-life you either have come to accept the fact that your mate is different from you or you've allowed differences to eat a hole in your marriage relationship. Differences are no longer funny or interesting. They are maddening irritations that can drive you apart.

You Both Have Changed

At each transition time in life, the marital relationship will likely need to be readjusted. The adult years have several reassessment times; thus, over the course of life there will be many realignments in a marriage.

The first adult adjustment comes in the early twenties when individuals establish life dreams. You ask: *Who am I? What shall I do with my life? With whom shall I relate?* Most people marry during this early-twenties adjustment period.

The late-twenties and early-thirties era is another important evaluation time when you ask many of the same life-direction questions, but now you question from the viewpoint of, *How am I doing with the choices I have made? Am I progressing fast enough? What are the areas that need to be corrected in order to accomplish my life goals?*

Mid-life is another serious evaluation time: late thirties or early forties for women; generally early-to-mid-forties for men. Again, you ask the same questions, but this time your perspective is, *Life is running out too fast. I need to make corrections NOW! I only have twenty to thirty more good years left.*

The next major reevaluation time for women comes at menopause and when the nest empties. It can be a time of affirming the directions established earlier, but this time may be complicated by physical and emotional problems brought on by estrogen depletion.

Preretirement is the next reevaluation time. Now you question with a strong backward view: *Who have I been? What have I accomplished? With whom have I related? How have I been relating to God?* But your assessment contains some future dimension with questions such as: *What do I still want to accomplish and what kind of person do I want to be during my retirement years?*

Another evaluation time comes when your mate dies. A spouse's death causes a serious assessment of life's past and a reassessment of the remaining years regarding further accomplishments, personhood, and relationships.

A final evaluation takes place just before your own death. There is a tying up of loose ends, a sense of coming to terms with life, a final reflection on life's value. The view now is definitely looking backward: *Who have I been? What have I accomplished? How satisfying were my relationships?*

Potential Peril. All except the last two of these developmental reevaluation times can have a serious impact on the marriage. Risk is involved as a person thinks through life, especially if the marriage relationship does not match with the person's life goals.

For example, a mid-life wife may feel that her husband is keeping her in a mother-only role. Their children are probably in high school or moving out of the nest, and her mothering job is ending. Her role loss, affecting her self-identity and worth, may breed resentment toward her husband if he wants her to function only as a mother.

At mid-life, husbands quite often experience a shock of realism about their careers. For the first time they may realize they're not going to go as far as they had dreamed. Frequently mid-life men, who are angry about their careers or other facets of life, will project that anger back onto their marriages. They may blame their wives for the limitations and frustrations they are experiencing.

The developmental reassessments in life should be expected. You should also expect that your marriage will take on a slightly different form because of the personal growth of each of you at each stage.

Change Requires Accommodation. When we were first married, I (Jim) was very rigid about meals and mealtime. This caused some friction in our marriage because I demanded that the meals be eaten on a strict schedule. Lunch had to be more than soup and a sandwich and was to be served at 12:00 sharp.

Now, some thirty years later, I frequently skip meals or eat a meal early or late. I'm a different person. I don't need as much food and I don't want to be tied down to a rigid schedule. Just the other day Sally said, "You were the one in our early marriage that *demanded* we have our meals on schedule. Now *you* want to change."

The "hang loose" part of me that is changing causes problems for Sally—and for me—sometimes. One part of me is very structured, organized, workaholic, obsessive-compulsive, competitive, and slave to everyone else's opinions. But there's another part of me that sings the words from "Sailing on the Tide," sung by the late Karen Carpenter.

She sings her feelings about being confined in the city with neon lights. She wants time in the sunshine. She dreams of her island in the sun where the pace is slow, where you don't make plans, you just "play it by ear."

Doesn't that sound great? The older I get the more appealing these thoughts become. I'm continuing to change. Your life situation and your needs have changed. Some couples forget to take an emotional update on each other and learn what the other one needs in his or her new circumstances.

We have come to realize more and more as we talk with people all over the country that mid-life marriages stay together because both the husband's and the wife's needs are being met. That may sound selfish, but good mid-life marriages are made of couples who have learned to accommodate each other and to understand each other.

The bottom line is the question, Is there more satisfaction if you stay in your marriage relationship than if you were out of it? Actually the bottom line is your **answer** to the question!

Avoidance Becomes a Pattern

Poor mid-life marriages seem to be marked by avoidance. Both partners use ingenious devices to successfully keep from communicating with each other about who they are and the needs they have. Favorite avoidance tricks are spending too much time away at the job, raising children, being occupied in church or community activities, being a "couch potato" in front of the TV, or working extra to pay off a house mortgage or to buy a second car, a boat, or a cottage at the lake.

Sometimes people feel avoidance is a way of protecting their partner. They think that talking about their marriage will be too painful or that it will get better by itself. Avoidance is usually not a deliberate plan at first; it just becomes an easy pattern.

Walt had avoided talking to his wife about some of his needs for years because he didn't want to upset her. In reality, he was afraid of her. On one occasion when his children encouraged him to talk to her, his response was, "No, I don't want to. You know how easily Momma gets mad."

The author of *The Wonderful Crisis of Middle Age* told of a woman who discovered that her husband was having an affair after twenty-five years of marriage. "He was finally forced into admitting some of the negative feeling he had had about their relationship all along: the times he felt he was being manipulated; the times he became utterly weary of her histrionics; the times he had felt imprisoned by her dependency and proprietary attitude. [The wife] said, 'He kept telling me that he hadn't wanted to hurt my feelings—so instead he took the chance of destroying our marriage.' "[5]

CULTURAL PRESSURES

Now that we've looked at some of the internal factors that may cause marriage problems at mid-life, let's look at cultural stresses that impact marriages.

Life Expectancy

Unhappily married fifty-year-olds in past generations figured they didn't have many more years to put up with each other. Today's dissatisfied fifty-year-olds know they may have twenty to forty more years of potential marital misery.

This century has seen a dramatic lengthening of American life expectancy. As recently as 1900, the average length of life was only about forty-nine years of age. In the eighties, however, average life expectancy rose to over seventy years.[6]

At the beginning of this century people married at an older age, generally in their mid-twenties. Presently a segment of the population is delaying first-time marriage, but the average couple in the United States still marries in their early twenties.

Shifting Marital Needs

For centuries marriage meant physical survival; then it became a primary unit for economic survival. Some sociologists feel that in many primitive cultures there might not even have been a word for *love* in marriage because couples united for other reasons.[7]

In our culture people don't marry so they can have children to work the land or for economic or political advantages. Most people marry for love, companionship, and a secure relationship in the midst of a lonely and uncertain world. We expect so much of marriage today: romance, sex, companionship, communication, career income, and a home. Changing expectations in marriage, coupled with earlier marital age and longer life expectancy, mean that we expect more from marriage—and for longer.

Today's mid-life married couples not only have to be concerned about being very successful in career and involved in the community, they also have to be good listeners, sensitive, caring, understanding, and terrific sexual partners with great looking bodies! A contemporary marriage partner has to meet many of a mate's needs that in past days were met by the extended family or by church and community friends.

Everyone's Getting a Divorce?

In addition, the mid-life marriage is being barraged by "everybody's doing it." Supposedly, everyone is playing around and everybody is breaking up. Some cynics are claiming, as they look at the high mid-life divorce rate, that expecting one marriage to last a lifetime is a bankrupt idea.

Even many Christians have adopted a self-gratification philosophy. They feel if their mate doesn't make them happy, they are justified in leaving the marriage or having an affair. One man told us, "My wife hasn't understood my basic needs for the last five years. So, of course, I got involved with another woman. After all, what does my wife expect? It's really her fault I had the affair, you know."

It's interesting to notice that even though the divorce rate is hovering around the 50 percent mark in the United States, marriage is extremely popular. A greater percentage of our population is married today than ever before.[8]

Against the Current

The mid-life marriage partners, in order to hold together, must swim upstream. We discovered from our national study of mid-life couples whose marriages had survived that the successful couples were willing to say, "We don't care what everyone else is doing, we're going to make this marriage work." Our couples made this pronouncement in spite of the fact that the divorce rate for married persons forty to sixty years of age rose more than 50 percent between 1968 and 1978.[9]

The apparent dissatisfaction with mid-life marriage is not a new phenomenon. A Detroit study done in the early 1960s showed that only 6 percent of the wives were satisfied with their marriages after twenty-two years.[10]

Also in the sixties, psychologist and columnist Dr. Joyce Brothers stated, "Marriage is a 'quiet hell' for about half of American couples. . . four of twelve marriages will end in divorce, while another six become loveless 'utilitarian' relationships to protect children, property, shared concerns, and other goals."[11]

Another study of 2,000 married couples, as reported by Richard Strauss in 1973, showed 60 percent of the men would not marry the same partner if they had it to do over.[12]

Some writers are indeed pessimistic about the future of our Western society in general and marriage specifically,[13] but in spite of these gloomy views, there's been a definite turn from *me* to *we*—from the seventies' "me-ism" to concern for the group and marriage and family. That's good news!

POSITIVE EXTERNAL FORCES

Several forces are at work that indicate hope for the future of mid-life marriages. These encouraging signs reinforce our belief that your marriage can survive mid-life crisis.

Changing Attitudes

In the eighties a remarkable change took place in the type of articles published by magazines. A growing sympathy developed for homemaking and mothering roles. Fathers and husbands were encouraged to get involved in home relationships and responsibilities, including the raising of children.

Yes, illicit affairs were still discussed in the magazines, but the stories were enlarged to show the problems of being involved in an affair. In the seventies affairs were presented as all fun and games, and everyone needed one. In the eighties the negative side—the loss of the marriage relationship—was also discussed.

The mood of the nation has changed so that traditional family values and long-term marriages are again socially acceptable. Even popular music, such as "What's 'Forever' For, Anyway?" presents a heartbroken longing for commitment to a marriage that lasts a lifetime. A 1986 Chicago *Sun-Times* survey found that 77.1 percent of first-time married men would marry their same wives if they had it to do over,[14] and a 1984 *Reader's Digest*/Gallup survey showed that 85 percent of those polled would marry the same person if they could make the decision again.[15] This is quite a contrast to the 1973 Strauss study where 60 percent of the men would not marry the same partner if they could relive their lives.[16]

Not Either/Or

Unfortunately, marriage is too often portrayed by the media as one of two opposite extremes, neither of which is valid. If you believe most television programs and movies, you'll be convinced that every family is broken, most children are being raised by single parents, or, if the parents are married, they are involved in an affair.

The other extreme is the image that families are only made up of a husband who goes off to work each morning, a wife who stays home to keep house, and two or three happy children—a "Leave It to Beaver" type of family. The illusion is that after marriage, everything is stable for the rest of life and all families are "normal" husband-wife-and-child families.

The Good and the Shaky

Our survey of mid-life marriages showed a picture somewhere between the opposing extremes of chaotic and serene. We found some surprises. At times these marriages had been threatened with breakup, yet they hung in there.

One of our secretaries working with the data compilation commented that these marriages were really in trouble. She was shocked when we told her that these were the **good marriages;** the people with bad marriages didn't participate.

This secretary is young and just recently married. She went on to say, "Boy, I hope my marriage isn't like that."

Stress and struggle are normal in the mid-life marriage, but our couples revealed a great deal of strength as they talked about the stresses they had gone through. One man we interviewed shared some of the frustrations about his marriage. He said he'd hoped when he first got married that the romance they felt would always be there. But he discovered after a few months of marriage that real life is not always perfect.

He went on to say, "You know, after being married twenty-seven years, I'm finally facing the fact that I'm never going to have an A-plus marriage. In fact, our marriage is probably just a *B-minus.* I don't like everything about her or the way we function together, and she certainly doesn't like everything about me. But that doesn't mean we're going to get a divorce. We'll continue living together, knowing there is more good in our marriage than there is bad, and the 'more good' makes it worth staying together."

After one conference a woman described some of the problems she was experiencing because her husband had always jumped from job to job, never really communicated with her, and always forgot her birthday and their anniversary. Just recently he had spent money on a fishing boat when they needed to pay bills that were embarrassingly overdue. Then she quoted that classic line, "I've never considered divorce. **Murder—yes!** But, divorce—no!"

HOW DO MARRIAGES SURVIVE?

The overall question we asked in our survey was, "What is it that has enabled your marriage to survive?" We wanted to discover the common factors that held marriages together. We also wanted to learn the biggest problems couples faced, the solutions they found effective, and the most helpful resources for making their marriages strong.

The people in our study were self-selected from across the United States, basically well educated, of mid-life age or a little older, and most of them were Christians. The couples each filled out an eleven-page questionnaire. In addition to the surveys, we also gathered information from private counseling, from the thousands of letters we receive from people who have read our books or heard us on radio or TV, and from talking to people who attend our seminars.

Our survey couples classified their marriages into one of the following categories:
1. Stable, but with ups and downs
2. Threatened, with one partner periodically wanting out
3. Injured by an affair
4. Separated and reunited
5. Divorce-threatened or pending
6. Divorced and remarried to the same partner

We divided the survey couples into two main groups. The first we called Stable Couples, those who had experienced the normal ups-and-downs of marriage but still considered their marriages happy. Couples in the last five categories were the

Threatened Couples. The two groups were different from each other in some significant ways.

> ► The Stable Couples had very strong commitments to remain married to each other no matter what happened. In contrast, Threatened Couples had a weakened sense of commitment to remain married or of thinking of their marriage as a priority against competing forces such as career or their own personal needs.
> ► In the Stable Couples, leadership was shared rather than by husband only.
> ► The Stable Couples reported better communication with each other than did the Threatened Couples.
> ► Friends were a negative influence on marriage for the Threatened Couples.

Other interesting conclusions regarding marriage stability can be found in the reference notes.[17] For information about other studies of mid-life marriages, also see the reference notes.[18]

Survival Traits

The following ten traits were listed by the mid-life couples in our survey as the crucial keys for holding their marriage together:

> 1. **A commitment to stay married and to keep their marriage as a high priority**
> 2. **Ability to communicate**
> 3. **Personal spiritual life**
> 4. **Resolving conflicts**
> 5. **Relationships with other people**
> 6. **Sexual intimacy**
> 7. **Sharing fun, leisure, and humor**
> 8. **Realistic expectations**
> 9. **Serving each other and sharing leadership**
> 10. **Growing personally**

Each of these ten keys to a lasting marriage as identified by our survey couples will be discussed in depth in upcoming chapters. We will also be telling you how each of these traits can be part of your marriage. We hope that this book will be used by mid-life people and by young couples to help develop a lasting marriage.

A word of caution: Don't be overwhelmed by these traits and feel you are failing if you're not reaching 100 percent in all of them. You are doing O.K. if these traits are working at all in your marriage. Say to yourself, *We are doing great! We are about 20 percent on communication, 30 percent on sexual intimacy, 60 percent on realistic expectations, and 10 percent on fun time.*

Congratulate yourselves on your current achievements. Be glad you are doing as well as you are and read the next chapters to improve your success rates.

Facing
Major
Problems

It was Saturday afternoon. I was a young graduate student who idolized Reverend Jordan. He was a brilliant preacher, a great Bible expositor, and senior pastor of a growing, dynamic church. I always looked for opportunities to talk to and learn from him, since I wanted to be the good preacher he was.

On that Saturday afternoon I stopped by the parsonage to pick up a book he was lending me. He greeted me at the door, but tension was written all over his face. As I stepped inside, a short burst of anger exploded from his wife in a distant room. She evidently didn't know I was there. The tension on my pastor's face turned to a flushed embarrassment. He hurriedly excused himself and went into the other room.

I sat down in the living room and felt sick to my stomach as I experienced the process of losing a hero. I could hear them arguing viciously in the back room.

After a few minutes Pastor Jordan emerged with the book he was lending me and hurriedly ushered me out the door. On other occasions he had taken extra moments with Sally and me, coaching us on being effective Christian leaders. Now he almost pushed me out the door.

In the following months the disruptive pattern taking

place in our pastor's marriage was revealed. We were stunned when we learned the sordid details of his involvement in an affair. Even though he and his wife had showed a lot of affection publicly, a growing distance had developed between this mid-life couple. After the affair, they separated and ultimately divorced. We were devastated.

Over the years we have had many of those "sick stomach" experiences when we begin to sense that a close friend or an admired leader is having serious marital trouble. We have often felt so helpless in those moments.

Is Anyone Happily Married?

Why are more and more marriages having trouble? Sometimes as we look at middle-generation couples, we are tempted to ask, "Is there any marriage that isn't in trouble?"

Barbara Fried, in her book *The Middle-Age Crisis*, talked about twelve mid-life couples she knew at a seaside colony. One or both of the partners in the marriages were having extramarital affairs. One woman summarized what was happening: "Well, I look at it this way. There was a year when it seemed that everybody I knew, including me, was getting married, and now there's a year when it seems everybody I know, including me, is getting divorced."[1]

By mid-life, married couples often have developed many critical problems between themselves. In this chapter we will discuss the three most prevalent—loss of intimacy, conflict over money, and affairs.

INTIMACY LOST

Many of the mid-life marriage problems are directly tied to a loss of intimacy. These people don't really know each other or care. They are living together with the same hopelessness as if they were two people who both have terminal cancer and neither has energy to care for the other one.

The need for intimacy, which starts very early in life, is the need to be close to someone else, to feel secure, and to know that you are significant to another person. In childhood terms, intimacy means someone with whom to play and share secrets.

One year when our family was considering a move to a house in the country, one of our young daughters asked, "But who would I play with?" She was afraid to lose her opportunity for intimacy with other playmates.

A push-pull goes on in each of our lives, however. We have a strong drive to relate to others, to belong—to feel a sense of home and have at least one person with whom we can verbalize our feelings, aspirations, and life goals. We also have a driving need to be individuals—to achieve, to make a mark in the world. Unfortunately, this very drive for individual success forces us into isolation from other people and into competition with them.

During childhood we want to be close to our parents, yet we want to be independent. In our teen years we have a strong push toward individualism, but we want our family roots and intimacy with our peer group. This tension continues throughout all the stages of life.

During our years of pastoring and teaching, we have watched many young adults have a series of dating relationships. They want to be close to someone, but when the relationship becomes too close and intimate, they back off. They need more space and freedom.

A similar reaction happens when people marry. Through the dating and engagement period, they enjoy the intimacy and openness with each other. After they marry, however, they discover that *every*thing is known to this other person. In their small apartment, one knows when the other burps or uses the bathroom. Each knows when the other acts crazy, cheats and lies, is depressed, or is lazy.

Many marriages suddenly have too much closeness, and couples may feel the marriage was a mistake. It wasn't a mistake to get married, but it was a mistake to think they could be endlessly intimate without meeting their other need for individuality. It's good to have some separateness. Years ago Gibran wrote, "Let there be spaces in your togetherness."[2]

Intimacy does not mean abandoning personhood, losing privacy, or sacrificing creativity. Intimacy means sharing with another person any part of you that you are willing to reveal. True intimacy in marriage was best expressed by several of our survey couples as they referred to each other as "my closest friend."

When we see the outward signs of conflict, an affair, separation, or divorce, we can tell a marriage is in trouble. Before the symptoms are outwardly visible to others, however, a loss of intimacy has already occurred within the marriage.

When sharing of the deepest self with the mate begins to be lost, often external forces—such as the children, the house, or the couple's reputation in the community—are all that hold the relationship together. The emotional bonding, or glue, between the couple is missing.

Imagine that you've dropped one of your finest coffee cups on the floor. You want to salvage it because it's part of a set you inherited from your parents. Imagine further that you don't have any glue, so you fit the pieces together and put rubber bands around the cup to hold it together. The pieces are held together because of the pressure of the many rubber bands, but the broken fragments are not adhering to each other as if they had been glued.

Carry the image a bit farther and imagine that you're serving hot coffee in that cup to a guest. Your friend is trying to drink, maneuvering her mouth around the rubber bands while coffee drips from the cracks in the cup. We would all say that the cup really isn't a cup anymore.

How Intimacy Is Lost

Intimacy—the sharing of our deep selves with each other—is the glue that bonds us together, seals up the cracks, and helps us to become one. In our survey and from a lifetime of working with couples, we've discovered several things that can have a negative influence on intimacy.

Faulty Childhood and Adolescent Patterns. Some people enter marriage not having learned to be vulnerable and open. They don't know how to share their needs and feelings or how to hear the same from another person. They may have come from a home where there was a lack of touching, expressing love, or sharing needs, feelings, hopes, and failures. Thus, they have no example to follow. When they consider a marriage relationship, they may experience a great deal of insecurity or even terror.

Passive Husbands. Eda LeShan in *The Wonderful Crisis of Middle Age* has said, "The women who were the most unhappy in middle age were those with passive husbands. . . . the happier wives were married to men who had minds and wills of their own. The wives with the most complaints . . . were married to passive men who seemed to be devoting their lives to trying to make their wives happy."[3]

Men learn passivity. Men usually do not learn to be intimate as children. They are told by their parents or other adults, "Be a big boy and stop crying. Men don't cry."

Many men, therefore, enter marriage not knowing how to share their feelings, unable to communicate about their inner world, and only able to talk about their external successes, such as in their career or an athletic event. Most men will tell you *what* they do, not *why* they do it or *how they feel* about what they do.

Sharing will get a wife. A young man is told, "If you want to get a woman, you need to pursue her, be romantic, and share your feelings." The young man does what he has to do to win a woman, and the woman thinks he is like that all the time. After they are married, however, he drops back into his normal male approach to life, discussing only externals instead of internals.

The wife is pushy. She doesn't mean to be pushy, but she can't understand why they shared so many feelings before they were married and now he won't share. He isn't treating her the same as he did while they were dating. She doesn't interpret this as a regression into maleness but that he no longer cares for her. So, she begins to push him to become a more internal, feeling-oriented, and sharing person.

He realizes he's not very good at this and feels inadequate and inferior to his wife in this area. Like any human being, he retreats from areas in which he is not having success, and so he shuns dialogue with his wife. By mid-life, when they go out to dinner with another couple, the two women do all the talking while the men carry on small talk related to what each is doing in his business.

He is preoccupied with his career. Men often view marriage and family as pieces of a puzzle to put in place. As each piece is in place, the man moves onto another piece. That other piece is usually his career. He spends the majority of his adult life putting pieces of his career puzzle together. Each piece is interrelated for advantage, advancement, financial gain, and prestige. He keeps moving on to new accomplishments, ignoring the family pieces of the puzzle already in place, just as a person constructing a jigsaw puzzle moves on from the pieces already joined together to the next pieces to be found and fit together.

All of life for the man is objectified. In a sense, he is not a participant in life; he simply manipulates the characters—the pieces of the puzzle—around him. He doesn't see himself as part of the puzzle. The puzzle is the product of his life, always objective and detached.

A woman, on the other hand, doesn't view marriage as just one piece of life's puzzle. She thinks of her marriage as a cake. The ingredients are gathered together to make a perfect batter. It is properly mixed, baked, cooled, and frosted. But the full enjoyment is not only in making the cake but also in eating it and serving it to others.

For the man, the challenge of life is not the completed puzzle but the excitement of putting the pieces together. The woman enjoys putting the pieces together and savoring the product.

In some ways, the husband is only passive in relationship to past accomplishments, but he is not passive to the process. He can become very energized and involved when there are new challenges, experiences, or achievements.

"I Won't Make Waves." Sometimes when a couple's relationship is on shaky ground, one or both of them are afraid to express real feelings, either positive or negative. They are afraid that an argument might develop or, even worse, that the marriage might break up.

The unwillingness to risk or to press the border of honesty certainly keeps things more pleasant at the moment, but in the long run, the marriage problems won't go away. In fact, they probably will grow.

The two of us have watched a number of couples gradually settle into patterns of avoidance over the years. The avoidance becomes so extreme that the married partners even tell their children which topics to avoid with the other parent.

Intimacy is essential to keep a marriage functioning properly, but intimacy always involves a risk. After years of counseling and from our own marriage, we would say that as people risk and talk to each other about their needs, goals, and aspirations, they usually will be drawn closer together, not pushed further apart.

Intimacy is worth the temporary discomfort caused as you resolve problems, especially when you realize that creeping isolation is the only alternative.

Intimacy Found

When you first met each other, you went through an unconscious checklist of whether or not you wanted to get to know this person. You decided this person was generally the right age, your body type, and had an interesting personality, all of which attracted you.

As you got to know your future mate better, you continued working on that unspoken checklist. "Does he or she have the same values I have? Are his or her goals and aspirations similar to mine? Do we have compatible backgrounds? Is this person tolerant of my idiosyncrasies?" Finally, after going through hundreds of items on your checklist, you both concluded that you were right for each other.

Recognize Changing Needs. The problem is that you don't stay the same. You change, and life around you changes. As a result, you need to continue to ask, "What are my mate's needs and what can I do to meet those needs?"

We're convinced that most people stay married because there is more satisfaction in staying together than in separating. The key to building intimacy, then, is to understand the continual changes in your mate and to meet those needs. At the same time, you must communicate how you are changing so your mate can meet your needs.

If intimacy goes out of a marriage, the natural magnetism for staying together also leaves. It's like an old piece of Scotch tape that had mended a torn page in a book. It has yellowed with age, the glue is gone, and when you turn the page, the tape falls off.

A woman at one of our conferences wrote about her struggles with her breaking marriage and the loss of intimacy:

——— ▼ ———

The tears well up. Can I face the inner fears of what's happening to me in the middle years? I'm feeling sad, out of touch, dissatisfied, and in need. My mate and I are separated, both struggling to be freed from the tensions we have created. . . .

I want to feel again, but I'm afraid of intimacy, for then I'm vulnerable to hurt, and I don't heal easily. Each time that I do overlook the previous pain, I end up hurt once more and the process starts again. How do we change and stop this eventual end? It's not enough to say, "I'm sorry," and repeat yourself again.

——— ▲ ———

This wife recognized that she and her husband were different from when they first married and now she wondered, "How do we get started toward renewal of the intimacy we once had?"

Feelings Follow Attitudes and Actions. The difference between the succeeding and failing marriages, which we have studied, is that couples who survived mid-life crisis recognized when a distance was growing and were willing to talk and work at maintaining intimacy.

Developing intimacy demands courage and vulnerability. We would suggest that you not say to yourself, *I would open up and talk about myself if he or she would also open up.* Someone has to start; someone has to risk. You must say, *I will make a start. I will be vulnerable.*

When you've had a breakdown of intimacy, you can repair the damage by carrying out right actions and cultivating the necessary attitudes. As you talk honestly to each other and work at meeting each other's needs, you'll find that the **feelings** of closeness and intimacy will come.

Your marital closeness should be helped as you read the **ten keys to an intimate marriage** in the following chapters. Next, however, we will consider the two other major marital problems—money and affairs.

TENSION OVER MONEY

Money was the most frequent cause of marital conflict for couples in our study. Often money problems were because of a lack of intimacy. In some cases, money conflict caused other serious problems, including communication breakdown, affairs, separation, and divorce. The handling of finances has been a problem in marriages for a long time, as pointed out by many studies.[4]

It's fascinating, however, that few of the young adults we've known talk about money during dating and engagement. They talk about many very personal things, including previous sexual experiences, but discussing how to handle money seems to be off limits. After all, money is not romantic to talk about. Discussing your net worth or how you spend money seems crass.

Since money management is the number one irritant in marriage, it must be talked about in order to reduce conflict. A couple needs to talk about who will earn the money and how it will be managed and spent.

These topics require that the individuals think through their value system about money. Any conflict they have over finances is probably not over money itself, but over what money *means* to them.

People frequently report that they don't have enough money. When we ask them, "How much would be enough?" they then begin to see that the question is not the amount of money but what it means and how they use it. This was the case with Barry and Priscilla.

Barry was raised in a lower income family which never had enough money for extra things in life. In high school Barry envied the richer kids and wanted the power that money gave to rich people. He was not exceptionally bright but found it easy to compete by using his physical ability and good looks. These became his lever to move the world and attract wealthy girls.

Barry dated Priscilla, not only because she was good-looking but also because of her family's wealth. After they were married, they frequently fought over money. Money was no big deal to Priscilla. She didn't want to climb the social ladder. She was already there. But to Barry, money was a means of getting up the social ladder. Where they lived, the kind of cars they drove, and his four-hundred-dollar suits were all part of the status that he needed. Priscilla liked to give away money, but Barry felt that giving away money reduced his potential to be successful.

When they came for marital counseling, it was obvious that their problem was not the amount of money they had, but their meaning and use of money. As each of them came to understand how and why they differed in their view of money, they were able to work out a resolution.

The Meaning of Money

As mid-life couples wrestle with the money issue, the concepts of power, self-image, and trust keep bubbling up. These ideas are not always immediately obvious to the couple, but almost every financial disagreement can be boiled down to one or more of these three topics.

1. Money is power in a relationship. Often an unspoken attitude is that whoever earns the most money has the greatest voice in the family. This power usually applies to all decisions, not just to how the finances will be used.

Wives who don't work for money outside the home may have little power in the marriage relationship. On the other hand, wives who work and are too successful may be a threat to their husbands. Husbands usually are pleased about the extra money their wives' jobs provide and they may value their working wives more, but if wives earn more money or have more prestigious jobs, husbands often are unhappy.[5]

One wife, responding to a *McCall's* magazine survey, said, "My marriage [is] in trouble. I was pushed into being a working 'mother' because my husband said he needed help to get the financial start we 'had to have.' I managed to move up the ladder and am now earning more per year than he. This has caused resentment and has placed [a] wedge between us."[6]

Americans still think that the husband should be the major provider in the family and ought to have the most significant job.[7] It's O.K. for the husband to be a doctor and the wife to be a nurse or for both of them to be teachers, but couples often feel uncomfortable when the wife is the doctor or the school principal.

2. *Money also influences self-image.* A couple of years ago I (Jim) parked our 1978 Pontiac under some olive trees in the faculty parking lot at Biola University. After teaching my class, I came out to find my car splattered with fallen olives and friendly deposits from the birds who had been eating the olives.

I started home, feeling very conspicuous in my dirty, aged car. On the way, I stopped to visit an old friend at his plush office to ask about his health. He is very successful, with two Mercedes, and a luxurious condominium with a view of a golf course and the mountains.

After my visit, I got into my bird-and-olive-bespeckled car and was even more aware of the chipped paint on the hood, the dents, the worn seat cushions, the hundred thousand miles on the odometer, and the squeaking speedometer needle that jumped up and down the gauge as I drove home. I felt crummy.

Sally and I had talked about eventually replacing this car, but suddenly I wanted to do it *now*. I was ready to spend money to improve how I felt about myself. I was willing to go into hock so that when I drove to business meetings, I wouldn't have to apologize for my old car, telling people I keep it because it's comfortable on long trips.

Money has a direct bearing on your self-image. Both you and your mate are using money to control what you think of yourselves and how you want others to think of you.

3. *Money involves trust.* I (Sally) remember the awkward feeling I had about opening a joint checking account shortly before we were married. I had been teaching school and had earned most of the money we were depositing. We were going to use it to live on as Jim went to seminary.

It was strange to put my money where someone else had equal access to it. On the other hand, I wanted to give my money to our account, because shortly we were going to be giving everything to each other.

The value that you place on money and how you use it in relationship with other people could indicate your trust factor in marriage. Our study revealed that the more committed the couple is to staying married, the safer they feel about trusting money to each other.

American Couples quotes Cindy: "Either you are married or you are not. It's very simple. You either make a commitment or you don't. Some of my friends made specific contracts about whose money was whose before they remarried again, which strikes me as setting up the end before you have tried to make it last forever. My husband did not make a commitment to me in my first marriage. I am not going to let that sour me. Whatever I bring into this [second] marriage, I share, and I know Bill feels the same way."[8]

Trusting each other in the money area will develop as you believe the other person will not ignore your viewpoint or take advantage of you. Trust can be built by explaining your concerns and ideas and by listening to your mate's insights and goals about money.

4. *Money and work are related.* The use of money and the work done to earn it are closely tied to each other. So are the marital arguments about money and work. Conflict over work usually centers around the amount of time the husband spends at work, the husband's focus on work rather than on the family, whether or not the wife should work, and who will raise the children if the wife works.

By 1976 only 40 percent of the jobs in this country paid enough to support a family. Instead of children being the reason for women to stay home, the expense of rearing children was the reason mothers had to go to work. Demographers forecast that soon the number of women will surpass men in the work force. They also estimate that, before long, over 55 percent of all women over age sixteen will be working, including half of the mothers of young children.[9] At the same time, more than 60 percent of husbands and wives feel that a mother of small children should not hold a job.[10]

If both husband and wife are working, the marriage may suffer because neither has the time or the energy to make sure the relationship is doing well. This can be compared to our automatic washer, which is designed so that if a wash load gets too far out of balance, a loud hornlike buzzer goes off, producing an irritation for any human nearby. It continues to blare until the problem is corrected. The washer works properly when it's balanced, and so do marriages.

When work—either yours or your mate's—begins to drain energy from the rest of life, trouble will result. Someone will begin to yell or to act in strange ways. It's then time to balance the load—to take a good look at where you both stand on the value of money and its use.

SEXUAL BREAKDOWNS

Although the most frequent marital problems are related to money, our studies show that the problems causing the most intense hurt and grief are affairs. In our survey of married couples, sexual problems that resulted in affairs were ranked as the second biggest problem for all the marriages combined. For marriages where an affair had occurred, the affair was the number one problem.

By mid-life, most serious sexual difficulties are directly related to intimacy. Couples who achieve true emotional intimacy are usually able to work out any mechanical problem related to their sexual experience. If intimacy doesn't develop or is not sustained, the likelihood of an affair increases.

Rob and Sandy, like many dating couples, had a strong physical attraction to each other, which made it difficult for them to build the psychological and spiritual dimensions of their relationship. The physical always crowded out meaningful dialogue and understanding. As Rob described it, "Even though our Christian ethics said we shouldn't, we repeatedly went all the way before we were married."

"Now [at mid-life]," Rob said, "I don't even want to touch her. We avoid each other around the house. I am repulsed if I happen to bump into her in bed."

Rob and Sandy had thought of intimacy as a sexual expression rather than a deep sharing of their emotional and spiritual lives. Their marriage is now so barren and distasteful, they are both prime candidates for an affair.

To have true intimacy and a good sexual relationship, you need to talk to each other about what you think and feel about all of life. This openness will encourage the growth of intimacy.

In a sense, it's the old dog-chasing-its-tail routine. As intimacy is experienced in all areas of marital life, sex becomes more satisfying. If sex is satisfying, intimacy is more easily achieved in other areas. If intimacy is totally missing in the marriage, someone else may fill the gap.

The enjoyment of sexual intercourse is not a complete indicator of whether a marriage will last. Marriages stay together because needs are being met and intimacy is present.

Cause or Result?

Unfortunately, an affair, separation, or divorce is usually viewed as the problem in a marriage instead of the result of the earlier problem, which is emotional separation. Affairs, separations, and divorces are different from each other, but only in the degree of separation.

Letters and calls to our office are often from a hurting person like Angie, who asked, "How could my husband do this to me after all the years we've spent together?"

Angie's questions and confusion poured out as she cried over the phone, "I've found out that my husband has become involved with another woman. I don't think they've actually had sex yet, but I can't let him sleep with me now that he wants to be with her. I'm going to file for a divorce, but how do I go about it? What do I tell our children? How do I live alone after spending my life with him for twenty-seven years?"

She was asking all the wrong questions. Instead of focusing on what they had lost in their relationship and correcting that, she thought that the situation was hopeless and that she had to get out as quickly as possible. She didn't understand the real issue, which we learned when we talked to Fred on the phone later.

As we explored the situation with him, we discovered that he had met an old girlfriend and feelings of their former love were rekindled. Even though they both were unhappy in their marriages, the two of them decided not to pursue an affair but to try to make their own marriages work.

Fred told us, "But I just feel that Angie doesn't care about me anymore. She is more interested in her career than in spending time with me. We never have an evening together, and we never go out. I feel as if I don't exist as far as she is concerned."

We encouraged Fred to tell Angie what he had told us. We assured Angie that Fred's attraction to the other woman didn't automatically mean she had to divorce him. Their last report to us was that their marriage is better than ever. Fred has been learning to communicate his needs and feelings, and Angie has been working to meet them.

Reasons for Affairs

An old Scandinavian proverb says, "If you want to count the causes of infidelity, count the leaves of an oak tree."[11] One study of affairs reported that people's reasons for having the affair were poor sexual adjustment in marriage, the "other person" was a challenge, they were "in love," their mate was unaffectionate, or their marriage was never any good.[12]

The reasons people get involved in affairs are numerous, but all the reasons seem to point to a feeling that something is missing in the marriage or the individual's life. If your marriage is being threatened by an affair, remember not to focus on the affair but on your mate's needs. Ask yourself, *What are the reasons for my mate being drawn to another person? Where has our marriage lost intimacy?*

Wives in Affairs

USA Today reported, "Women have extramarital affairs mainly because they want deeper emotional intimacy; they select empathetic men, and most don't feel guilty. . . . Women call emotional communication the affair's greatest reward. If a partner doesn't express his emotions well, listen and empathize, women end the affair. . . . Men are always asking me what they can do to prevent their wives from having an affair. I say, 'Talk to her.' "[13]

Anne Kristin Carroll, an Atlanta marriage counselor, puts it bluntly: "What most women are looking for is appreciation, a reaffirmation of herself as a woman, not as the children's mother, but as your woman, personally, as a living, breathing female. If she isn't reassured *verbally* and *nonverbally*, she will find that in time appreciative looks from other men become more and more appealing. She may try to shake the feeling off, but if she is continually ignored, if her feminine needs for appreciation, affection, romance, quiet talks, etc., aren't met, she may in time secretly turn to that man who has noticed her *as a woman*."[14]

Magazine articles about unfaithful wives and promiscuous women all point to the same kinds of human need for intimacy. We also know this from the women having affairs who write and call us.

Husbands in Affairs

Obviously, women aren't the only ones drawn into affairs. The most numerous letters and calls in our office are from wives who tell us their husbands are having an affair. The husband is talking divorce and the wife doesn't know what to do.

We tell her to learn what the other woman is like. What is there about the other woman that meets the needs of her husband? The other woman probably knows the husband's interests because she works with him or she wants to learn what he cares about so she can talk about it with him. She also knows how to listen and to hear what he says. She probably also is not a mother, but a girlfriend, to him. The wife should begin to include these qualities in her life as she relates to her husband.

How Both Mates Feel

The recurring theme of the mate having the affair is, "I feel insecure, lonely, unstimulated, not needed, sexually unsatisfied by my mate, and confused." The mate who is being rejected by the one having an affair feels like the lettuce at the bottom of the dish after all the goodies have been eaten out of the chef's salad—abandoned, used, exploited, and insecure.

Each mate feels misunderstood and unsatisfied by his or her mate. The one is unsatisfied and gets into an affair, while the other one is unhappy because of being rejected.

Married people usually presume too much about each other. They think they are meeting their mate's needs, but they have never bothered to ask. Test yourself on these points:

- Is your mate really sharing with you the deepest part of his or her inner self?
- Do you understand your mate's personal goals and aspirations?
- Do you grasp the full intensity of the things that make him or her disappointed, angry, discouraged, happy, hopeful?
- Are you helping to facilitate his or her growth?
- Are you genuinely interested in him or her, or just projects in which you are jointly involved?
- If you were not married to each other, would your mate want to go on a date with you?

The Cost of an Affair

A few years ago when we wrote an article for *Today's Christian Woman* about why people get involved in affairs, we invited people to write if they were in an affair and wanted help. The large volume of letters surprised us. People wrote who had been carrying the guilt and hurt of affairs in their hearts for years but had never found anyone with whom they could share their pain.

We discovered similar hurts in our national survey of marriages. The couples talked about the searing pain of affairs, separation, and divorce. Even though these couples had now worked through the problems and had re-established intimacy—in some cases remarrying each other if they had divorced—the scars would always be there.

All the parties in an affair get hurt. A Christian leader in her midthirties told us the story of the tremendous agony experienced by everyone involved in her affair. All four adults, their children, both churches, friends, relatives, and the community at large bore a part in the pain.

She expressed her personal feelings as the affair ended by saying, " 'Thus began several months of pure hell which I am not sure is finished yet. The tears that began that night did not cease at all for ten days. They flowed like water being poured from a pitcher. I took a bus back to my hometown, not so much because I wanted to go there, but because I did not know what else to do. More like a zombie than a human being, I moved through the next few days until my husband and a pastor friend checked me into a psychiatric ward of a local hospital.

" 'I really didn't care whether I lived or died, but if I could have made a choice, it definitely would have been for death. I could neither eat nor sleep. I had staked my life on the gift God gave me in Bruce [the man with whom she had been involved], and now that gift was no longer mine. . . .

" 'Not an hour passes when he is not on my mind with both love and pain. Meanwhile I have no choice but to continue to go through the motions of living. . . . Indeed life is hell.' "[15]

Alternatives to Separations and Affairs

When one mate "wants space" or gets into an affair or talks of getting a divorce, a clear signal is being given that needs are not being met. Instead of the drastic experiences of divorce, separation, or affairs, some better alternatives are available.

1. Separate from some of life's pressures. You and your mate together should plan how to separate yourselves from stress rather than each other. Ask yourselves some of these questions:

> ► Could we legitimately get away from some of the pressure to let our marriage heal?
> ► Could we plan several weekend get-aways?
> ► Could we quit serving on boards and committees and cut back on our business workload?
> ► Could we reduce our lifestyle and living costs so that financial worries are lessened?

A lawyer, whom we know, worked six days a week and developed a very large practice, but he cut back his work so he could enjoy his wife and children. A doctor's family was willing to move into a smaller house so he could drop his overload at the hospital. In both cases, the income level was lowered, but the marriages—which had been seriously threatened—were strengthened.

2. Build breaks into your routine. Use the drive home from work to unwind. If you work at a desk, occasionally look out of a nearby window or walk outside on your breaks. I (Jim) find it helpful to take just five minutes and go look at my flowers outside.

When I used to have a heavy counseling load, I took a five-minute break between sessions. I stretched out on the floor and fell sound asleep, knowing that my secretary would buzz me when it was time for the next appointment. Those mini-breaks kept me going.

3. Use separation within the house. If your relationship is very stressed, it might be helpful to give each other separate space and privacy within the house. If one of you is under a great deal of pressure in your work, you may be driven by the need for more aloneness when you are home. Temporary separation within your own house may help meet your need for space so that a more disruptive separation is not needed.

When I (Jim) was in the deepest of my mid-life crisis, I desperately wanted to escape. I needed time to be alone. I repeatedly thought of driving away in the car. Sally's sensitivity to my need and allowing me to be alone watching TV provided the necessary release so I didn't have to run.

4. *Plan temporary physical separation.* Perhaps it is possible to have a legitimate short-term separation for emotional healing for you and your mate. This temporary separation should not disrupt the normal flow of life or signal to the community that you are in danger of a divorce.

The husband might take a fishing trip, go backpacking, or attend a work-related seminar. The wife might also attend a seminar, visit a sister, or go on vacation with an old college roommate.

IF BAD GOES TO WORSE

If the situation has become so bad that one of you needs to move out, don't make a big once-and-for-all cleanout of your closets. Rent a room and move only a few of your things. Keep both your names on the checking account. Wear your wedding ring. Remember, the more bridges you burn, the more you will need to painfully reconstruct later. Things always look worse in the heat of an argument than a few days later when everything has quieted.

Sometimes couples who are having marriage trouble skip over all of the smaller steps and jump to a permanent separation. In anger they may shout, "I never have loved you! We never should have gotten married, and I'm never coming back!" They grab all their belongings and look for some place to set up their new lifestyle. Or, they may just quietly move out and send the legal papers later.

The most successful separations are when a couple recognizes the need for space, but the separation is *not* a preparation for divorce. The separation should be a time of healing, planned for the purpose of restoring the marriage. The need for separation is simply an indication that stresses have built up, which perhaps can be relieved by time apart to get a fresh perspective. Counseling during this time may also help you to understand and meet each other's needs. Reading the next chapters about the **ten keys to an intimate marriage** will also help your marriage survive.

PART TWO

▼

Ten Keys
to an
Intimate
Marriage

CHAPTER

4

Key #1
Commitment
to Marriage

A commitment to stay married was one of the three most important factors for making marriages last, according to the couples in our study. More than 94 percent "strongly agreed" or "agreed" when asked if they viewed commitment to stay married an important part in holding them together. Most of them wrote additional comments to support their views. Here is a sample:

▼

"**Commitment is the basic shelter without which a marriage freezes to death.**"

"**Single strongest factor to hold us together through the rough times.**"

"**A commitment to stay married settles it and makes for no other choice.**"

"**The idea of divorce is simply not an option.**"

"**Never entered our minds that we could even walk out of a marriage—a vow seemed binding.**"

▲

Commitment Is a Priority

Couples in our first group (Stable Couples) had a very strong commitment to remain married regardless of the pressures of life or competing factors such as career and raising children. The couples in the other five categories (Threatened Couples) consistently placed a lower priority on commitment. This lower view of commitment frequently opened the door to serious marital problems.

Psychologist Joyce Brothers, who knows the pulse of American families because of her many years of counseling experience, has said, "There is currently a very strong interest in commitment. . . . One of the top priorities in life for young people is a happy home and family life."[1]

Commitment was also found to be crucial by three doctors who studied 6,000 marriages and 3,000 divorces. They concluded, "There may be nothing more important in a marriage than a determination that it shall persist. With such a determination, individuals force themselves to adjust and to accept situations which would seem sufficient grounds for a breakup, if continuation of the marriage were not the prime objective."[2]

Commitment: Doggedness or Joy?

Our couples' answers revealed many different definitions of commitment, some not as positive as we had expected. One man said, "I'm committed to marriage as an idea. I intend to stay married all of my life." Even though marriage seemed to be an impersonal concept to this man, he was willing to stick it out no matter what happened.

One wife who had been married twenty-eight years said that her commitment to marriage had been because of "fear of disobeying my vow and fear of failure in a personal way."

A husband said, "This commitment began in the wedding ceremony and is considered a sacred promise before God."

The wife of a couple who had separated for a time and were now reunited said her commitment to stay married was because of her "abhorrence of divorce [a child of divorce knows]. I am a child of divorce."

We chuckled over what one wife said about her commitment. Her husband had had an affair, gone bankrupt, found it difficult to communicate, and always wanted to be the winner in any conflict. She said, "I promised God to 'hang in' for better or for worse, and worse it was!"

To others of our couples, the sense of commitment was more than just an obligation or an idea, it was to their individual spouse—getting to know him or her, adjusting, growing, learning to be a more effective marriage partner and a more mature person.

A husband said, "When I finally realized my wife needed me just to listen to her without giving her solutions, I determined to meet her need in that way. I am committed to understanding her."

A woman whose husband threatened to leave reported, "I think I kept my husband because I *grew*. I *wanted* to be different."

A wife who felt her marriage had always been stable said, "Being willing to allow my husband 'humanness' and to remember that his love and commitment to me is a real gift has been important."

Unequally Committed

Often, of course, one mate is more committed to make the marriage last than the other one is. Our daily work in our organization, Mid-Life Dimensions, is with couples whose marriages are coming apart, and usually it is only one of them who wants to try to save the marriage. The one who wants to try is the one who contacts us for help.

When answering the survey question about whether or not a commitment to stay married had helped hold their marriage together, one husband said, "Especially my wife's! There were times when my commitment wavered—hers never did, even when I was most unbearable."

This man, with a graduate degree and a high income, had suffered from such severe emotional problems during mid-life that he separated from his wife and was finally hospitalized with a breakdown. During his hospitalization, his wife visited him faithfully and did all she could to aid his recovery. After his release, they were officially reunited and have now been married a total of thirty years.

The wife of another couple married twenty-eight years

wrote this about commitment, "It was the main thing, *but* it was my commitment. My husband was not strongly committed." The husband wrote, "I *fought* very hard the commitment to stay married—wanting it *vs.* not wanting it."

This couple had separated because of the husband's affair but are now reunited. Throughout their questionnaires they talked about the stresses they had faced and survived. The husband said, "It's worth it. I'm glad my wife didn't give up—today we still have each other."

Because commitment was such a strong factor among the couples we surveyed, it's important to understand what commitment means and how we can implement it in our lives.

WHAT COMMITMENT IS NOT

Commitment Is Not Self-Fulfillment

We sometimes hear people say, "I am committed to make my marriage work." By that they mean, "I am committed to make my marriage work for *me* so that *I* am happy," not, "I am committed to make *our* marriage work so *we* are happy." In marriage the *I* must become *we*. Individuals should be happy in marriage, but commitment doesn't imply that everything in the marriage works only for one partner's benefit.

A wife who was faced with her husband's threats to leave her said, "I had to change some things about myself. I decided I had to learn just what he wanted in a wife and try to be that kind of woman so he would want to stay. I knew I wanted our marriage to last."

Commitment Is Not the Spontaneous Response That Occurs When Everything Is Going Well

Some couples say their marriage lasts because they have an equal amount of problems and love in their relationship. We ask, "What happens when there are more problems than love to cover their problems?"

Every one of our survey couples reported that they had had difficult times. The problems most mentioned by the Stable Couples were parenting a difficult child, death of parents, illness, work situations, and financial problems. Threatened Couples reported the most stressful event to be an affair or separation, followed by the items listed above.

It is important to point out that *all* of the marriages had stresses, yet they overcame those problems and stayed together. Many of the survey respondents wrote comments which indicated that their commitment to stay married was what helped carry them through the hard times:

——— ▼ ———

"Commitment is truly the only thing holding my marriage together now."

"Without a commitment, my husband would have quit long ago."

"Determination backed with Christian principles is the glue that is holding our marriage together."

"Because of a deep-seated value for keeping my marriage, I have stayed when I would rather have thrown in the towel at times."

——— ▲ ———

Obviously when circumstances are not going well is when a couple needs to deliberately commit themselves to work at keeping their marriage strong.

Commitment Is Not Simply a Tool to Avoid the Embarrassment of a Failing Marriage

Commitment only for commitment's sake is negative and selfish. What good is it if people just grit their teeth and suffer in a stalemated condition? Enduring just to prove that you're tough is the opposite of the positive commitment that causes each person in the relationship to grow and to enjoy the marriage.

Another woman said, "If I didn't hate divorce and its tragic results, I would have left. Also I didn't want to upset our extended family." Unfortunately, this woman was committed because of outside pressure, rather than being committed to her husband.

Commitment Is Not Holding on Only Until Someone Better Comes Along

Donna often talked to us about how unhappy she was in her marriage. She could never get Barney to talk to her when he got home from work. Instead, all he wanted to do in the evenings and on weekends was sit and drink beer and watch TV. He paid no attention to their two children except to yell at them or hit them. He didn't give her enough money for groceries but expected good meals. She tried to give him what he wanted sexually, but he never cared about what pleased her.

Late one night she came running to our door in her robe and slippers. They had been arguing again and this time he started to beat her. When she was calmed down and was sure Barney would be asleep, she went back home.

As she talked to us a few days later, she said, "Many times I would have left for good, but I guess I'm committed to my marriage just because I'm afraid no one else would want me. Even though this marriage is bad, I wouldn't want to live alone. It would be great if I could find someone else, but until I do, I'm committed to staying with Barney." This woman is committed by default. She is just marking time in her present marriage, hoping she will meet someone better.

COMMITMENT IS A CHOICE

To us commitment is positive, not negative. We believe two people make a positive decision to:
1. Stay together
2. Love and affirm each other
3. Grow as persons
4. Make their marriage an expression of their desire for each other's happiness

One of the strongest needs in the human personality is to be valued and loved. Our definition of love is **a desire to understand the other person's needs and a willingness to give energy from your life for that person's highest fulfillment.** Our concept of commitment is tied closely with our concept of love.

In essence, each person in a healthy marriage is saying to

the other, "I'm concerned about you—what you think, your values, your goals, your dreams. I appreciate the unique way God is working in your life and the positive difference you are making in the world. I want to do what I can to help you achieve your fullest potential."

We see that the choice to be committed includes some of the following ingredients.

A Choice to Be a Caretaker

When we commit ourselves by choice to each other, we each automatically become a **caretaker** for the other as well as for our marriage. The massive study reported in *American Couples* found that wherever there was no caretaker in the marriage relationship, the marriage fell apart.[3]

Someone within the marriage must be concerned about maintaining the relationship. Strong marriages are those where both partners assume the responsibility of caretaker for each other and the marriage.

Phil and Nancy have been married ten years and have a strong marriage even though, during most of the ten years, one or the other has been in a heavy graduate-school program and their financial earnings have been low. Their income has kept up with their expenses only because they budget very carefully and buy very wisely.

While most of their peers now own homes, have at least two luxury or sports cars, and take expensive vacations, Phil and Nancy live in a modest condominium, drive a small, old, carefully maintained car, and take two-day camping vacations.

Their school and work schedules are very demanding. Yet Phil and Nancy have fun. They plan their weekends and most of their evenings so that they can do things together. They surprise each other with love notes and gifts or inexpensive "adventure" trips to the yogurt shop, an art exhibit, or the arboretum. They are fully behind each other in their work and school. Phil shares in the household work, and Nancy helps with their car maintenance so that they can be together.

If one or the other is under a particular strain with a certain work or school project, the other pitches in and carries more of the load at home for a while. They deliberately choose to nurture each other. Their relationship is a refreshing model to us and to others.

Commitment is a choice to invest, unconditionally, in the well-being of the other person. It is the determination to hold steady when the temptation might be to run from a difficult situation. It is a willingness to go that extra mile, or ten miles. Commitment gives a person staying power.

A Choice to Be a Bonder

Bonding is a term used to define the united force between two people. We know that the bonding between an infant and his or her parents is important for the baby's emotional and physical health. Bonding between husband and wife also causes a marriage to flourish. We believe that commitment is one of the essential ingredients necessary so that marital bonding will take place.

Donald Joy has helped us discover the depths of bonding in his two books: *Bonding* and *Re-Bonding*.[4] He defines bonding as "the mystery of human attachment between two persons . . . so profound . . . that it cannot be understood merely in physiological terms. It includes biological, psychological, spiritual, even ethical dimensions. By pair bonding, I wish to refer to that exclusive, lifelong, mutually attaching relationship in which a woman and man form one new entity. . . while each retains individuality and integrity as a separate, distinct person, they together form a 'persona' both greater than and different from the sum of the two parts."[5]

Bonding may seem mystical or psychological, but its results are very tangible and visible. One of Webster's definitions of bonding is "to join securely." When you say you have strong bonds with someone, you are talking about ties that link you together. You share common interests. You have a history with each other.

Bonding is a process and takes time. It doesn't occur in an instant and doesn't necessarily happen because of repeating vows, having a sexual experience together, or growing up in the same neighborhood.

Marital bonding is special in that it also contains *exclusive* and *lifelong* in the definition. That's why the choice to stay married includes doing all you can to strengthen the bonds between you and your mate. It does encompass vows, a sexual relationship, and compatibility in as many areas as possible.

You can develop your marital bonds by deliberately looking for all the areas you have in common, rehearsing your history together, recounting your pleasant memories, promoting positive attitudes of love, and carrying out jillions of actions of building and affirming. The two of you together truly are, then, more than the sum of the two of you separately.

COMMITMENT IS TRUST

Masters and Johnson, internationally known for their study of human sexual behavior, define commitment as "a pledge to do something. One person tells another, 'I promise,' and the promise is kept, the obligation fulfilled. Trust has been asked for; trust has been given, and trust has been repaid. This is the basic meaning of commitment. It is the cement that binds individuals and groups together. Without the ability of one person to rely on another, the social bond would not exist."[6]

The marriage relationship is a legal bond, but it is much more. We commit ourselves and trust each other, not so much because of the legal contract of marriage, but because we have made a previous choice to be committed to this person. We are trustworthy because we care about the other person.

Lack of Trust Is Learned

Babies are born trusting. Distrust and untrustworthiness must be taught. Great-grandpa Conway used to tell a story that portrayed how a child's innocent trust can be broken.

A father put his three-year-old son on the kitchen table, then stood about three feet away, and said, "Jump to me, Mikey." The boy smiled and leaped out toward his father. But the father stepped back and let the boy fall flat on his face on the floor. The father picked him up, put him back on the table, and smiled pleasantly at his crying son as he urged, "Jump to me, Mikey! Jump to Daddy!" The boy jumped again, and again his father let him fall on the floor.

The father put his son on the table a third time and begged him to jump. The boy was puzzled and said, "Don't drop me this time, Daddy, O.K.?" The father said, "O.K., Mikey. Jump to me. Jump to me." The boy leaped toward his father again, and the father stepped aside, letting him crash to the floor.

The father picked the boy up, stood him on the table once more, and said, "Son, I want you to remember this lesson. Don't ever trust anyone, not even your father."

Blatant experiences such as this, or insidious, subtle ones, eventually teach us to be wary. Each of us enters marriage with our past experiences of "trust betrayed" and "trust honored." Some of us have had more good encounters than bad, but even one traumatic time of broken trust can influence feelings and attitudes in marriage.

Arlene told us that she had been very much in love with Vinnie when she was in high school. They had been going steady for several months. Then she learned that on the nights when she wasn't out with him, he was dating Martha from another high school who also thought they were going steady. Arlene felt heartbroken and betrayed. She grieved for months. Her hurt was two-pronged: He wasn't really hers as he had let her think and she felt she looked like a fool to her friends.

Although it is many years later and she is now married to a trustworthy man, she said she often struggles with feeling suspicious of her husband. She finds it easy to be jealous of any other woman in his life, no matter what the reason is for her husband and another woman to have contact.

Being the one who is untrustworthy can be a problem too. Somehow, through inadequate training experiences in life's early years or through poor choices as an adult, some people develop a habit of letting others down. This pattern of being unreliable can carry over into marriage in spite of good intentions to be different.

By mid-life most marriages have experienced some breakdowns in trust. They may have occurred from small things such as not keeping a family secret, forgetting a birthday, or not remembering to cancel the onions on your wife's hamburger order.

On the other hand, trust may have been more severely violated by your taking that drink you said you wouldn't, flirting at a party, having a full-blown affair, or taking money needed to pay bills and using it for your own interests. Whatever the case, it's necessary to **work** at trusting your mate again and to **work** at being worthy of your mate's trust.

Marriage demands commitment, and part of commitment is trust. Trust can't be ignored. It would be like saying, "Oh, I don't mind if the car doesn't have any spark plugs. I have all the other pieces." Without spark plugs, the engine just won't run. Without trust, your marriage won't function as a marriage.

The good news is that if you have learned not to trust or not to be trustworthy, you can unlearn those negative traits and replace them with positive ones. If your trust problem in either area is severe, you may need professional counseling to help you break old habits.

You Can Learn to Be Trustworthy

Reliable, mature friends and/or your mate can also help you become trustworthy, especially if you ask them to help you be accountable. Ask God to help you be honest. Then deliberately decide each day to practice keeping your word, as Kent did.

After Kent and Bonnie had been married a few years, they began to realize that Kent had a problem with being completely honest. He didn't deliberately plan to be dishonest, but he often shaded the truth to his advantage and frequently broke his commitment for meeting certain responsibilities. His employer also began to call to his attention that he didn't always keep his word.

Although Kent had this problem, he also was a sensitive, conscientious person and wanted to change. He and Bonnie talked about it and decided that they both would pray every day for God to help him. He asked Bonnie to show him areas where he wasn't as dependable as he should be. In return, she was generally very gentle when she pointed out what she saw as dishonesty. Because she knew he was working on the problem, she was more forgiving if he had a momentary relapse.

Kent even got up the courage to share his problem with his pastor and a small group of men who met weekly. They agreed to pray for him regularly and to encourage him. The day came when Kent could say, "I am now a dependable person. Sometimes I slip back into my old habits, but I'm improving."

If you need to strengthen trustworthiness in your life, try reading a few verses from the book of Proverbs each day. Apply those principles that day. When you finish the entire book, you will be surprised at how much more you know about reliability and honesty. Those qualities will start to become a natural part of your life.

You Can Learn to Trust Your Mate

If you're having trouble trusting your mate, keep a list of all the positive reasons you have for trusting. List specific occasions for trust in the past. We suggested that Arlene (the woman whose trust was destroyed by her high-school boyfriend) do this so that she could begin to feel confident in her husband. We also have suggested this to people whose mates, because of an affair or other betrayals, have given them concrete reason to mistrust them. As you see the list of trust experiences growing, you will gradually have your confidence rebuilt.

From T*he Living Bible*, read chapter 13 of 1 Corinthians several times. Especially let verse 7 sink in: **"If you love someone you will be loyal to him no matter what the cost. You will always believe in him, always expect the best of him, and always stand your ground in defending him."** That is **love!** That is **trust!**

We also suggest reading books such as *Healing for Damaged Emotions, Healing of Memories,* and *Forgive and Forget.*[7]

Of course, the ideal solution is for you and your mate to discuss the lack of trust in your relationship and work at it together. That takes time and a willingness to be vulnerable and open to change. There may be pain, but the results are worth the effort. (In the next chapter we will talk about how to communicate better.)

COMMITMENT REQUIRES ENDURANCE

In high school and college I (Jim) ran track: the half-mile, mile, and two-mile. I never did like to run, but I started running in high school as a way to impress a girlfriend. Even though I hated it, it was a way for me to have the acceptance and success I so desperately needed.

I particularly disliked running the mile. The first lap (a quarter of a mile) was easy to do, because, basically, I was running on adrenaline. I usually felt like I was flying around that lap. The second lap was even more fun. My body was not stressed and I was not overcharged.

Halfway through the third lap, however, it seemed as if the race would never end. My heart was pounding, my lungs were burning, and my legs were beginning to feel like rubber. It was a dreadful feeling to finish the third lap, realizing that I had a full lap to go before the race was over.

As the fourth lap started, I usually experienced a momentary surge of extra adrenaline. My pace picked up. But halfway through that lap, with every ounce of my energy depleted, my legs really turned to rubber. My lungs felt as if they were raw, and my heart wanted to explode out of my chest. Yet I knew that when I got two-thirds through this last lap, I was supposed to accelerate and run faster than I had through the whole race.

Again and again the debate would rage within me as I neared the halfway mark on the fourth lap. My mind would say, *All right, Body, in just a few more yards I'm going to ask you to really pour on the steam and run as fast as you can.* My body would respond in disbelief, *You're out of your mind, Mind! I have poured out every ounce of energy and strength that I have. What do you mean, run faster?* The discussion would rage within me for about fifty yards, but as I started the third turn, my mind would say, *Now, kick!*

The minds of the other runners were also forcing their bodies to run faster. We each drew energy from some unknown resource and began to run faster and faster so that those tired, exhausted bodies, which couldn't even feel the track beneath them, were now running at their maximum speed, each hoping to be the first man to cross the finish line.

Where did that extra energy come from? Our bodies and personalities have an extra source of physical and emotional energy that we ordinarily don't use. Under circumstances of challenge, we are able to draw on that hidden source to finish a task that we have committed ourselves to carry out. The capacity to finish a task that may seem superhuman, or above and beyond the call of duty, is called **endurance.**

True marital commitment must have a dimension of endurance, the ability to stick with the relationship through thick or thin. The difference between endurance and commitment only for commitment's sake, as we discussed at the beginning of the chapter, is the motive. Endurance sees the positives in the relationship and in the mate. The person with endurance focuses on the big picture and knows this present problem is not all there is.

Marital commitment may need to call on hidden resources to go through what might seem to be hell itself. Many husbands and wives who learn their mates are having an affair tell us they are surprised at their reaction. They find a strength they didn't know they had. Instead of unraveling, they are able to assess the situation and start taking action that will help correct the situation.

Ways to call on these hidden resources might involve stepping back to take an objective look at all your mate's good qualities, taking a break to do something energizing for yourself for a few hours, or looking for new ways to affirm your mate and finding yourself also nourished in the process.

Tapping your unseen assets might mean getting serious with God in a way you never have before. You might find that earnest prayer and reading the Bible really do have something to offer. As you get your fresh perspective, you will find you have a strength to endure that you didn't know you had.

Endurance is like the material in a man's socks. They are made of 80 percent high bulk orlon and 20 percent nylon. The nylon is a webbing that holds the high bulk orlon in place. Have you ever noticed the heels and toes where the orlon has worn away? There isn't a hole; the material is just thin. The nylon is still there.

In a sense, endurance in a marital commitment is like the nylon webbing in a sock. It doesn't wear out. Everything else around it may go, but it's still there, doing its job of holding the marriage together.

COMMITMENT TAKES TIME

Building commitment in your marriage requires spending time together. We strongly believe that **marriages are held together by understanding and meeting each other's needs.** That understanding comes through taking sufficient time with each other to discuss problems, joys, dreams, goals, decisions, family matters—to know how each thinks and feels about all areas of life and to keep up with the ways each is growing and changing.

Couples who habitually dash past each other in the bedroom and bathroom as they hurriedly dress for work, or quickly gulp dinner standing at the kitchen counter before they rush off to separate meetings, or fall exhausted into bed late every night without energy to talk, cuddle, or make love, are not building commitment. They are building disaster.

Researchers have proven a phenomenon that we all know is true, if we think about it. It's a simple principle. Generally speaking, couples who get divorced have spent less time with each other than have couples who stay married. Communication and compatibility are important to marital success, but taking time to be with each other has been found to be more important.[8]

We are deliberately using the term **taking time,** because you do have to **"take"** the time from all the other forces in your daily lives that squeeze in on your marriage relationship. We have found it helpful to schedule times with each other, which we view as important as any other calendar appointment.

We also have small daily times with each other that we keep strictly for each other—eating, reading the mail together, taking walks, chatting before going to sleep. You should build in "together" times with whatever works for you. Remember, aside from spending time with God, spending time with your spouse is the most important thing you have to do.

In a later chapter you will find some more specific ideas on how to spend time together as we share what we have learned from our survey couples and others.

COMMITMENT INVOLVES SELF-DEVELOPMENT

Commitment in marriage is a commitment to continue to grow as an individual, so that year by year we can more fully enjoy who we are, feeling successful and productive in life in general and in our marriage.

Mid-life people frequently comment that their marriage is stale and boring. A serious commitment to marriage means that we will find ways to grow so we can offer to our spouse a person who is fresh and on the cutting edge of life.

One man answering our survey said, "Life cannot be static. Growth should be a better description of one's progress through the different stages of life." In other words, we shouldn't just get old; we should be growing and developing more completely as we move through life. Personal growth is one of the ten keys to an intimate and lasting marriage to be considered in more detail in a later chapter.

CHOICE BUILDS COMMITMENT

We said earlier that commitment is a choice. In fact, all of life is made of choices. We can choose to be committed to our mate, to grow as an individual, and to count our blessings. We are really as happy in life and in our marriages as we want to be. Think about that!

We know many people whose marriages, by all external appearances, could be rotten and unfulfilling. Some have drastic physical limitations, a traumatic past, or other difficult circumstances. Some of these people are devastated and defeated; others are joyful and reach out to help others. Why the difference?

The Wilsons and the Palmers are a study in contrast. Both couples started out marriage in a low income bracket. Then Carl Wilson began to advance quickly in his job. The promotions meant their family could move, and they chose a larger house in a more affluent neighborhood of the same city. The Palmers also made a move about this time, but to a different state. Each couple had two children.

Shortly after the Palmers moved, they were pleasantly surprised to learn that they were going to have an unplanned baby. The Wilsons, too, learned they were going to have an unexpected baby—and they were horrified.

Soon after the Palmers' baby was born, Brenda Palmer discovered she was in the beginning stages of rheumatoid arthritis. Caring for her children and house became very painful, but Brenda did it cheerfully most of the time. Kevin arranged his work schedule so he could give her as much extra help as possible, but she still had to carry on as a mother and homemaker many hours when it would have been easier to worry only about herself.

In the meantime, at the Wilson household all was not going well. No one was ill, but Sue Wilson was resenting Carl's working long hours, leaving her with the new baby and managing the home alone so much of the time. The more she complained, the more Carl stayed away. He didn't feel he had any responsibility for helping her carry the load. Eventually the Wilsons' unhappiness grew to such a level that they divorced.

The Palmers, on the other hand, have now been married twenty-six years and are a strong family. Their two older children are grown and gone; the younger one will graduate from high school soon. Brenda's arthritis is very advanced, but she doesn't let it consume all the family's attention and energy.

Of course, many factors are involved in why one couple divorced and the other did not. We cannot make simple judgment calls, but we do know enough about both families to detect that part of the difference was in the choices that each couple made. The Palmers chose to work together and support each other when the surprise baby arrived and Brenda's illness struck. Carl and Sue Wilson chose to defend their individual interests and did not see the other one's needs as something they could at least emotionally support with empathy.

We can determine to make the best of our problems, or we can allow the same circumstances to demoralize and destroy us. It is a choice we each make with each event that comes into our lives.

Years ago Dr. Viktor Frankl said, "Everything can be taken from a man but one thing: the last of the human freedoms—to choose one's attitude in any given set of circumstances, to choose one's own way."[9]

When you choose to be committed to a specific marriage partner, you should be making that choice on the basis of several rational facts. Of course, some irrational, emotional things may also be part of your decision, but it's helpful to think through the specific reasons why you are choosing to be committed to this marriage partner alone.

In fact, you might want to stop right now and make a written list of those reasons. Leave it where you can keep adding to it over the next few days. You might be surprised at the long list you compile.

In the process of evaluating your reasons for the choice, you, no doubt, will be confronted with the losses you'll experience if you commit yourself only to this person. As you think these through, you will probably say, "There are losses, but they are less important than the gains. The positive benefits outweigh the negatives." If your list of negatives is longer than your list of positives, go back to your power of choice and decide that you are going to focus on positives instead of negatives. Lasting commitment is a rational as well as an emotional choice.

PROBLEMS CAN BUILD COMMITMENT

A test will probably challenge your commitment. The test may be another person or the compounding of many forces: troubles at work, difficulties with the kids, pain-in-the-neck in-laws, illness, or lack of emotional support from your mate. Instead of helping you, sometimes the people around you may seem hell-bent on irritating you to the point of insanity.

Your instinctive drive may be to run away, to escape the overpressured situation. Or you may want to retaliate and get even: "You're hurting me. I'll hurt you back."

Perhaps your instinctive drive is for self-gratification. You may see in a third person the potential for a very fulfilling relationship. Unconsciously, you have slipped back into your mother's arms, seeking love, care, and nourishment.

You may be asking—and perhaps very justly so—"Why do I have to put up with this? It's time I get some of my own needs met instead of always giving to others."

A word that describes why, as well as how, you should "put up" is **sublimation.** Sublimation means **the redirection of instinctive drives on the basis of self-chosen principles for the purpose of fulfilling long-range goals.** This means you deny those immediate, pressing drives and redirect them so the goals you want to accomplish in your life and in your marriage are really achieved.

In practical actions, sublimation means you don't physically or verbally abuse each other, because you know that will not accomplish your long-range goals. You don't threaten each other by withholding sex or by flirting with someone else. Those actions will make your mate feel less confident and will erode your marriage relationship.

In other words, you're not going to allow your instincts to pressure you into a momentary gratification that ultimately will have damaging effects on your long-term marriage relationship. Sublimation will enable you to be committed.

We build our marriage by the choices we make day by day. A marriage relationship is not just saying one "I do" at the wedding ceremony. Instead the relationship is formed by the many small "I do's" and "I don'ts" each day, which become an accumulation of hundreds of thousands of "I do's" and "I don'ts."

A wealthy man was concerned about the financial plight of a homebuilder who was a fellow member of his church. The rich man went to the builder and asked him to build a house. He wanted nothing spared in the quality of materials and the workmanship.

The builder was grateful for the job, but he saw an opportunity to increase his profits by using inferior materials and cutting corners on the quality of craftsmanship. None of the shoddy work or cheaper materials showed, but the builder knew things were not built as they ought to have been.

When the house was completed, the rich man said to the builder, "I've been concerned for you. I want to help you get back on your feet. As a result, I'm going to give you this house to own for as long as you live in it."

As you can imagine, the builder was astonished. He was also very sorry he hadn't built a better house.

In a sense, each choice we make for our marriage is like an extra nail or a reinforcing piece for a house. It's either built with quality materials and high craftsmanship or with just enough materials and quality to get by.

Key #2
Good
Communication

An Indian legend describes creation and the first communication problems between man and woman. The Creator made woman and presented her to man.

After one week man came to the Creator and said, "Lord, this creature that you have given me makes my life miserable. She chatters incessantly. She never leaves me alone and wants me to talk to her all the time. She takes up all my time and cries about nothing. I have come to give her back again as I cannot live with her."

So the Creator said, "Very well." And he took her back.

After another week man came again to him and said, "Lord, I find that my life is very lonely since I gave that creature back to you. I do not like all the silence now that she is gone. I remember how she used to dance and sing to me. Her laughter was music, and she was beautiful to look at and soft to touch. Give her back to me again."

So the Creator said, "Very well." And he gave her back again.

Then after only three days, the man came back to him and said, "Lord, I know not how it is, but after all, I have come to the conclusion that this creature is more of a trouble than a pleasure to me. So please take her back again."

But the Creator said, "Be off! I will have no more of this. You must manage however you can."

The man said, "What is to be done? For I cannot live with her or without her."[1]

It's Not Easy

Adjusting our expectations and needs so we will be comfortable with our mate's expectations and needs has been the big challenge through the centuries. To do so requires good communication so that each one has expressed his or her thoughts, feelings, and desires in a way that the other hears and understands.

Successful communication builds and maintains successful marriages. That sounds simple, but it's not. One of the complaints we hear most often is, "He just won't communicate. I've tried for years to get him to talk." Or, "It's impossible to understand her. We're just not on the same wavelength, so I've given up."

Several couples reported that their communication had changed over the years: "During our mid-life crisis years we had a minimum of communication. But now that things are good it really helps to share."

Some of the couples had great insight into themselves and the whole communication process. A husband married thirty-eight years said, "We have learned to express our feelings and thoughts as our own, without intimidating or putting the other person on the defensive."

A husband married forty-two years put it clearly, "Every solution that is a right solution is born of communication."

This man really has it figured out. Their marriage has not been easy. They've struggled all their married years with differing views on money. They have also had a difficult time with her sexual coolness after menopause.

He sums up his comments with a classic statement, "Many conflicts (or differing opinions) will never be resolved, but communication is what has held us together."

The Missing Glue

A major key in helping our survey marriages was that the couples communicated, although some of our survey couples still had trouble in that area. Usually the communication difficulties have developed from some common, basic problems through the years, as in the case of Dan and Grace.

Dan's financial success in his business was evidenced by his new cars, luxury home, and retreat home in the mountains. But he would not talk to his wife, Grace. At least, that was her report to us.

Grace felt that Dan lacked empathy and understanding. He apparently wasn't interested in what was happening in her life, and he didn't share what was going on in his. She knew little or nothing about his business and, from her point of view, he didn't seem to care that she didn't.

When she came to talk about her marriage problems, we found that a negative pattern had evolved through their married years. At first they had good communication, but it gradually disappeared. Each one had become preoccupied with what they were doing—Grace in raising the children and Dan in making his business a success.

When they did attempt to share their concerns with each other, the other one seemed disinterested. On many occasions one would say directly to the other, "Well, you take care of that. It's your area." Gradually their lives separated emotionally so they had nothing to talk about. They really had nothing in common.

We Don't Know How

Their situation is not uncommon, according to other counselors and psychologists. Dr. Roy Rhodes, a Dallas psychologist, has said, "The average couple married ten years or more spends only thirty-seven minutes a week in close communication."[2] Other counselors and researchers report slightly different amounts of time, but everyone is agreed that couples do not spend enough time communicating with one another. The greater problem is that most people don't even know how.

Communication difficulties are a rather recent concern. Dr. David Mace reports, "I once made a survey of what I considered to be the twenty-six best books on marriage published between 1930 and 1970 in order to find out how they treated the subject. Most of them scarcely mentioned it at all. Of those that did, only a few had any real perception of its importance."[3]

Even though the number of books and seminars on communication skills has increased greatly since 1970, communication is still a major problem in homes today. In a 1983 study reported in *Traits of a Healthy Family*, Dolores Curran, educator and syndicated columnist with over three million weekly readers, surveyed over 550 marriage and family counselors. She discovered that communication was identified as the number one family problem.[4]

As we said earlier, our forefathers married to insure physical and economic survival in the remote and rugged territories of our developing country. Today, however, marriage partners also expect a meaningful relationship and companionship. These new needs demand better communication.

Many people, especially men who lived by the old standards, were not prepared for these rapidly changing marriage expectations of communication and intimacy. They think that all a woman wants is a macho man who provides money and gives her a hug now and then. Unfortunately, most men were not taught communication skills as children or teenagers, and they have not cultivated them as adults. In fact, the sensitive characteristics of understanding and intimacy are often mocked by the man's peers.

Roommates or Intimates?

Whenever the topic of communication comes up in our seminars, we can almost feel the audience polarizing. To women, communication means sharing themselves, their life's dreams, aspirations, joys, and problems. They want to understand the other person in the same terms. Women view communication as a way to arrive at companionship.

Men think of communication in terms of solving problems, making choices, giving advice, or discussing plans. Men are good at communicating as long as the topic has little or nothing to do with their value systems, feelings, hopes, or fears.

A man in our study, married thirty-four years, confessed, "My wife always listened to me. However, I often considered her conversations 'small talk' and did not listen to her like I should have."

Communication breakdown in a marriage frequently has nothing to do with the ability of both people to talk, but with **what they talk about.** Women are willing to disclose themselves; men generally are not. Many men view the marriage relationship as being **roommates,** who never talk about deep stuff, but women think of it as **intimates,** who share their innermost secrets.

Language Problems

Communication is not simply the ability to talk to someone; it also implies that you are understood and accepted by the other one. We live in a world with thousands of languages, but in reality we have nearly five billion languages. That is, each person has his or her own language composed of the way he or she uses words and the unique meanings he or she gives to those words.

Being able to speak and understand English does not necessarily mean that I can communicate with someone else who speaks English. Communication includes a willingness to share myself with another person and a desire to understand that other person.

This is illustrated by the woman who went to see a divorce lawyer.

Frantically, she said, "I *must* have a divorce from my husband immediately!"

The lawyer asked, "Is he beating you?"

"No," the woman replied. "I get up before he does."

"Do you have grounds?" the lawyer asked.

"Yes, about five acres," she answered.

"I mean, do you have a grudge?" the lawyer questioned.

"No, just a carport."

Exasperated, the attorney demanded, "Madam, why do you want a divorce from your husband?"

"Because it is impossible to communicate with that man!"

REASONS FOR NOT COMMUNICATING

Why don't we communicate? As the two of us have observed our own communication and have counseled with people over the years, we have come to believe that there are several major reasons why people don't communicate effectively.

Afraid of Rejection

If I open up to you and let you see my joys, fears, values, goals in life, you might reject me. If I only show you a mask and you reject it, I can say, "Well, you rejected the mask, not the real me."

One man said, "If I tell my wife that her being overweight really turns me off, then she will feel rejected and attack me. We are so afraid of hurting each other or being rejected that we never get near the truth. We just sweep our emotions under the carpet with all of the ignored truth of other years."

Wary of Criticism

If I share a part of myself with you that isn't up to your standards, you might criticize me. You might jab where I am most vulnerable. Therefore, I am guarded about what I disclose. If I only talk to you about surface matters, I never have to share the deeper part of me or any of my ideas that are only in the thinking stage. Since I'm never sure what you'll criticize, it's easier not to talk at all.

Intimidated by Advice-giving

Let's imagine a scene in a typical home: A husband and wife get together at the end of a hard day. The wife begins to share how burned out she feels, trying to keep up with her part-time job, the kids, and all the housework. She is appealing for understanding.

Instead the husband may treat this as a problem-solving opportunity and, without much thought, jump into the role of a time management expert. He might say, "You know, you could save yourself a lot of time if you'd put bigger loads in the washer, if you didn't fold the towels in thirds, and if you'd make the kids clean up their rooms so you didn't have to do it."

All of that may be true, but that's not really what his wife needed. As a result, the wife who receives advice instead of understanding will shy away from sharing the next time. Advice-giving just compounds the problem. She now has all of her work, plus the feelings of inadequacy and being misunderstood.

She is perhaps also angry at her husband, because he doesn't help with the work.

Each of these three reasons for communication breakdown are fears that have a common thread going back to a person's self-image. A person afraid of rejection, criticism, or advice may not be emotionally strong enough at the time to handle these reactions from the mate. Furthermore, each of these responses puts the second person in a one-upmanship position over the one who wants to communicate. Not many people are able to share openly with another person who is looking down on them. When equality is lost, so is communication.

Burned Out

Another reason for communication breakdown is fatigue and burnout. If either of you is tired, your ability to understand and make yourself understood is impaired.

When Jim was going through the worst of his mid-life crisis, I had to accept the times when he just could not give himself to good communication with me. He was burned out from giving himself to other people for many years as a caring pastor/counselor. Some evenings he would just sit and stare at the TV, no matter what was on.

Our three daughters and I were also part of his problem. He had been pouring himself out for everyone, including us, for a long time. When some family decision needed to be made, he simply didn't have the emotional energy to talk about it.

I remember once when I asked him if Becki could go to a certain movie, he defiantly responded, "You decide. Don't lean on me! I don't have the energy to think." Later, when his physical and emotional health began to be restored, he could communicate again.

If you or your mate is burned out, you need to patiently work on getting physically and emotionally restored before you try to improve communication. Interestingly, as your life becomes better balanced and renewed, you will be able to communicate better.

Distracted and Disinterested

Other communication obstacles may be from straightforward causes, such as an event or problem that commands more attention at the time, or a lack of interest in the subject the mate wants to discuss, or perhaps even a lack of interest in the mate.

The possibility of disinterest in the mate is a threatening thought, but even that can be corrected. Remember, people are drawn to someone who understands them and meets their needs. As with any other relationship deficiency, both people involved need to work to bring about healthy communication. We hope the following ideas help.

ELEMENTS OF POSITIVE COMMUNICATION

Communication is a complex process, but perhaps it will help to look at several aspects of this process of exchanging information and understanding between marriage partners.

Do's and Don'ts in Communication

Sometimes we learn what to do by understanding **what not to do.** We have listed some don'ts, and we have also listed their positive counterparts. Check yourself against this list to see how healthy your communication is.

Don'ts	Do's
▶ Don't be judgmental.	▶ Be accepting and tolerant.
▶ Don't expect too much from one session.	▶ Be planning to talk again.
▶ Don't bring up your mate's past.	▶ Be forgiving.
▶ Don't butt in or be rude.	▶ Be as courteous as to a stranger.
▶ Don't overstate by saying, "You always . . ." "You never . . ."	▶ Be accurate by saying, "Sometimes . . ." "Many times . . ." "To me it seems . . ."

▸ Don't lose your temper.

▸ Be in control of yourself.

▸ Don't pout and give the silent treatment.

▸ Be positive, outgoing, and unselfish (even when you don't feel like it).

▸ Don't tell endless stories.

▸ Be concise.

▸ Don't compete.

▸ Be seeing yourself as an equal partner.

▸ Don't think in terms of winning and losing.

▸ Be cooperative and noncombative.

▸ Don't belittle your mate.

▸ Be affirming and building.

Communication Is Dialogue

Communication is more than dispensing information. It is dialogue, an exchange of ideas and opinions in an atmosphere of acceptance and understanding.

John Powell in *The Secret of Staying in Love* says: "Dialogue is to enable the partners to come to a deeper knowledge, understanding, and fuller acceptance of each other in love. Dialogue is always moving towards encounter, towards the mutual experience of each other's person through this sharing of feelings .... No one ever needs a reason, excuse or explanation for the way he feels. It's okay to feel whatever we feel. The only real danger is to ignore, deny or refuse to report our feelings .... True dialogue is characterized by a sense of collaboration not competition .... The only valid motive for dialogue is this desire to give to another the most precious thing I can give: myself in self-disclosure, in the transparency achieved in dialogue."[5]

Dialogue will fall apart when one person tries to use words—or the lack of words—to control the other person. Sometimes I (Jim) will push Sally into a corner with logical arguments that she can't answer. She may break down and cry, feeling that I don't really care about her. The truth is that I just want to win the argument.

At other times I won't talk. In a subtle way, I'm using my

silence as a power over her, almost as a punishment for some injustice I may feel. Sometimes Sally will tell me to quit sulking and feeling sorry for myself. Frequently that drives me deeper into a hole. In a sense, both of us are using words to manipulate each other, and when we do this, we are not drawn closer to each other.

Communication Is Self-disclosure

In order for two people to effectively communicate with each other, they must be willing to open up to each other. When we expose ourselves to another, we are risking damage to our innermost self. Yet, without disclosing ourselves, we are not genuinely communicating.

After *McCall's* magazine published an article entitled "When the Man You Love Can't Show His Feelings" in November 1980, thousands of women wrote to the editors, affirming that their husbands were silent and passive. They said their husbands were good fathers and providers but did not know how to develop an intimate relationship. One woman said, "I do not feel loved. Now should be the time when we are getting closer together and finding new ways to make life interesting. But there is no communication, only criticism and silence. Is it too late to make a change?"[6]

Without a degree of self-disclosure, we cheat ourselves from the benefits of good communication. John Powell explains, "To the extent that I have hidden myself from you, the meaning of your love will be diminished. I will forever fear that you love only the part of me that I have let you know; and that if you knew the real me, all of me, you would not love me. Love follows upon knowledge, and so you can love me only to the extent that I let you know me."[7]

Communication assumes disclosure to yourself as well as to the other person. In fact, you cannot reveal yourself with integrity to another person if you don't also honestly acknowledge to yourself who you really are, with your strengths, weaknesses, failures, potential for growth, and all that makes you "you."

Honest disclosure *will* result in personal growth. Every time you encounter another person—by understanding and being understood—you are changed. You see life in a slightly different way. Therefore, when you involve yourself in communication, you will experience personal growth because you have opened yourself up to the other person and to yourself.

Communication Is Hard Work

Obviously, communication is not an easy process, and on some occasions it could be highly threatening. Communication takes effort. It's very different from sitting back in the Lazy-Boy chair with a remote control in your hand, passively watching TV. You don't have to move, think, or interact with TV. You're never actually exposed to those people. Your ideas, feelings, opinions, and values can be kept to yourself. No one is going to come out of that tube and challenge you or ask you to enlarge on what you're thinking.

True communication takes energy. You have to think about how to take emotions and translate them into words in such a way that the true impact of your feelings can be understood by the other person.

Accurate communication may demand that you take past patterns and adjust them to your current values. In the process you may have to throw away old feelings and expressions and use more appropriate words that indicate where you are today.

Arlene, the woman mentioned in the previous chapter whose marriage was being affected because of the betrayal of her high-school boyfriend, Vinnie, had to learn new ways of thinking and talking. We coached her to reprogram her mind so that she did not view her husband as her teenage boyfriend. She had to tell herself that all men were not the same; her husband was not going to leave her.

She also stopped using phrases such as "You're just like Vinnie!" Arlene needed to live in the "now" with her marriage and not impose old patterns onto her husband.

An effective communication encounter between you and someone else is hard work and should cause your adrenaline to go up, your heart rate to increase, and your palms to perspire slightly. To some degree, it may wear you out, but the overall process should be exhilarating because you were able to share a part of yourself with another person. That person also shared a part of himself or herself with you, and both of you have more fully accepted each other as you really are.

By mid-life most couples settle into a pattern of communication, or lack of it, that meets their needs. However, when one or both of them has a mid-life crisis, they usually experience a collision that forces them to start talking to each other.

One woman said, "Before my husband had a mid-life crisis, we didn't hear what the other one was saying. He thought he told me but I had no recollection."

Another couple after a mid-life crisis said simply, "Now, he listens, I listen; he hears, I hear."

Caution: If you have not effectively communicated with your mate in recent years, the experience may not be fun at first. But keep at it, because your understanding and relationship will improve.

Communication Takes Time

Dr. Paul Tournier has said, "It is impossible to overemphasize the immense need humans have to be really listened to, to be taken seriously, to be understood. No one can develop freely in this world and find life without feeling understood by at least one person."[8]

Being understood by another person will not happen with one rushed experience of communication. You need many encounters in a relaxed atmosphere even to begin to know and understand each other.

If people never changed, you would not have to keep working at the process of understanding. The truth is, however, change is taking place every day. Unless you take the time to understand your changing mate, at mid-life you may be living with a stranger.

A wife in our study who was married twenty-six years said, "It takes time together to feel secure enough to bring up emotionally charged subjects."

Communication Should Reveal *Your* Perspective

Instead of a declaration of "truth," you should express your feelings, thoughts, and observations as **your** perception. This attitude then allows the other person to have his or her perception also.

You should not make pronouncements such as, "You are a careless clod because you forgot my birthday!" It would be better to say, "I feel you don't care about me when you forget my birthday." This allows you to express your feeling of being neglected, but you are saying it is **your feeling** without accusing the other person of intentionally hurting you.

Instead of making statements like, "You are thoughtless and always make the whole family late by never being on time for dinner," try saying, "It seems to me that you are often late for dinner, and that is very inconvenient for the rest of the family's schedules."

In place of "You try to make me feel stupid by always butting in and finishing my sentences," say something like, "I feel very put down when you interrupt what I'm saying."

The idea of using "I" messages has been recommended by communication experts for many years, but we still don't find that many couples have put the skill to work. It takes practice, but it's worth it. Just begin your sentences with "I" rather than "you."

When you say, "I feel," "I perceive," "I think," you are owning the thoughts and feelings as your point of reference. This allows for your mate's point of reference to be credible while still maintaining your credibility. Your feelings are truly yours, but your mate won't need to feel he or she is being attacked. Complete communication has taken place when your mate has also used "I" messages to express his or her point of view and you both are working on a solution.

Communication Requires Courtesy

Isn't it odd that we are usually more polite to a total stranger than we are to our husband or wife? The one we vowed to love and cherish often gets the leftovers of our civility. We certainly should be able to let down, relax, and feel at home around our spouse, but that doesn't mean we act rudely.

We've noticed that one mate will frequently interrupt or speak for the other one. This was part of the communication problem with Dan and Grace, the wealthy couple we mentioned earlier who faced their responsibilities separately rather than together. When we would look at Dan and ask him a direct question in a counseling session, invariably, Grace would answer. Or, if Dan started to make a comment and paused a moment to think exactly how he wanted to say it, Grace would interrupt and finish his sentence.

Answering for Dan or finishing his sentences had become such a habit for Grace that Dan didn't need to talk. In fact, Dan didn't even need to think while he was at home. Grace did all the thinking and the talking. Dan was conditioned by Grace not to communicate. By the way, this is not uncommon for married couples. The wife who complains that her husband doesn't talk frequently falls into this pattern of talking for him.

Other couples are bluntly frank with one another. They quote the Bible, saying, "We're to 'speak the truth in love,' "[9] but they put the emphasis on speaking the truth and forget the love part. Speaking the truth is to be balanced with loving, and speaking the truth is to include the positive and the affirming as well as the negative. Not many of us say the positive and encouraging things that need to be said. More often, we generously list criticisms and complaints.

A good rule to follow is, "Be kind to one another, tenderhearted, forgiving one another, just as God in Christ also forgave you."[10] When we remember how much God has had to erase in his pardoning us, we should do nothing less than be courteous and compassionate to our mate. Many couples' communication problems could be eased by practicing common courtesy, built on truth spoken kindly.

Communication Involves Body Talk

It's surprising, but true: Your body communicates more information to people than your words do. Communication researchers find that only 7 percent of our communication is actually in the content of what we say. An additional 38 percent is communicated through the tone of voice we use. An additional 55 percent is communicated through our overall body: a twitch around the mouth, a slight wrinkle in the forehead, narrowing or widening of the eyes, tightening of the jaw muscle, dilation of the eye pupils.[11]

An outsider may not notice these movements, but spouses understand. Subtle changes in the face indicate something's going on inside. Of course, overt actions, such as a yawning, glancing at your watch, or leaning forward to be nearer the person, are obvious signals that anyone can interpret.

It's important to remember, therefore, that you cannot rely only on what you say in communication. Your tone of voice and your body *must* agree with what you are saying, because your mate is picking up all of the signals.

Take a moment right now to evaluate a recent communication time with your mate. How much did you depend on your words? Was your body saying anything different from your words?

Now think about the messages you'd like your body to send the next time you communicate with your mate. Plan to look directly into your mate's face. Have your whole body in an attentive position. Lean slightly forward. Your body is now focused for real communication.

Sit close enough to your mate so that you can touch. If the discussion becomes threatening to your mate, reach out and give a touch of encouragement. You don't have to say a word, but your touch says, "I'm concerned. I accept you. You're O.K. I want you to continue. I'm glad we're talking."

Communication Must Be at the Right Moment

We do not learn at an even pace, nor do we communicate at a consistently high level. There are moments in our lives when we are more open to learn and to communicate. These are teachable moments or communication moments.

Usually these moments are directly related to events taking place in our lives or to new insights we have recently gained. We said earlier that we are continually being changed by our experiences and the events around us. Each of these change events not only changes us, but also presents a new opportunity for communication.

Since the most effective communication takes place at the right time, the one wanting to communicate must sense when this is. You can often aid in setting the right time by alerting your mate that you want to talk. You may need to make an "appointment" for a convenient time. Forcing communication when there isn't sufficient time or interest may damage the overall outcome. If your mate wants to talk when you're not ready, be courteous enough to set a later time. Then prepare yourself for a positive and profitable encounter.

Communication Succeeds with Positive Regard

We may learn many communication skills, such as courtesy, proper language, use of "I" messages, openness, vulnerability, and accurate body language, but the most important ingredient for effective marriage communication is **positive re-gard.** This was verified by a study that explored various communication attitudes and how much each contributed to marital satisfaction. Positive regard was found to be *the most significant attitude.*[12]

Positive regard means, "I prize you, I value you. You are different but that difference is a plus not a negative. I not only value what you do for me, I also value the qualities you have as a person."

Often Sally and I remind ourselves of how much we mean to each other. I am grateful for Sally's sensitivity to people, her wit and humor, her attention to detail, her deep commitment to God, and her unselfish service to me and our family.

I value Jim for his spiritual insights, his caring for me and treating me as an equal, his thoughtfulness and sharing of household work, his caring for our family and other people, his humor and intelligence, and his business wisdom. He is also a great . . . . (oh, well, I'm not going to share *everything* with you!).

You may have all the communication skills in the world, but if you don't value the other person, skills won't help. Or to quote the Bible, "If I . . . could speak in every language there is in all of heaven and earth, but didn't love others, I would only be making noise."[13]

The question is, How can we improve positive regard? A partial answer is that we generally like people we understand. We also tend to like people who like us and who accept, appreciate, and admire us. We also like people who meet our needs, who want us to grow, and who want the best for our lives.

If you want your mate to like you, you need to pattern your life so that it's easier for him or her to have positive regard for you. You need to help your mate understand you, and you need to be the likable person who can be affirmed.

You can build your positive regard for your mate if you begin to focus on his or her strong points and good qualities rather than the negative ones. You will like your mate better as you understand and express appreciation for who he or she really is and as you begin to invest yourself in meeting his or her needs. As you value your mate, communication will be easier.

A simple principle from the Bible is that our hearts follow the investment of our lives. (Where your treasure is, there will your heart be also.)[14] Invest in your spouse, and your heart will follow.

Key #3
Vital Spiritual
Life

We were getting acquainted with some of the people at a week-long conference when Bud and Helen began to share their story with us. We were attracted to them because of their optimistic, outgoing attitudes that easily integrated their vibrant Christian faith with everyday life.

Had we known them when they were younger, we would **not** have had the same high opinion of them. When they married, their lives were tangled with several complications, including Bud's drinking problem. Almost immediately their marriage was on the rocks.

Rigid Parents

Bud was still rebelling from the rigid control his parents held over him as a child. Although his family was wealthy and he enjoyed the luxuries, he resented his parents' domineering ways. They were inflexibly austere in their relationship with him.

He ran away from home at age sixteen and lied about his age to get into military service. He began drinking and often was insubordinate to his superior officers.

His parents were very embarrassed because he had dropped out of school and was often in trouble in the army. They didn't disown him, but they did cut off their flow of money to him and stopped having much contact with him. He was glad to be free from them.

When Bud was discharged, he wasn't sure what he wanted to do for a living. He had no special training and no money. He drifted from city to city, trying different jobs. He was involved with many women but none he cared to marry. He didn't have money to get married anyway; in fact, he was heavily into debt for a car and was always behind in the rent on his dingy little apartment.

New Hope

Then he met Helen. She was pretty and outgoing, and she seemed to love him enough to put up with his faults. She thought the drinking and his financial troubles could be straightened out once they married.

Helen actually was still reeling from a broken engagement and Bud offered the love she was seeking. He had a charming way about him and did a good job of convincing her that he was the security she desired. She felt he just needed someone to help him settle down.

They actually loved each other very much when they married, but Bud didn't settle down—at least, not the way Helen expected. She didn't mind working to help pay expenses, but she did resent his using her money for alcohol. She began to nag about it, and Bud felt she was becoming oppressive. He drank more; she nagged more.

Bud couldn't hold a job. He didn't like having Helen be the one making the living most of the time, but he felt she didn't understand that he just needed to find the right job. Helen felt it would help if he just stuck with one thing for a while, even if it wasn't what he really wanted.

Bud began making sure he wasn't around the house when Helen came home from work. Instead, he usually hung out at his favorite bar. Helen was often in bed when he staggered in late. Then she was up and gone to work before he dragged out of bed the next day. He kept excusing himself about not having a job and he couldn't see that he was drinking too much.

Frightened—Angry—Lonely

Where is the security that marriage was supposed to bring? Helen wondered. She was lonely, tired of that cramped little apartment in a bad part of town, and disgusted that Bud couldn't control his drinking and hold a job. She was scared too. What was he really doing those nights he wasn't home? Did he have another woman?

Whenever Helen tried talking to Bud, he would get angry and accuse her of being a watchdog over his life. Finally one day, he screamed at her, "My parents dictated every move I was to make, and you're trying to do the same. Well, you know what I did to get them off my back, don't you? Do you want me to do the same to you? I'll just leave and you can be rid of me. And I can have some peace."

He didn't leave, but Helen did. She had felt humiliated before when her former fiancé had broken their engagement, and she wasn't going to be the one to be abandoned again.

Helen and Bud didn't have many friends because Helen had tried to hide Bud's drinking problem, but she did have one girlfriend from work who let her move in with her temporarily. Helen was uncomfortable there and missed Bud terribly, even though she wouldn't have seen much of him if she were at home.

A Turning Point

Bud was furious because she left, but he wouldn't let her know he cared. When he was stone drunk one day, he had a car accident which wasn't too serious, but he did have to be taken to the hospital because of broken ribs. The hospital notified Helen at work.

Helen wasn't sure if she should go to see Bud in the hospital right away. During lunch she talked with Margaret, a Christian who worked in the same office with her. Because of all that had happened, Helen was open to listening to Margaret explain God's love for her. She began to see that the love and security she had been longing for could only come from God. She wanted the personal friendship with God that Margaret talked about.

She gave her life to God as she and Margaret prayed, and immediately she felt at peace. She even had hope that God could do something about Bud.

The New Beginning

As Bud sobered up, he could feel the pain of his broken ribs. He also began to think more clearly about Helen and the way he had been treating her. He was miserable—in pain and out of a job, he now had an uninsured car smashed up and a wife who had left him and hadn't even come to see him yet—and no one would bring him a drink.

By the second evening, Bud was sure Helen was never coming. He was still in pain and was experiencing alcohol withdrawal. Tears came easily. How could he have been so dumb about himself and his job hopping? How could he have trampled so stupidly on the only person in the world who loved him?

By the time Helen did walk in the door that evening, he was a very open and tender man. He was so glad to see her he cried. As they talked, she shared with him about her new faith in Christ and the peace she was feeling. She had been reading the Bible and couldn't believe all the wonderful things she was learning.

Before the evening was over, Helen, with the little bit she knew, helped Bud make the same commitment to God. They hugged each other and cried together. Now they both felt clean and hopeful about the future.

By the time Bud was released from the hospital, he had dried out. He was determined that, with strength from his new relationship with Christ, he could stay free from alcohol. In time, he found a sales job that really suited him.

Helen and Bud started attending the church where Margaret went. They were like dry sponges, soaking up the love the congregation extended to them and learning all that God had to say to them in the Bible. In the months that followed they attended classes and seminars that provided growth for them.

As they grew spiritually, they found that they were also improving financially. They were eventually out of debt and into a small house of their own. Today, after several profitable financial investments and years of growing together, they say, "God has really blessed us!"

The most beautiful results are seen in their strong, loving marriage and the ministry they have together of helping others get their lives on solid footing. They shared with us that through the twenty-six years they've been married, they have had many hurdles to cross, but their relationship with Christ was what carried them through.

A commitment to Christ also strengthened the marriages of many of the couples in our survey. A wife whose husband had an affair, declared bankruptcy in his business, and turned away from God, said, "I never could have made it without God." She held on to God and the couple is now reunited. Another woman who had been married ten years said, "We'd be divorced if we hadn't become Christians."

RELIGIOUS VALUES—ARE CRUCIAL

A vital spiritual life was ranked as one of the three most important keys for a lasting marriage by the couples we surveyed. I (Jim) had anticipated that people would say the most important trait was a romantic feeling as expressed in the Sonny and Cher song "Love Will Keep Us Together," but they didn't.

A National Concern

It is true that those who filled out the questionnaire had religious affiliations, but our findings are consistent with other studies on marriage and the family. In a study of healthy families by Dolores Curran, two of the top fifteen traits (out of a possible fifty-six) had religious or spiritual dimensions. They were "a sense of right and wrong" and "a shared religious core."[1]

Another national study of family strengths completed in the seventies at the University of Nebraska pointed out the evidence of a link between religion and success and happiness in all phases of an individual's life.[2] George Gallup, Jr., in a 1979 survey of parents, discovered that 63 percent felt religion had greatly strengthened their family relationships.[3]

The people in our survey said a vital spiritual life provided them with an avenue for strength, hope, and stability. They saw God as a friend who cared about what they were going through, a person they could talk to, and one who was making a difference in their lives and marriages.

Many of these couples described very intimate and personal communication with God. This may sound mystical, but we repeatedly heard people saying that God was touching them in the innermost part of their being where no one else could. God was nourishing them, giving them a strength to go on, to grow, to have hope that they had not found in any human source.

One wife who had been married twenty-two years said, "A quiet time and Bible study are important to me—just 'Jesus talking to my heart' has helped." Her relationship with her husband was good, but their children had physical and learning problems, which put a strain on the marriage.

Your Personal Meeting with God

What we are talking about can be illustrated by author and seminary professor Lewis Smedes, as he writes about one of his spiritual experiences with God:

"I was alone in a plain red cottage on Fox Island, not far out into Puget Sound . . . . I had no radio with me, no television, and no stereo . . . . I took no newspaper, had no magazines, and read no books . . . . In the middle of the second week, on a Wednesday afternoon, long about four o'clock, I felt the presence of God . . . . The key is feeling: we will discover him, I dare say, only as we feel him.

"Being alone, shorn of my assorted psychic crutches, was just a way of clearing the decks. Aloneness is no magic entree to God; it is just a way of cleaning out the clutter that tends to clog the valves of deeper feelings. . . .

". . . to feel yourself in God's hands in the pit of your personal hell is to know it is all right when everything is totally wrong. . . .

". . . I began to feel as if all those human hands, . . . were taken away from me . . . . It was as if my closest friends, the ones I needed most, were saying, 'Sorry, we cannot reach you there. We cannot help you.' . . . All the hands I needed were drawn away. . . .

". . . I discovered, all by myself, in touch only with my final outpost of feeling, that I could be left, deserted, alone, all my scaffolds knocked down, all the stanchions beneath me pulled away, my buttresses fallen, I could be stripped of human hands, and I could survive. In my deepest heart I survived, stood up, stayed whole, held by nothing at all except the grace of a loving God.

"I was in the hands of God.

"I could live by grace.

"I could lose all human support and not fall down."[4]

Our survey couples reported similar experiences that had given them strength when all of life was crashing down around them. Many people have told us they had thought they had faith until they experienced a severe crisis. Then they found that faith in something vague and undefined didn't work; they learned they needed God in a personal way.

Fran said, "I can't believe I grew up in the church, was confirmed, married in the church, and did all the right things, but didn't know God. When my husband had his heart attack and nearly died, I had to have something **real.** It was then my teenage son told me I could know God personally."

Levels of Commitment

Spiritual life is quite different at various ages in our lives. Children tend to have a naive, almost gullible faith. They accept the faith of others. Teenagers are inclined to have a hero-type faith. They follow the leader or the group. But it may be a faith without much personal commitment.

The young adult tends to have a questioning type of faith. "My parents believe this, my teenage group believed that, now what am *I* going to believe?" This is an important process. Without this questioning period, the person may end up attending a certain church or ascribing to certain beliefs simply because his or her parents did or because he or she became integrated into a youth group as a teenager.

The adult faith is marked by a commitment and understanding of who God is, his love, Jesus' sacrifice, and the Holy Spirit's power. The adult makes a deliberate commitment to follow God and to live out the teachings of Scripture. The adult intentionally invites God into his or her life.

These levels of faith are not totally age related. Sometimes a child or a teen can have a very mature faith while some adults may have a very immature faith or none at all.

This deep, personal, adult commitment to God changed the lives of such people as the Apostle Paul, Augustine, Martin Luther, Mother Teresa, Billy Graham, Chuck Colson, and millions of others, including Jim and Sally Conway.

RESULTS OF A VITAL SPIRITUAL LIFE

Our society is strongly affected by the philosophy of looking out for number one. People ask, "What is the bottom line?" When it comes to marriage, partners frequently are asking, "What do you do for me?"

Marriage Stability

A spiritual life that is strong and alive gives people a different perspective. The Bible teaches servanthood, sacrifice, trust, esteeming others as better than ourselves. The Bible speaks of forgiveness, love, affirmation, flexibility. When a person is living in vital relationship with God and expressing that relationship in practical terms, a degree of stability and a positive life view result.

Since the natural tendency of most people is to be self-centered, it is likely that most marriages will experience stress. A vital relationship with God and a deliberate determination to live out biblical principles will counteract that native tendency toward selfishness.

One man who had been married thirty-two years said, "I came to the Lord many years after my wife and our kids, but since then I have become much more sensitive to the needs of my wife and only because of the Lord."

A living relationship with God should serve to temper potentially rash decisions and verbal explosions. One woman in our survey told us that a daily time of quietly reading the Bible helped her to focus on bigger aspects of life rather than on her stress of feeling exploited by her husband during his mid-life crisis.

A vital relationship with God kept our couples from getting into trouble in their marriage relationship and also provided a way out of any trouble they had gotten into. By confessing wrong, granting forgiveness, and praying together when marital trouble had erupted, our couples had powerful resources for repairing damage. They were not left in a stalemate with each person expecting the other to make the first move, but they each initiated reconciliation.

The two of us are both assertive, strong-willed people

with definite ideas of how things should work. As a result, we often "knock heads." Usually, as the conflict begins to cool a bit, one of us will say, "You know, the devil wants to distract us from the good we're doing by stirring us up to fight with each other—(long pause)—I'm sorry." "So am I," the other says. Then we hug, with a realization that God is in our marriage with us, even though the devil will continue to try to break us up.

Protection from Mistakes

A number of individuals in our study shared with us that God kept them from making bad decisions, restraining them when they were faced with a choice between right and wrong. Beth told us that in her early married years she never noticed other men. But in her late thirties, with trouble in her marriage, "Suddenly the streets were full of attractive men!"

She kept fantasizing how she might bump into some handsome man when she was out shopping for groceries, buying clothes for the kids, or just walking in the mall. She hoped maybe a salesman would come to her door or an old college friend would drop into town and look her up. She wanted some man to notice her and care for her.

A couple of times she found herself flirting with men who flirted back. But she remembers how she felt when a good-looking man invited her to go for coffee. Suddenly she sensed the arms of God holding her. "It was," she recalls, "as if God were saying to me, 'I know you're hurting, but this man is not able to help you. Trust me to help you.'" She was able to tell the man no with a deep sense of peace.

Through the years we've seen that a strong spiritual life has added a dimension of stability, hope, and power for change that's not commonly found in people without faith.

COGNITIVE FAITH OR PERSONAL FAITH

What kind of faith are we talking about when we say "a vital spiritual life"? We mean a faith beyond ourselves, a trust in a personal God who loves us and is concerned for our best. This faith is a personal relationship, as opposed to accepting of a certain creed or belonging to a religious organization.

Both of us were taken to church when we were very young. We attended faithfully with our parents. Our parents' Christian concepts were not our experience; they were only ideas. These ideas had not yet become our personal commitment nor was God our personal friend. Instead he seemed to be a distant judge or heavenly boogeyman looking over the banister of heaven, waiting to catch us in some evil deed.

In our early teen years we each went through training classes and joined the church where our parents were members. It was not until we were in our late teen years, however, that we moved from a "concept" relationship with God to a "personal" relationship. We asked God to forgive us for keeping him out of our lives and claimed Christ's death on the cross as his provision for our sins. We wanted the Holy Spirit to live in us and direct our lives.

For me (Jim), this decision came one spring night as I knelt at the altar of Independence Road Methodist Church in Cleveland, Ohio. It was during our annual revival meetings, and I felt God drawing me to himself in an even stronger way than I feel drawn to a cozy, warm fire on a cold, raw winter evening.

I told him that night that I was sorry for keeping him out of my life and sorry for sins I had committed. I asked him to forgive me. I thanked him for sending Christ to die on the cross for me, and I asked him to enable me to live for him.

My (Sally's) decision came when I was a college freshman. My parents had given me excellent Christian training, but when I arrived on the Sterling College campus, I noticed that my new college friends had a closeness to Christ that I didn't have. He seemed real to them. I thought I was a Christian, but I wasn't sure and went on a search about the matter. After listening, watching, and talking to many people for several weeks, one night at an evangelistic meeting I made a specific, deliberate commitment to Christ. Now there was no doubt! I, too, felt God's realness.

New Friend

After our commitment experiences, God was no longer distant or a threat; he was now a personal friend who had created us, wanted the best for us, and who was going to develop the potential of our lives to help many people.

If you would like such a relationship with God, begin by confessing to him the areas of your life that you know to be wrong. In the Bible wrong is called sin, which means "a missing of the mark." If you shot an arrow at a target but didn't hit the bull's eye (righteous living according to God's standards), you would miss the mark, or sin. Confess your missing of the mark to God.

Now specifically focus on your marriage. Look at what you've done wrong. Also admit the things you've not done that you could have done to make your marriage relationship stronger. These are called sins of omission. These acts of omission usually haunt people when there is an affair, separation, or divorce or when a mate dies. You might say to yourself, "If only I would have . . . ." Tell God now that you're sorry for your errors in the relationship between you and your mate.

Confess to God that you also have a desperate need for the future of your marriage. You need to make certain changes and take specific actions, but you can't pull them off without God's help. Tell him that. You don't have to be holy and pious. Just lay it flat out, "God, I'm a mess. I'm in trouble. Our marriage may collapse unless you intervene, and I'm helpless to do anything in this particular area." What you're really doing is hollering for help. And that's all part of a vital walk with God.

Chatting with Your Friend

As you are walking with God, you will want to interact with him throughout the day. Talk to him under your breath while you're working, while you're eating—whatever you're doing. You can do this because of your amazing mind which can be involved in two or three activities at the same time.

Sometimes Sally and I will be talking as we drive with the radio on. Suddenly one of us will say, "Quiet a moment!" We stop our conversation and focus on what we're hearing on the radio. The truth is, we've been sorting out what we don't want to pay attention to on the radio, but when something of interest comes on, we focus our full attention on it.

You can do the same with God. You can have a running dialogue with him while you're going about your daily activities. As you hear a song, listen to a bird, look at the sky, talk to a friend, or do your work, you can also take a moment—a millisecond—to reflect with God, "Well, what do you think about that, God?" Or, "Hey, God, that's terrific. I'm glad you made that bird."

It's important to see God as awesome, mysterious, all-powerful, all-wise; but it is also important to realize that he wants us to view him as a friend. Not everything in the movie series, *Oh, God,* was on target, but a very positive point portrayed was the friend relationship between God and a human being. Scripture, especially the Psalms, shows us that we can have such a friendship. Jesus said, "I don't call you servants . . . I call you friends" (John 15:15). God wants to be a friend with us moment-by-moment through our lives.

Enjoying His Leadership

Finally, commit your next steps to God. The Bible says, "Commit everything you do to the LORD. Trust him to help you do it and he will" (Psalm 37:5, TLB).

Maybe I (Jim) am different from other people, but the experiences of my life continually reinforce how desperately I need God. I have never come to the place where I don't do or think something wrong during each day. Nor can I really control what is happening in my life or my future. Even as Sally and I work on this book, I wonder if anybody will buy it. Who really controls what will happen?

The book of James says that we are foolish if we think we control our future. Our lives are just like a morning fog rising off a pond. We are here for a little while, and then we vanish with the rising sun (James 4:13–15).

I have found that some of my accomplishments have been initiated by God through his people, not by me. For instance, back in the fifties a woman named Jesse in our church in Newton, Kansas, urged me to start writing. *Who would want to read anything I wrote?* I asked myself.

Still God planted a seed through Jesse and others who encouraged me to write a few articles. In the seventies a young woman named Barb, who had been a part of our church in Urbana, Illinois, became a staff writer for *HIS* magazine. She asked me to write a monthly column, which I did for five and a half years. Many of those columns have been reprinted in magazines all over the world and later resulted in my being asked to write books for various publishers.

Who made all that happen? Not me. God in his sovereignty brought those people and events together in my life. All I did was depend on him to help me meet each event as it occurred. That is why it is so important for you and me to commit our lives to him. We need to say very directly to him, "God, here is my life. Pick out what you want and throw away the junk. Steer me so I will be the most effective person I can be in my marriage, my contact with people, and my career." Such a prayer doesn't eliminate us from acting, thinking, or planning. Now, however, we act, think, and plan under the guidance and leadership of God.

Choosing the Maker

Imagine that you've just dropped your three-hundred-dollar camera. As you pick it up, you notice the lens is cracked and the shutter doesn't work. Who are you going to ask to fix it? Are you going to do it yourself? How about the auto repairman down at the corner gas station? If you had a chance to have it repaired by the man who made the camera, wouldn't that be a wiser choice?

You have one life to live. Who will you trust to make it the most effective life? Yourself? The government? Dear Abby? Your boss? Your mate? Each one of us is forced by life to trust someone. Why not the one and only God who created you?

CHAPTER

Key #4
Effective Conflict
Resolution

One summer our family went camping in the upper peninsula of Michigan. We never imagined that we would get an effective lesson in facing problems and resolving them, but we did. The location was beautiful, an isolated campground with a terrific view of a magnificent lake. Tall trees were all around us. Unfortunately, we had chosen a week when it rained constantly.

On the first day of rain, we noticed that our borrowed tent leaked. Well, that was no big deal. We just moved our gear into the middle of the tent away from the outside walls and the one corner where water was dripping in.

The second rainy day we noticed that water was starting to leak in other spots. We kept piling up our gear until we hardly had space on the floor for our sleeping bags. But we were survivors. We were tough. We weren't going to let a little rain get us down.

By the fourth rainy day, water was dripping into the tent in several places, but we drifted off to sleep that night with a sense that we were in charge and were going to beat this rain.

The next morning, it was still dark and still raining. Now all our sleeping bags were soggy. Our clothes were soggy. We'd been sleeping in water which had come up through the floor of the tent. Our little trenches around the tent had overflowed. Everything was a soggy mess. We finally made the decision to move from the tent.

We settled into the unoccupied park shelter after a kind ranger said with a grin, "I can't say you have permission to stay here, but I'll be at the other end of the campgrounds and I won't be back to check." So we pulled our soggy gear into the shelter house, built a cozy fire, dried things out, set up "camp" in different style, and enjoyed those last wet days together.

Problems Don't Just Evaporate

Many mid-life marriages are just like that camping experience. When a few difficulties are raining on your marriage, they're pretty easy to ignore. You avoid them. You don't talk about the difficult subjects such as money, sex, career, or in-laws. In fact, you may not talk at all. You keep moving from one part of your marriage to another, seeking safe spots where you don't have conflict.

Eventually, however, problems accumulate. Everything gets soggy, miserable, and ugly. Effective conflict resolution seems impossible. You may come to the point where you're ready to abandon the marriage. Or perhaps you'll restructure your marriage so that it is something you both greatly enjoy.

Ignoring marital problems will lead to a paralyzing condition that Sheldon Vanauken called "creeping separateness": "Finding separate interests. 'We' turning into 'I.' Self. Self regard: what *I* want to do. Actual selfishness only a hop away . . . . The failure of love might seem to be caused by hate or boredom or unfaithfulness with a lover; but those were results. First came the creeping separateness: the failure behind the failure."[1]

How much better to squarely face the problems and begin to work on them. If necessary, a professional counselor can help define the problems and decide on solutions. One mate may have to do it alone for a while. If that's you, we suggest you read *How to Save Your Marriage Alone*.[2]

It's time for you and your mate to pick up your soggy, miserable marriage patterns and move to dry quarters. As you do, you'll find you're making some adjustments. At first they may feel strange, but if you work at accommodating each other, you may like the new structure much better.

PROBLEM SOLVING IS NEEDED IN EVERY MARRIAGE

Most marriages begin with conflicting desires. Two people are attracted to each other, but they have differing tastes, preferences, opinions, habits, life perspectives, standards, and values. Even after twenty-five years of marriage, the question may be, What do we do with conflict? Understanding why conflict arises and learning how to handle it are important in building a strong marriage at mid-life.

Who Gives In?

In our survey of couples whose marriages were surviving the mid-life years, several questions tested this area of problem solving. Comments from the survey couples showed us that they had learned how to handle conflict, or at least how not to allow problems to continually disrupt their marriage.

One woman said, "My husband never thinks anything is worth arguing about unless it involves money or his work. I have learned to 'let go' easier."

Another woman said, "We do best if we do it his way." We smiled as we read what a man married thirty-four years said: "My wife never allowed us to have differences."

Some of these comments sound as if one of the couple just gives in. That's one way to resolve conflict. It takes two to fight, and if one won't fight, there isn't a conflict (unless the other one gets mad because the first one won't speak up).

There were some positive comments such as, "We solve problems by talking it out before they become real problems."

A man married twenty-one years said, "I try not to allow small things to cause me to get mad. I try not to do little things to irritate her."

Marriage Doesn't Eliminate Problems

It's important to remember that these same successful couples had actually faced all kinds of problems: money, career, children, in-laws, sex, affairs, physical illness, and dozens of other struggles. A successful marriage is not measured by the absence of conflict but by the presence of conflict resolution.

While Bob and Jan were dating, they were actively involved in getting to know each other and learning how to resolve problems. Some of those times were very agonizing. They felt threatened as they talked about their differences and wondered if they were so different that their relationship would collapse.

After two years of getting to know each other, they decided to get married because they felt they were similar enough. Besides they loved each other. But problems arose when they stopped the negotiating process. They anticipated that their strife would be less because they were married. In reality, because they *were* married and had closer involvement with each other, they had *more* conflict.

Unfortunately, some couples conclude that their marriage was a mistake because they have conflicts. As a result, they don't focus on developing resolution skills and their marriage deteriorates as Bob and Jan's did.

Joint Assets

In the 1983 study discussed in *American Couples*, researchers Blumstein and Schwartz wanted to learn how married couples and cohabiting couples handled making decisions and resolving problems. The couples were asked what they would do if they were given six hundred dollars to spend on themselves.

The researchers reported that the married couples tended to view the six-hundred-dollar gift as a joint possession and assumed they would decide together how to use it. The cohabiting couples, on the other hand, viewed the money as something to be split fifty/fifty. Neither had any say in the use of the other person's share.[3]

The partners in unsuccessful marriages tend to react to life as if they are only cohabitors. In our studies we noticed that successfully married couples tend to view their possessions, time, and energies as joint assets rather than as separate, personal possessions.

Two contrasting couples in our survey point up this fact. One couple, in their early forties, said about conflict, "We hardly ever argue—I'm not sure why—we try to talk things over."

As we looked at other parts of their survey we could understand why. Under leisure they said, "We spend every Thursday evening together *without* our children. We need time alone together." About money they said, "We both feel that God has given *us* this money and it is extremely important that we manage it well." Another comment was, "I know who my husband is and how he operates; therefore, I don't expect him to act differently than he does."

In contrast, the comment of the wife of the second couple was, "I just give in." Their survey showed that their marriage was threatened. They had already experienced a separation.

Under the section on leisure she said, "Not enough. We spend most of our leisure time separate." Regarding money she said, "We have not worked that one out yet!"

We wondered what held them together. Then we noticed she had written, "Commitment was the only thing."

PROBLEM SOLVING CAN MEAN GROWTH

Couples don't like to have problems in their marriage. No one prays, "God, problems are so much fun. Please send us some more." Problems aren't funny. They cause stress and anxiety.

Problems can, however, become opportunities for growth. Remember, every time your pattern of life is challenged or upset, you have the potential for growth.

The next time your mate gives you static, you can say to yourself with a grin, "My world is being challenged and this is an opportunity for me to grow." Actually, you *will* grow. You *will* change. You will become more or less like the person you want to become. The direction depends upon your response to the problem.

One morning as Jim and I were harried with many business and ministry details, I was editing this section of the book, which Jim had written months earlier. While I was working with these thoughts about conflict resolution, I was also handling several other important interruptions. Jim was working on details for future conferences, and he was frustrated with the computer, which was threatening to crash and lose everything in our system.

Because we were both under pressure, we bumped heads with each other over several matters. It was just one of those days when, no matter what we said to each other, it came out sounding crabby and bossy.

Later that morning, once we were feeling calmer, I told Jim, "During some of our fussing I wanted to remind you of the sentence you had written: 'My world is being challenged and it's an opportunity for me to grow,' but I was afraid you'd throw the computer at me." We laughed, and he told me I could share this with you.

Growth Means Saying, "I'm Sorry"

We have learned to expect more conflict when we are tired or under a lot of pressure. We also know that a little cooling-off time or space makes the resolving of problems easier because we both can be more objective and less emotional.

We also have learned that it's important for each of us to take responsibility for settling the conflict or tension. Two magic words, "I'm sorry," work wonders for us, especially if they're followed up with a touch or a hug.

Sometimes couples try to separate the activities of their lives in order to eliminate problems. *If we can put each segment of life into a separate, antiseptic container*, they think, *we won't have any conflict with each other*. But marriage is an intermingling of two persons in the totality of their lives. You can't isolate the individual parts.

A marriage is more than a legal contract, it is a relationship of common values and a shared life. Yes, problems are unpleasant, but they also provide an opportunity for the couple to understand each other more completely, if they work at resolving the problems.

PROBLEM SOLVING IS A PREDICTION OF SURVIVAL

Frequently in premarital counseling I (Jim) ask couples to talk about the problems they've experienced between themselves and how they've resolved these conflicts. If the couple can walk through several of their problem experiences with me,

I can help them understand the process they have used to re-solve them. How they solve problems now is part of the guaran-tee of their marriage survival later. If they say they've never had a conflict, I respond, "Then one of you is a nonperson, and the other is probably arrogantly dominant."

One couple resolved a severe problem when both sets of parents originally objected to their marriage. Carlos was Cuban and Lynne was Chinese. They delayed their marriage for more than a year while they listened to their parents' objections. They spent time with their parents, giving them the opportunity to change their thinking and to get to know their potential mates as they knew each other. The couple had a few stormy scenes with their parents, but patient talks and repeated family times finally won the parents' approval. Carlos and Lynne married with all parents' blessings.

I told Carlos and Lynne, "Since you've been able to get all of your parents now to agree to your marriage and have helped the two families put aside their differences, there's a high likeli-hood that you'll be able to handle the toughest marital prob-lems of the future."

Every problem you and your mate have resolved is part of the confirmation that your marriage will survive. The next time you have conflict, draw on your previous experience of problem solving to be a help. If your past record isn't so good, don't give up. Keep learning.

PROBLEM SOLVING REQUIRES PROBLEM RECOGNITION

The two of us have had lots of practice in learning how to resolve conflicts in our thirty-three years of married life! Some of the reasons for our conflicts are that we are both firstborn children with strong leadership qualities, firm convictions of rightness, and a highly protective sense of our rights. In addi-tion, we are perfectionists who are also workaholics. We grew up with many similar values, but the dissimilar ones are poten-tial conflict spots.

Although our conflicts have been in many areas of life, each of us recognizes that they aren't because the other is a bad person but because he or she is different. We see that our conflicts seem to come from four main causes.

1. Differing Viewpoints of the Same Issue

Neither viewpoint is right or wrong, just different. But sometimes it comes out, "I'm right and you're wrong."

Example: In deciding when to go to bed at night usually Sally would rather go early; I would choose to go later.

2. Pressure of Our Busy Life and Schedule

We each work about 80 to 100 hours a week, teaching seminars, counseling by letter and telephone, managing our office, making radio and TV appearances, and writing. In rushing to care for many details, we sometimes end up speaking hurriedly to each other and it can come across as snapping at each other.

Example: We are under terrific pressure to get the manuscript for this book cleaned up and to the publisher so that it can be released on time. The other day I (Jim) ran out to the bank and the copy shop. The errands took longer than I expected. When I got back, Sally asked, "What took so long?" To her innocent question, I snapped, "You're always making sure I'm still working! I don't like being mothered!" At a more relaxed time, I wouldn't have been bothered by her question.

3. Differing Tastes

Earlier in our marriage our taste differences were sometimes used as put-downs or resulted in one of us feeling that the other was selfish.

Example: When we have an evening to relax, I would choose to watch TV and Sally would choose to read. If we watch TV together, usually Sally would rather not watch tense spy movies that I would enjoy. Our solution is to take turns with TV program choices or to have Sally read while I watch a program she doesn't care to see.

4. Attacks from the Devil

We have come to see that we are often in conflict with each other just before we are to make a public appearance. It's almost as if there is a planned evil attack to make us less effective as speakers and to rattle our marriage.

We are not alone in recognizing the devil's power. M. Scott Peck, M.D., in his book *People of the Lie* and *The Road Less Traveled,* has made it acceptable, even fashionable, to talk about the power of evil.[4] Current movies and TV programs abound with satanic influence as a topic. Of course, the Bible has always acknowledged the presence of evil.

When we recognize the pattern of the special attacks on us, we stop, hold each other, and pray for God to restrain the devil and to help us be kind to each other.

Not only should you recognize that a problem exists and identify the source, but also ask yourself, *At what point does a problem become a serious problem? Are we having a temporary difficulty with money, or is this a long-term problem we need to work out?*

The same questions may arise in any area: stress with our children, couple communication, intimacy, sex, career, in-laws. When is a problem really a problem?

Successful couples are able to say to each other, "This is a problem; we need to talk about it." When a couple starts to bury their problems and tries to ignore them, they're moving into an unhealthy relationship. Yes, bringing problems into the open can cause conflict, but it is likely that the relationship will improve as the conflict is resolved.

Nick Stinnett, a dean of Pepperdine University, discovered two important factors in his study on healthy families: "First, they had the ability to see something positive in every situation no matter how bad, and to focus on that aspect. Second, they joined together to face the crisis head-on."[5]

PROBLEM SOLVING—HOW TO DO IT

1. Talk About It

It sounds so simple, and it really is. One of our survey wives, married thirty-two years, said, "Many times I just *wouldn't* let my husband stay mad. I made the overture to 'talk it out.'"

When you recognize there is a problem, talk about it. It's important for you and your mate to understand that everything in life can be talked about. True, each of you can be responsible for handling some matters alone and other things can be completely ignored. Otherwise, your life could become a nonstop talk session. Somewhere a balance must be found between the two extremes of talking about every tiny detail and not talking at all.

Sally and I usually approach conflict resolution very differently. I tend to be the turtle type. It's easier for me to crawl into my shell and wait for the storm to blow over. Sally, on the other hand, can't function effectively when there are bad feelings or misunderstandings. She tends to press on toward a solution as quickly as possible so that life can be stabilized again. We'd like to share with you some of what we've learned about resolving our conflicts over the years.

Let's start with a typical problem that we have and work it through. We generally agree on money, but we do have one basic difference. Jim likes to put as much as possible into house payments, causing us to run short of available cash for other items. I (Sally) would rather have a little more money to use for necessities now than to have the house paid off early.

Following are some of the ideas and feelings we try to talk about as we resolve conflicts.

a. Think of we versus the problem, not "That's your problem, you solve it." Part of your marriage vows probably included the phrase "for better or for worse." That means that your lives are unalterably linked together. You each assumed the benefits of being with the other—and also assumed his or her problems. When there is a problem, it's not your problem or your mate's problem alone; it is **our** problem together. **We** have a problem.

How shall **we** solve our problem with money? It's not that Sally has a problem because she wants to enjoy money now or that Jim has a problem because he wants to invest; it's that **we** have a problem to work out together.

b. Focus on issues and facts, not on personality differences. When we focus on the other's personality idiosyncracies, we tend to say: "The way you're thinking is just like your mother's." "You're too emotional and you always want to keep a fight going." "You never want to work toward a solution. You just want to ignore things all the time."

Does this sound like your family, or are we the only ones who have said things like this to each other?

Focus on the issue. Sally doesn't accuse me of being a tight wad (although I really am), nor do I attack her personhood by calling her a big time spender who doesn't care about the future. The truth for the two of you is somewhere in the middle. Don't be distracted from the issue by attacking each other.

Is the contention about sex, in-laws, the job, division of jobs around the house, the dog, or leisure time? Talk specifically about the problem. Don't concentrate on the differences in each other's personality. Of course, your mate is odd, but so are you.

c. Understand each other's needs, interests, and feelings. Each of you approaches a problem with different requirements, concerns, and emotions. Work at understanding the other person's point of view in each of these areas. Be able to say to your mate, "Now let me see if I have this straight. What you feel about this situation is . . . ?"

I understand that Jim is anxious about our financial future. I try to feel his feelings of responsibility for us. At the same time, I have helped him to see that he shouldn't always live life in the future, but that some fun and necessities are important now.

d. Want your mate, as well as yourself, to win. Try not to get into a win/lose situation—"I win and you lose." Try to accomplish a win/win result. You bring that about by each person being able to express his or her needs, interests, and feelings. Each person has an equal opportunity for input into the discussion and into the final resolution. You each promote the other's high value and preserve the other's dignity.

Our solution to the money problem has been to compromise. Because we both feel that the other one understands how we feel, we can meet part way. It's not that one of us wins; we both do because we have both owned the problem and worked on the solution together.

e. Own the solution. When you have identified the problem as "our" problem, think of several alternative solutions. Discuss how each of those would work.

How to spend our money is **our** problem. Together we have looked at many alternatives for solving it. We've chosen the best alternative. Now we will lay out specific steps to resolve it. We each recognize our part, our ownership, in the steps toward resolution.

Our solution is that I (Jim) have scaled back my ambitious timetable for paying off the house and Sally will continue to be thrifty in her use of money now. We both have agreed that Sally will help keep me mentally healthy by reminding me to plan less demanding work schedules and more times for fun. We both have agreed upon the solution and the consequences. And we are each benefitted by the influence of the other.

2. Use a Variety of Methods

What are the typical responses when you're first aware of a conflict? When you're halfway through the conflict? When the conflict is resolved? Each of us reacts differently at different stages of the conflict. We also generally follow the same pattern each time, even though that pattern may not be the most helpful.

For example, an abusive husband tends to respond to conflict initially by feeling that his authority is challenged. He begins to feel insecure, and he asserts himself by raising his voice and trying to pressure his wife into submission.

The wife might eliminate the problem by reassuring her husband when his ego is threatened. If she doesn't give in, he becomes more agitated, perhaps pacing the floor and hitting something. If she still doesn't react exactly as he wants, he beats her.

After he has beaten her, there generally is some degree of separation between them. During this separation he becomes reflective, is sorry for what has happened, and goes to his wife, promising her that he will never do it again. But *he will do it again*, and again, and again, until he and she learn other ways to resolve conflict.

Notice that the problem is not just his. It's also his wife's. There are a lot of *ifs* in this scenario, and the wife's response to the situation could have helped the husband move toward a better resolution. Perhaps she could have given in if the issue was not important. Remember, you don't have to fight over every issue.

After a conflict is over, ask some questions:

a. **What could I have done in the early stage to eliminate the conflict?**
b. **How did my mate feel?**
c. **Can I put myself into the thought and feeling process of my mate?**
d. **Was there a solution of compromise that would have helped us both to win?**

Some people respond to conflict with anger, others overeat, some drink, and others go into hiding. But better methods can be used to resolve conflict. Sometimes it's best to ignore it, try to quiet the situation, divert it by changing the subject, negotiate—"I'll do this if you do that"—put up with the situation as it is, or assert your rights if the issue is crucial. Maybe you need to fight over the issue. Trying different methods may help you to discover a new method that will make the process of conflict resolution move more quickly.

3. Get Outside Help

Your outside support network could be a professional counselor, your pastor, someone in your extended family, a neighbor, a friend from church, someone on your bowling team, or a person at work. Many kinds of support groups have been established by churches and communities for specific needs— alcoholism, drug addiction, caring for aging parents, physical and sexual abuse, career changes, as well as marital conflict.

It's O.K. to ask for outside help, whether from your casual support network or from a professional counselor. Only when you become God are you perfect enough not to need help.

Support systems are not there to tell you you're right or wrong. Rather these friends or professional helpers should be used to give perspective to the conflict situation and stability to your life.

4. Reduce Stress

We all accumulate about 10 percent more responsibility each year. The more our responsibilities build up, the easier it is for us to have a stress overload. Sometimes problems are created, not because they are genuine problems, but because we are so stressed out that little matters appear to be giant problems. Molehills become mountains, as the old saying implies.

Rod and Marcia Hart are a typical couple whose marriage was nearly ruined by a stress overload. Three of their four children were on their own. Gary was living at home and going to a community college.

One of their daughters was married, had a baby girl, and lived nearby. Marcia planned frequent family gatherings so that she could be with her granddaughter. She liked having the entire family together because it reminded her of the days when she was a young mother and everyone was at home.

Marcia had gone back to her career as a school nurse, and she also was very involved in several church and community activities. Rod was in advertising and had a good position with Sterling Advertising. He had begun to realize that he wasn't going to go much farther in that company, so he started his own enterprise on the side, planning to leave Sterling in a few years.

He had good plans, but the economic recession kept his company, Hart Advertising, from prospering as he had expected. In fact, he could not afford to hire other employees and was still doing most of the work himself, which meant working at nights and on weekends. Marcia had some secretarial skills and was willing to help, but she already had so many other obligations that her help was sporadic.

The Pressure Builds. Rod's position with Sterling began to be threatened with cutbacks, and he found himself feeling very competitive with the other men, angry at his superiors, and irritated that everyone around him seemed inefficient and disloyal. He wanted more help from Marcia in Hart Advertising, but she was tired, too, and felt that weekends should be for family and friends.

In order to fulfill her obligations as a school nurse, help Rod, and keep up with her church activities, entertaining, and family, Marcia had to be very disciplined in her schedule. She had lists, with her hours of the day and week carefully planned. She couldn't afford to have anything happen unexpectedly or take longer than she had planned. She became very tense.

Rod began to object to having their family over for Sunday dinners or Saturday barbecues. "I have to spend my extra time developing Hart Advertising," he blustered. He crabbed at

Gary for not doing his share around the house and yard. He frequently made remarks that hurt Marcia's feelings. If Marcia didn't understand something he said, he felt she was just trying to give him a hard time. Why couldn't she just help him with Hart Advertising and not have to know why something had to be done a certain way?

They fought so often that it became a way of life. Neither wanted it that way, but each blamed the other. After months of war and emotional misery, they began to think of separating.

One Saturday they were both very tired and tense as they tried to get out a mailing for their advertising company before a group of church couples came for the evening. Marcia had to get the appetizers prepared and was feeling distracted about that. Rod had just discovered that Gary had taken off with friends for the day and wouldn't be there to mow the lawn. Rod would have to do it.

Volcanic Eruption. He exploded! He was already irritated at Marcia for having invited people over when they had so much to do. Now he blamed Marcia for Gary's irresponsibility: "That kid is getting away with murder, living at home for practically nothing and never helping with any of the work. If you didn't baby him, he wouldn't be so lazy."

Marcia jumped to Gary's defense, explaining that he had a heavy load at school and that he was working hard to pay tuition. She went on to say, "You are hard-hearted just like your dad. You don't care about the family and what's really going on with us."

Rod accused Marcia of being self-centered and not understanding the realities of their economic situation. She said money wasn't all there was to life. They ended up screaming at each other and stomping out separate doors.

When they each had cooled down, they realized that their real problem wasn't Gary or Rod's tendency to be like his father or Marcia's financial insensitivity. They were *too busy*. They were trying to function as machines instead of as humans.

Rod and Marcia decided to scale back their lifestyle and expectations. Gary also began to take more responsibility for himself. Their move into a smaller house allowed them to have more leisure time and less pressure. All of these decisions had a positive effect on their marriage.

Carefully look through your activities and responsibilities. Prioritize them according to importance. Now chop off the items at the bottom of the list. You may think you can't do that, but you must. If you get rid of some of your obligations, you will be freer to handle the real problems.

5. Be Flexible

Successful couples in our mid-life marriage study tended to be flexible and adapted to changing life circumstances. Some marriages that stay together are very rigid, but the mates have learned what not to talk about and how to survive in the same house without irritating each other.

Challenge yourself to grow in the areas of toleration and flexibility. Ask "what if" questions: "What would we do if I lost my job or were offered a great job in another part of the country? What if our house burned? What if I had lung cancer? What if we got an extra $5,000? What would we do with it? What if . . . ?" Discuss each of these questions with a goal of improving your ability to adapt.

Incorporate change into your daily life. Do some things that you've never done before, such as:
- Take different roads to work.
- Shop at different stores.
- Eat at new restaurants.
- Visit a very different church.
- Learn to sail.
- Take a canoe or backpacking trip.
- Attend a live symphony performance.
- Learn to paint or pencil sketch.
- Visit a drug rehabilitation center.
- Take a poor family on a picnic.
- Spend an afternoon visiting in a retirement home.

Exposing yourself to new experiences and people will help you become a more adaptive person and a better problem solver. You will be able to see more options, see the other person's point of view, and see that life is not just black and white, cut and dried.

6. Yield

Kenny Rogers' song "The Gambler" is about an old man teaching a young man how to play a card game. A couple of phrases say, "Ya' gotta know when to fold" and "when to walk away." In problem solving you have to learn when to yield, when to give in, when not to press your point.

Remember that you're trying to work toward a win/win situation. That means, in most instances, neither of you will achieve all of your goals, but each of you can achieve some of your goals. As you come to compromises and submit to each other, you'll actually feel fulfilled, because you've helped your mate also meet personal goals.

By now you realize that the two of us haven't had a marriage without conflict. Perhaps because we're both leaders, we have had even more conflict than many couples. But we've learned much about resolving and reducing conflict.

Don't be afraid of conflict. You can have a higher quality marriage because you have not dodged disagreements but have met them head-on. Successfully resolving conflict nourishes the conviction that the two of you will be able to cope with whatever may come next.

Your ability to cope with the bad times will be the proof of your marriage. One insightful person has said, "A family doesn't prove itself through having a good time together. Your worst enemy will be willing to have a good time with you. You need your family when things are rough . . . . to bind up the wounds, particularly the psychic ones. Realize that you can prove your worth to your mate only when things have gone wrong by sticking together and making things right."[6]

Key #5
Impact from
Other People

"**K**aren, you've just got to do something about the way Ted treats you! You're being used. You can't go on being a doormat. If I were you, I'd set him straight about putting his work ahead of you and your family. He leaves you home all those nights, caring for the kids by yourself. You need to confront him."

Karen hadn't even talked about this problem to her friend Joyce, but Joyce's remarks began to influence Karen's thoughts of and actions toward her husband. For the first time, Karen started to resent Ted's work. She was not a confrontive person, but she tried to follow Joyce's counsel. As a result she and Ted began to have arguments.

"Ted, you're just using me. I stay home and take care of the kids and the house while you're out eating dinner with all your precious clients. When do I ever get a break and have some fun?"

Ted couldn't understand the change in Karen. The fighting between them increased until Karen suddenly realized how Joyce had been influencing her. True, she didn't want to be a doormat, but she hadn't been unhappy about Ted's work before. After she put the kids to bed those evenings, she had used most of the hours for her ceramics hobby.

As she thought about it, she began to see that Joyce really was projecting on Ted's business how she felt about her husband's traveling. Once Karen had that perspective, she settled back into her original acceptance of Ted's schedule.

The married couples we surveyed reported that other people influenced their marriages. That influence could be positive or negative. Karen's friend had a negative influence, but often other people not only enrich a couple's relationship but are also a holding force in times of extreme stress.

A woman from our survey, who had been married for twenty-two years and whose husband had several affairs before they both decided to work on improving their marriage, said, "Some friends stood by us through the worst of times. Had they all deserted us—like most did—we might have given up."

We have frequently had the delight of meeting that type of special friend at one of our seminars. Someone will joyfully introduce his or her friend as "the one who helped me through the worst time in my life. I would have divorced my husband (or wife) if it hadn't been for Mary's (or John's) encouragement to hang in there."

We were surprised to discover in our survey that a couple's extended family had little or no impact in stabilizing their marriage. The people who had the greatest influence for marriage stability, according to our couples, were (a) the spouse, (b) their children, and (c) friends. Relatives were generally a negative force for marriage stability for both the Stable and Threatened couples in our study.

HOW OTHERS HELP

People vary in how they help. Some launch a direct frontal attack to others' problems, while other people try to help by listening, being available, and expressing care.

Confrontation

Some couples reported that confrontation by a mate, child, or friend was a help and caused them to think seriously about their marriage. One woman reported that when her husband had an affair, she wanted to give up on the marriage. But two strong Christian friends arranged a special meeting with her and "encouraged me to hold onto my marriage."

One man in an affair was caught at a restaurant with his girlfriend by an old friend of his who told him, "It's not worth it. I know, I was there five years ago." This friend's comment helped break up the affair.

Other couples said that confrontation was unhelpful, causing them to harden their position and forcing them to justify themselves. Confrontation is one kind of help, but it must be used very judiciously. Friends need to understand the situation and emotions of the people they plan to confront.

The purpose of confrontation is to help the other person, not just to make the confronter feel righteous. Helpful confrontation is always given in small doses along with a great deal of love.

Availability

Being available to talk or to do things together was one of the ways other people helped strengthen the marriages of our couples. A woman married nineteen years said, "I've been helped by having other women to talk to. It's good to know others are struggling with problems and how they're solving them."

Having a group that meets for regular companionship or study was very important. These groups, however, must be more than a Sunday school class meeting to discuss doctrine or Bible characters. The activities must relate to immediate life situations and the couple's current marital needs, whether it's the study of Scripture, stress management, or financial planning. People going through a crisis can be helped if they have a readily accessible friend or group of friends.

Practical Help

A married couple's needs can be met by friends in practical ways—by the friends' babysitting so they can have time alone, providing a mountain cabin for a getaway, paying a marriage seminar registration fee, or bringing in meals if the wife is ill. Actions can help more than words in many cases.

THE BEST KIND OF HELP

The best kind of friends in or out of the family have some of the following personality traits and perceptions on life.

Positive Attitudes

People who had the most impact on strengthening the marriages of our mid-life couples were encouragers. They identified strengths in each of the marriage partners and talked up those strengths to the other partner and to other friends. They were aware of problems and weaknesses in the individuals, but they chose to focus on positive strengths and to affirm those.

We have an uncle and aunt, George and Nell (real names), who are encouragers. They see the good in everyone. They affirm people and give them a sense of hope. On a recent visit to our home they carried out their quiet mission of encouragement, verbally praising each of us for our strengths. They praised the work we're doing together as a couple, the good job we've done in raising our daughters, and, in general, affirmed our marriage relationship. We never realized what they were doing until after they had gone and we reflected on how good they made us feel.

Positive helpers tend to give an optimistic focus to a mid-life marriage. By this time in life there can be many negative things to concentrate on, so an affirming word may be a breath of fresh air that will help to stabilize and fortify a marriage.

Unconditional Love

Most of us have primarily experienced *conditional* love ever since we were little kids. We learned it at Christmas time by being told that Santa Claus was watching us and the number of toys we received depended on whether we were "naughty or nice." We learned it as we were spanked for bad behavior and praised for good or cute behavior.

Unconditional love is the love we experience from God. God loved us "while we were yet sinners."[1] He didn't wait for us to be good and then love us. In fact, he loved us before we were ever bad. He knew we were going to do wrong, but he loved us and continues to love us.

When we talk about unconditional love, people almost always raise a question about confrontation. Does love mean that you ignore wrong in a person's life? Not at all. Unconditional love means you continue genuinely to love the person in spite of the fact that you recognize weakness and you might have to confront the person about wrongdoing.

Loving a person unconditionally means that you refuse to "yo-yo" that person by giving love and then withdrawing it. **Your love stays consistent even though the other person's worthiness of your love is inconsistent.** Unconditional love is not based on the other person's worth; it is based on your commitment to love that person no matter what. Here is a good definition of *genuine* love:

> Love is very patient and kind, never jealous or envious, never boastful or proud, never haughty or selfish or rude. Love does not demand its own way. It is not irritable or touchy. It does not hold grudges and will hardly even notice when others do it wrong. It is never glad about injustice, but rejoices whenever truth wins out. **If you love someone you will be loyal to him no matter what the cost. You will always believe in him, always expect the best of him, and always stand your ground in defending him.**[2]

Objectivity with Both Partners

Good friends of mid-life couples don't take sides. They don't hear the complaint of one against the other and decide the other mate is a horrible, incorrigible mess. If friends or family members take sides, they are not likely to help either of the people in the marriage.

We have a joke between us, arising from our early days of people helping. For months a woman had been depicting her husband to us as a horrible monster. After we met the husband, we said to each other, "He didn't have two heads after all!" He actually wasn't such a bad guy, and he certainly had his side to their difficulties. Whenever we are tempted to take one mate's side, we laughingly remind each other, "The other person probably doesn't have two heads!"

Helpful friends and family members *do* listen to the problems, but instead of reinforcing them, they encourage the complaining person to look at positive aspects. They suggest that the problem should not keep him or her from seeing the mate's strengths. They help each one toward a more positive perspective, thus keeping the door of friendship open with both mates.

Nonjudgmental

Nonjudgmental people are generally aware of their own frailties and personal potential for failure. That tends to foster caution about criticizing others. Judgmental people, on the other hand, have often classified wrongdoing into acceptable and unacceptable categories. For example, they decide it's unacceptable to drink wine, but acceptable to tolerate sexual lust as long as it isn't acted out. "Acceptable" and "unacceptable" are decided according to what the judge tolerates in his or her own personal life.

Often the question is raised, "If we don't condemn evil, who will?" While it is true that we must take a stand against wrong, we must be careful we don't define other people's wrong as evil, while *our* wrongdoings are behaviors to be understood with gentleness.

We must also be careful that we don't take the place of God. The Bible says that each person will "give account to Him who is to judge the living and the dead" (1 Peter 4:5 NASB). Ultimately God is the judge of every man and woman. (For other Bible references on this subject of judging, see Romans 2:1–3, Hebrews 9:27, Galatians 6:1–3, and John 16:7,8.)

A nonjudgmental attitude actually flows out of the idea that we all have times of failure. As married couples we will have assorted difficulties and mistakes throughout our experience. Our attitude is not to be one of superiority, but of humility and restoration, realizing that we might experience a similar temptation.

Nonjudgmental people are not soft on evil, they are just soft on people. They may say to someone, as we often have, "You know we can't approve of what you're doing, and we sense that you don't approve of it yourself, yet we want you to know that we're your friends. We're going to stand by you through this time of confusion as you seek to work toward the right relationship with people and God, which you really want to have."

Empathetic

People who are helpful to mid-life couples generally possess empathy. Empathy is the ability to "feel with," or "feel into," other people's situations. Being empathetic enables you to listen effectively and to understand what people are feeling, rather than just what they're thinking. Empathy helps you to understand why they view life as they do and why they're considering certain plans of action.

A person can learn to be empathetic by repeatedly asking, "What would it feel like if I were in their shoes, having their experience? What can I learn from them so I can fully understand what it feels like to be where they are in life?"

You can develop your empathy skills while you read the newspaper or watch TV news. Imagine yourself in the situation of the people in the news. For example, suppose a famine is reported in some part of the world. Think what it would be like to be without food, to be slowly dying, to watch friends and family members die from starvation. How would you feel? How would you react to your government and to other nations? What would you think about God?

Any exercise in which you put yourself into the mind and situation of another person will rapidly develop your ability to be empathetic. Empathy will give you a fuller insight into the lives of people you're trying to befriend.

Recently I (Jim) answered the telephone and heard a crying woman on the other end. She was from the East Coast, her husband was having an affair, and she was coming unglued. What should she do now? How could she save her marriage and get her husband back?

It was important for me to feel what she was feeling. What was it like to feel rejected and betrayed? At the same time I had to use empathy to imagine what her husband was feeling. Why did he want to leave?

As I imagined what each was feeling, it was easier for me to stand in the middle and extend my hands to both of them. I could help each of them understand the other's need and help them work toward a solution.

I encouraged the wife to try to be more of a girlfriend than a mother to her husband. She was also willing to lose weight and to try to be more carefree. Her husband also began talking more about his needs to her. This couple is not out of the woods yet, but they've started.

When you use empathy skills, you must not take sides. You need to remain a friend to both. Commit yourself to pulling the marriage back together, not reinforcing the anxiety that one of them may feel.

Optimistic

People who are effective helpers to the mid-life couple have a sense of hope. They are not panicked or depressed by current difficulties; they see these problems as temporary. Good helpers see problems as opportunities to help the relationship develop and mature in ways that it might not without some stress.

In another recent telephone call a woman said to me (Sally), "My pastor and my counselor both are encouraging me to get a divorce because my husband has been involved in an affair." As we talked, I discovered she had already filed divorce papers. I also learned that her husband frequently stopped by the house to pick up a few items and would often stay for several minutes, talking and reflecting on some of the good times they'd had together. This was an indication that the relationship might be restored, but the other counselors were not seeing these hopeful signs.

When there is trouble in a marriage, it's important to focus on the power of God to bring about changes. If we focus on the problems and our human limitations, we are left with hopelessness. By focusing on God and asking him to intervene, we can have a greater degree of hope, even though there has been an affair, separation, filing of divorce papers, or actual divorce.

I suggested to another woman on the telephone, as we have to many others in similar situations, that she should delay the divorce proceedings and tune in to every positive thing that was happening between her and her husband. Sometimes those positive things may be very small, such as a kind word or a tender look, but if those are emphasized and nurtured, they can grow into a restored relationship.

Restorative

Friends need to help troubled mid-life couples "accentuate the positive and eliminate the negative." The negative is accentuated if the helpers are on the sidelines chanting, "Get a divorce! Get a divorce! You deserve better!"

Often we are asked, "Is there ever a time to give up on saving a marriage?" Yes, if you are legally divorced and your mate has remarried. But generally most people give up too quickly. People often say something like, "This has been dragging on for three months, so I'm just going to get a divorce," or "I've tried for two years to work this out, but I feel that it's hopeless. I'm giving up."

A number of research studies show that divorced people frequently have second thoughts and later wish they had tried harder in their first marriage. We often meet people like that.

Barbara was a dynamic woman and very successful in her work. She had been divorced and remarried. As she reflected on her marriages, she very frankly admitted, "Even though I deeply love Al, my second husband, I do believe that I did not try hard enough with my first husband. I wish I could do it over. I keep having these nagging feelings of being a weak person and a big failure. Perhaps my son Dirk wouldn't be going through such rebellion and destroying his life if I'd stayed married to his father."

By not giving up quickly and by making all the changes possible, regrets will be fewer later on if the marriage cannot be restored. A time may come when a mate, family members, or a friend can no longer help prevent a divorce, but three to five years of concerted effort needs to be made before that final decision. Good helpers don't rush people into separations or divorces.

Friends Hinder and Help. If you are tempted to make negative comments about one partner in a troubled marriage, remember the following story of Bill and Cindy. "Friends" almost destroyed Bill and Cindy's marriage by their negative actions and words. Other people, however, were true friends. They were optimistic encouragers, "the glue" that ultimately helped hold their marriage together.

Cindy had just turned thirty-eight and began to experience feelings of being left out. Bill was a nationally known motivational speaker who was continually being sought after, especially by attractive women. It wasn't that he flirted; he sincerely loved people. He was a tall, good-looking guy with a muscular body, a rugged outdoorsman appearance, and an infectious smile. He was also a caring, sensitive person, who was concerned about people's needs.

While Bill was building his career, Cindy was fully occupied and satisfied with caring for their three children and basking in the glow of Bill's fame. But as she got to her middle thirties, she began to realize that her mothering responsibilities were coming to an end. Bill was more preoccupied with his traveling and public speaking, and she was feeling isolated and neglected.

Six months earlier, a young married woman from Bill and Cindy's church was hit broadside by another car as she was coming home from shopping on a rainy evening. She lingered in a coma in the hospital for three days before she died.

Her husband, Dennis, was grief stricken. At age twenty-seven, he was left without his wife and had to be both mother and father to their two-year-old Amy.

Cindy stepped in to help with Amy, which Dennis deeply appreciated. Caring for Amy filled much of the emptiness in Cindy's life. Without expecting it, she also enjoyed the praise and appreciation from Dennis.

Needy People. At first, Dennis was only grateful to have someone really care for his daughter. Cindy was an older woman to him, and the thought of attraction never crossed his mind. But he began to notice and appreciate how much she knew about children and life. He also noticed that she was an attractive woman who kept her body in good physical shape. In fact, on one occasion when she came straight to the house from her exercise class, he found himself caught off guard. Before he realized it, he told her that she had a great-looking body.

These two needy people began to draw emotional strength from each other and to encourage each other. Their relationship of innocent help and appreciation, plus tragic need and loneliness, drew them together, causing a spontaneous combustion. Soon they were in a full-blown affair that neither of them, even in their wildest imaginations, could have anticipated.

Some months later, when Bill became aware that something was going on between Cindy and Dennis, he confronted her. Cindy abruptly reacted and told Bill if he didn't like it, he could move out. She had finally found someone who really loved her instead of his career. She was angry at Bill. In her mind, Dennis was an opportunity for her to start over.

Bill was devastated. He would lose his family, but it also would affect his career. How could he go on as an influential speaker when his personal life was anything but positive? In desperation, he turned to some of his friends and received a variety of responses.

Who Needs This Kind of Help? Ed was a college friend of both Bill and Cindy's. His marriage had broken apart about a year and a half earlier, and Bill thought that Ed might be able to help him. Ed verbally consoled Bill, but as soon as he was off the phone, he got on the next plane and went to see Cindy. Ed had always loved Cindy and was disappointed when she married Bill instead of him. He looked at this crack in their marriage relationship as an opportunity to win Cindy or, at least, to sexually meet her needs.

Ed's moves were totally rebuffed by Cindy, and Bill was infuriated when Cindy later told him what Ed had done under the guise of friendship.

Some women friends also started flirting with Bill. They expressed sorrow over Bill's marital stress, but he was startled at how aggressive they were with their suggestive clothing and words. He was especially shocked by one woman at the church who wanted to get together to "pray with him."

Other friends totally abandoned both of them. They treated Bill and Cindy as lepers. These former friends almost acted as if a continued friendship with Bill and Cindy would cause them to catch some marital virus themselves.

Positive, Healing Friends. Fortunately, there were other friends who continued a strong friendship with both Bill and Cindy. They didn't exploit the situation but believed the marriage could survive if some of the pressures were relieved.

These friends took Bill into their home when Cindy kicked him out. This gave Bill time to think in a peaceful environment without the fear of being exploited. When Bill was ready to talk, his friends helped him to understand why Cindy would be attracted to Dennis. Bill began to see that he had strongly contributed to the marital breakup, even though he originally thought it was all Cindy's fault. Now he understood that his drive toward fame had left her in the dust. Her situation and internal feelings had made her an easy target for another man's attentions.

At the same time, these special friends were talking with Cindy. They assured her that they didn't blame her. They helped her to see that a vacuum had been created in her life. The vacuum had become so strong and compelling that, if Dennis had not filled it, another man would have. As she understood the forces that pulled both her and Dennis into the relationship, she began to see that she had more going with Bill on a long-term basis than with Dennis on the short-term fling.

It wasn't easy or quick, but Bill and Cindy began to date each other again. Three months later, he moved back home into a separate bedroom. About six months later, with continued friendship support and professional counseling, their marriage was healed. Now they function on a different marital basis, with a more sensitive Bill and a more secure Cindy.

Perhaps you need to reflect on your friendships. What type of friends do you have? If they are not strengthening your marriage, should you look for different friends? What type of friend are you toward your married friends?

Friends rarely have a neutral impact on a marital relationship. They either encourage the couple to appreciate each other and strengthen their relationship or they become divisive, taking sides and even exploiting the weaknesses that are found in every marriage.

Key #6 Sexual Intimacy

You know we have to talk about sex in a book on marriage! It's not just a joke or gimmick to get you to buy the book. Sexual happiness is one indicator of marital health, and sexual intimacy involves all that goes on between a husband and wife, emotionally as well as physically.

"Lovemaking is an act of the human person, of intelligence and sensitivity, of gentleness and respect for one another, of struggle and of happy combat. The whole psyche is involved in it; one's skin, one's emotions, one's juices, one's mind, one's perceptions, one's freedom, one's aspiration. Animals have babies, but they do not make love. Human beings create an art of playfulness and make love, not when they need to, but when they wish. It is those who make love only in order to have children who mechanize and dehumanize the act of intercourse."[1]

People are drawn together into a marriage relationship partly to prevent loneliness, to be understood by another person, and to receive emotional and physical affection. They believe this other person will help them to feel loved and will provide satisfying sexual experiences through closeness, touching, and sexual intercourse.

The mid-life couples in our survey shared with us that a satisfying, active sex life is one of the other important ingredients that held their marriages together. Our survey did show some couples who were unhappy sexually, such as the man married thirty-three years who sadly wrote, "It's just fading away." Marriages where an affair had occurred generally had sexual problems. But most of the couples, even those well beyond the wife's menopause, were reporting sex to be getting better.

▼

A wife married thirty-nine years said, "It has grown from zero to *most* satisfying."

"Sex is a joy for both of us!" wrote a woman married forty-five years.

Another wife married thirty-five years said, "It's better with age."

A husband of twenty years insightfully wrote, "Our sexual relationship makes being in love a real pleasure."

▲

These couples enjoy sex. They are involved in experimentation and report that their sexual lives are more effective and satisfying than when they were first married.

One doctor tells of an older couple who had tapered off to having intercourse every four weeks or so. Then the wife became ill and they had no relations for about six months. When she tried to resume intercourse, the husband could not get an erection. So the wife went out and bought a book on sex, and read that if a wife fondled her husband's penis it helped him to have an erection.

One might think that this is common knowledge, but she had been taught that playing with sex organs was not something a decent woman did. She bravely tried it anyway and it worked. In fact she experienced their lovemaking as far better than thirty years ago, and her husband as a changed man, cheerful, optimistic, and vigorous. The wife then remarked, "Maybe I shouldn't admit it but I enjoy our relations more than I used to. I'm even thinking of trying some of the other things I read about in that book."[2]

STATE OF THE UNION

Later in this chapter we'll talk more about the sexual creativity that can keep your marriage alive and fun, but first we'll make some general observations from the couples we've surveyed and counseled.

1. *The Frequency of Sex May Decline for a Mid-life Couple, but Their Sex Life Is Not Less Satisfying.* Mid-life couples are tolerant about less frequent sex and report that it's due to physical fatigue or obligations of the family or career.

One woman said, "It's less than when we were first married because we were making love two or three times a week. Now it's once a week. I think it's the pressure. I used to think that he was less interested; now I think just some of the mystique wore off . . . . I say, 'O.K., just store it up and it will be more fun when it comes.' "

2. *Both Quantity and Quality of Sex Are Important to the Well-being of the Relationship.* Successful couples tend to keep more in touch with each other, not only about how often they want to have sex, but also about the quality—when and where they want to have sex, what position they'd like, how they want to be touched.

Kathy and Greg had been married twenty-two years and Greg had been involved in several affairs when they began to really work on their marriage. They started to talk about many areas, including their sex life which was in deep trouble. Their attitudes and satisfaction changed as they focused on each other's needs and talked freely about their own needs.

Kathy said, "I gradually became freed up to enjoy having sex instead of just enduring it to satisfy Greg. When I began to experience pleasure, Greg enjoyed it more too."

Greg's comment shows his growth: "Sex is more meaningful now that I can say, 'I love you.' Our sex life is much better now that I have opened up myself emotionally to Kathy."

3. *When the Nonsexual Parts of a Couple's Life Are Going Badly, It Tends to Show Up in Their Sexual Relationship.* "If you don't get along in the bedroom, you won't get along in the rest of your married life," an older, unhappily married man warned me (Sally) shortly before I got married. He wasn't giving me a tip for my happy marriage so much as he was giving a commentary on his own married life.

I doubt that this man's unhappiness was based only on the absence of the physical act of intercourse, but on the entire package of poor attitudes, inadequate communication, and lack of respect that existed between him and his wife.

Mid-life couples have discovered that sex is not only a physical relationship, but it is built on feeling loved. When sexual intercourse is pulled out of the loving context, it's reduced to only a skill to be practiced and improved, such as learning to play tennis or sail a boat.

To lower sex to merely the physical act of intercourse is to decrease it to an animal level. Dogs react to each other because of hormones not because of companionship, loving understanding, and commitment. Human sexual love is broader than the sexual act. For the act to be satisfying, the rest of the marriage must be meaningful.

4. *Partners Equal in Sexual Initiation and Refusal Enjoy Their Sex Life More.* The old stereotype that men are always the aggressors and women are passive is not an adequate description for many marriages and especially not for most of the successful mid-life marriages. Each mate feels free to stimulate the other mate through words, touch, suggestive looks, and little flirtations. Each mate also feels free to say "Not now, honey; I really need to get this project done."

When we were first married I (Jim) felt that it was my responsibility to set the pace for our sexual encounters. I didn't expect Sally to initiate, and as a good wife her job was not to refuse. Some years later I told Sally that it was a lot more fun for me if she also started some sexual teasing and touching. (We men like to be chased a little also.)

Our survey and other studies show that "equality in sexual initiation and refusal goes with a happier sex life. Going beyond equality to role-reversal makes couples unhappy."[3] If the wife does all the initiating and controls the sexual relationship, the sexual satisfaction for the couple drops. A balanced sex life doesn't mean that both of you feel or act the same way all of the time. It does mean that, overall, you are working toward equal levels of interest, initiation, and expression.

5. *A Healthy Possessiveness Is a Normal Part of a Successful Mid-life Marriage.* Married partners want to be desired by their mate, but we have noted two extremes. On the one hand, too much possessiveness is viewed as stifling and frequently causes friction. On the other hand, no sense of possessiveness indicates that the partner doesn't care if the marriage survives. The amount of possessiveness could be an indicator of the mate's attitude toward the future of the marriage.

ATTITUDES FOR A SUCCESSFUL SEXUAL RELATIONSHIP

To develop and maintain an intimate, exhilarating sexual relationship is a strong desire of most married people. We have found some practical ways to help that happen.

Maturity

To be able to love someone demands maturity. The greater the self-confidence, self-esteem, and sense of life success we possess, the greater is the likelihood that we will be effective lovers. If we are preoccupied with our own baggage—problems from the past, feelings of inadequacy or failure, feelings of exploitation or deprivation—we are not likely to be able to give ourselves fully to our marriage partner.

If you struggle with your personal maturity, you may benefit from reading chapter 13 entitled "Personal Growth." For now, store in your mind this concept: In order for sexual love to be satisfying, we each need to be mature individuals.

Giving and Caring

Effective sexual love in mid-life marriages is found most frequently when couples are able to focus on the satisfaction of their partner rather than on their own satisfaction. They each love with *agape* love, an altruistic love that is gentle, caring, and given without expectation of reward.

In a study of six different styles of expressing love in a relationship, researchers report that "the agapic is the most successful style . . . . No other lovestyle was associated with as many healthy indicators."[4]

This same study pointed out that lovestyles that tended to be only physical, or obsessive and jealous, or coldly evaluative of the partner's suitability were not as effective as the giving lovestyle. The people with an agapic lovestyle gave love without expecting a return and showed a great deal of care and understanding of the other person.

Our successful mid-life couples reported that there were two sides to their sexual relationship: giving love and receiving love. They each were able to understand the other person's need for sexual love and knew how to express that love. At the same time, they were able to allow their mate to love them sexually and not feel guilty for enjoying their mate's giving. They had a sense of freedom, both in giving and in taking love.

Vulnerability

Sexual love is also more satisfying as the partners are more vulnerable to each other, allowing both weaknesses and strengths to be seen. The successful mid-life marriages in our study had a growing sense of intimacy that was seen in their willingness to open up to each other. For example, men were willing to let their wives see them cry. They freely expressed emotions that generally are considered only a woman's domain.

Intimacy was developed as couples openly shared their thoughts, beliefs, attitudes, and feelings with each other. Less successful marriages were frequently marked by a lack of self-disclosure, openness, and vulnerability.

ACTIONS OF LOVE

As you already know, your sexual attitudes influence your sexual relationship. Your attitudes steer your actions. But the converse is also true; your actions influence your attitudes. As you focus on the actions of love, your feelings of love will grow.

Time

Couples in our study reported a strong correlation between feeling satisfied with each other and time spent together. A number of recent studies also show that not only quality time but also the quantity of hours people spend with each other is important in keeping a relationship flourishing. Time together in a relaxed atmosphere is crucial for the sexual dimension of the mid-life marriage.[5]

Anne Kristin Carroll says, "If you want to see femininity nipped in the bud, just show me a woman who is ignored, unloved, seldom sees any expression of affection—you might as well shoot her, because emotionally you've already killed her.

"Start checking yourself out. If your wife looks like warmed-over death, has severe nervous problems, seems to have lost that youthful spring in her walk, the glow from her face, and somewhere along the way, most of her self respect, in 99 percent of the cases you have a love-starved female."[6]

Some people think the Bible is a nonsex, monk-type book in which we are instructed only to spend time with God. However, the Scriptures direct us to spend sexual time with our partner: "The man should give his wife all that is her [sexual] right as a married woman, and the wife should do the same for her husband: for a girl who marries no longer has full right to her own body, for her husband then has his rights to it, too; and in the same way the husband no longer has full right to his own body, for it belongs also to his wife."

We are even cautioned that spiritual activities, such as fasting and praying, should be limited in order not to threaten the marriage by ignoring the sexual relationship: "So do not refuse these [sexual] rights to each other. The only exception to this rule would be the agreement of both husband and wife to refrain from the rights of marriage for a limited time, so that they can give themselves more completely to prayer. Afterwards, they should come together again so that Satan won't be able to tempt them because of their lack of self-control."[7]

Touch

The skin is the largest sensory organ in the body. A friendly touch has an amazing impact on our psyche. The touch may be only for a brief moment, but if it's from someone who cares, it's powerful.

Clint Eastwood is characterized as a tough actor with his outstretched hand pointing a massive gun at the head of some gangland villain and growling, "Go ahead and make my day." The rough approach may make Clint's day, but it won't make your partner's day.

Slipping your arms around your partner and holding him or her close for even ten seconds can drastically transform a crummy day into one of cheer. Touch is magical. You can work some loving magic every day in your life, and it will provide part of the basis for a positive ongoing marriage relationship, as well as a vital sexual life.

Hubert Humphrey was interviewed in 1977 when he was fighting his battle with cancer. He talked about his wife to whom he had been married for thirty-nine years: "Muriel and I were saying the other day, 'Wouldn't it be terrible if we really didn't love each other because in a sense we're compelled to be together.' I just can't imagine how miserable you would be if you had somebody you wish you weren't near, and that happens to people, in life. But she's been very tolerant of me and my ambitions, and now we have a sense of softness with each other, a tenderness that maybe we didn't have when we were youngsters first in love. Frankly, life is somewhat different for us because of my illness, and it's so good, so good just to have someone you can enjoy and touch."[8]

Words

The Song of Solomon in the Old Testament is a beautiful and graphic description by a married couple of their sexual attraction to each other. With words, they describe their fantastic sex life.

Usually it's harder for men to verbalize their feelings

about love. But spoken expressions of love and affection are very important to strengthen your sexual relationship.

Talking to each other about the sexual experience itself will also help to reinforce your relationship. Tell your partner that he or she is really good in bed and that you enjoy sex with him or her. "I like the way you touch me." "It is really fun for me to touch you." "Seeing your body is very exciting to me." "I like it when you _____." (Hey, we're not going to fill in all the blanks for you!)

As people go through mid-life, and especially during mid-life crisis, they may feel very inadequate and unsure sexually. It's crucial during this time for you to be giving your mate verbal reassurance that your sexual relationship is exciting and you're grateful to be married to him or her. Try every day, whether your mate is in mid-life crisis or not, to express appreciation. Say it, not only with actions, but also with words.

Physical Appearance

Sometimes our worst clothing is our underwear. Women wear old pinned together bras and saggy panties, and men wear holey T-shirts and shorts that ought to be thrown in the rag basket. Funny isn't it, that we wear our best-looking clothes for people we don't know, and we put up with junk for our most intimate moments.

When I (Jim) threw away my baggy white undershorts for some new, close-fitting colored ones, I was surprised by Sally's response: "I like to see your tight buns in those new shorts."

You may say to yourself, "It doesn't really matter." But it does. Attractive underwear is worth the investment. (At this point, our editor wrote in the manuscript margin, "This is one of those *great* truths very seldom expressed!")

Your physical appearance also includes those love handles at your waist, the cellulite on your thighs, the saddle bags on your hips, the bulging tummy, the extra chin, and sags where muscles used to be. We tuck it all in and cover it up when we go out to meet other people, but when we're around the person we most value, the flab hangs out all over. What a grotesque put-off for vital sex! One wife in our survey wrote, "My husband doesn't understand that flab looks horrible in a 'sexy' swimsuit."

It's worth a little exercise and weight loss to help your partner be stimulated more spontaneously. Paying attention to how you look will have a positive effect sexually and psychologically on both of you. As you feel you look good, you will also be more sexually aroused.

New Ways, Times, and Places

Most couples have sexual intercourse "same time, same station" again and again and again. It's usually in their own bed, late at night, in the dark, with the husband on top.

From a practical point of view, the end of the day when your physical energy is at its lowest point is probably the worst time to have sex. Why not think of some variety? Why not have sex when you first wake up or during the day? How about sex during the lunch hour or a surprise afternoon encounter or in the middle of the night?

Having intercourse in a different place can also be invigorating: the living room couch, the jacuzzi, the sun deck, your car in a secluded lover's lane after a nice dinner out.

How about spending a few hours listening to soft music or reading to each other in front of the fireplace? Then let your lovemaking flow into all types of kissing and touching.

Move into the bedroom if you care to or stay in front of the fire while you give each other a full body massage. If you like, use ordinary baby oil with the massage.

Warning: R-Rated

In the next few paragraphs we're giving somewhat explicit information about sexual creativity. It is not our desire to offend anyone but to offer help to those who want it. If our frankness would be offensive to you, we encourage you to skip to the subtitle "Potential Problems."

The following are some important guidelines that the two of you need to agree on before you consider sexual creativity.

▶ Anything that *both* of you *agree* to do or say *with each other* is permitted. You may decide to have oral sex (mouth to genitals) or you may want to have sex by massaging each other's genitals without the penis entering the vagina.

▶ Continue to experiment. If you don't like what you try, explore with some other ways. You aren't obligated to any pattern.

Now let's think about creativity with various positions. Have you tried. . .

1. Husband on top with the wife's legs widely spread and pulled up toward her breasts?

2. Husband on top, touching his wife's breasts with the tip of his tongue?

3. Wife on top, lying flat on her husband, or wife on top with her legs doubled up as if she is riding a horse? She can then lower her chest to her husband's face so that he can kiss her breasts and fondle them with his face or hands.

4. Both lying on your sides with the wife's leg over the husband? In this position, it is easy to stimulate each other by the husband massaging his wife's clitoris and the wife gently touching her husband's testicles.

5. Both lying on your sides with the husband curled around his wife? When the wife pulls her legs toward her chest, her husband can enter her vagina from the rear.

6. Standing in the shower?

Hey, the sky's the limit! Experiment and find the 500 best ways for you.

For clear step-by-step instructions on sexual techniques, we would encourage you to read "One Flesh: The Techniques of Lovemaking" in the book *Intended for Pleasure*, written by Ed and Gaye Wheat, a Christian medical doctor and his wife.[9]

Elizabeth Barrett Browning wrote, "How do I love thee? Let me count the ways." Think of different ways to touch each other, to express affection, to kiss and stimulate each other. Be creative and allow your creativity to bring a richness of pleasure and enjoyment to your marriage.

POTENTIAL PROBLEMS

Surprisingly, the biggest sexual problems in mid-life are not usually physical or mechanical but are the result of our thought processes, or the stress we're under, or the quality of our relationship with our mate.

Power Intimidation

A power struggle can be one restraint to a good sexual relationship. Tony Campolo in *The Power Delusion* says, "In both dating and marriage, each person endeavors to gain power over his or her partner. One way to do this is to withhold love. Therefore, the person who loves the least has the most power and the person who loves the most has the least power . . . .

"Think of some high school girl who is desperately in love. Her boyfriend, on the other hand, has only limited interest in her. In such a situation, he has great power over her and can make her do whatever he wants. She obeys his wishes because she is afraid of losing him. She may even submit to sexual relations with him, in spite of the fact that premarital sex is contrary to her religious convictions. Because she loves him so much, and he loves her so little, she is powerless. Because she desperately wants to continue the relationship, at all costs, she is vulnerable to his every whim."[10]

This power versus love struggle, described by Tony, continues in many marriages. Each mate is afraid to unreservedly love the other one because, in loving the other person, he or she becomes vulnerable and loses control. Then exploitation or hurt may follow. Sadly, some marriage partners withhold love from each other to retain power.

People who have been hurt in their family relationships or by other people unconsciously try to protect themselves. Yet they want to be close to people. So it's a constant struggle of trying to draw love from someone and still not give away too much love or become too vulnerable and get hurt.

We have frequently watched couples in counseling blame each other for their marital problems. At the same time, they both say they want it to be different. They're willing to make changes—if the other person will change first. This maneuver for the power position goes like this, "You change first, then I'll change. But I'll always change one step behind you so that I'm not the vulnerable one."

When you truly love someone, you disclose yourself. You expose yourself to potential exploitation. You are willing to do whatever is necessary so the life of the person you love is enriched.

Surrender of Power. This is what Christ's mission was about. Jesus came into the world and died for all the evil of all mankind, from all nations, for all of time. He didn't die for the sins of only the people who would respond; he paid the price of all of humanity's evil. He was willing to waste himself on some people who would utterly reject him.

True loving has that selfless quality about it. We are willing to be exploited if necessary. We will spend our love on a person who may not fully appreciate what that loving means or how much the sacrifice costs.

Frankly, selfishness has been a problem in my life (Jim). As a teen I felt more secure in a dating relationship if I loved less than the girl did. Some of that trait carried over into our marriage relationship. Yet Sally was willing to continue loving me, even when I was withholding love. I wanted to protect myself so that I'd never be in a vulnerable situation. I didn't want Sally to laugh at me because I loved too much. I'm grateful to God, Sally, and other people who have helped me to wrestle with this problem.

I have been able to give more in a relationship as my self-image has improved. Three factors have changed me:

1. **Daily Bible reading and regular prayer, which have assured me that God loves and values me. In that process I have also come to love God and to like myself better.**

2. **The affirmation of me by other people and especially by Sally. This has helped me to be more vulnerable and giving in relationships.**

3. **The support, encouragement, and openness of several small groups of people who have helped me to know that my inadequacies, temptations, and sins are common to everyone. The group support has helped me to accept myself and appreciate God's special gifting in my life.**

As I feel better about myself and my relationship to God, I am able to give love away to other people more easily. But I must confess that I still struggle with wanting to be secure and to love less in most of my interpersonal relationships.

Wife's Lack of Sexual Satisfaction

Some mid-life marriages don't have the fullest possible sexual relationship because the wife doesn't experience sexual fulfillment. The old illustration of the gas and electric stoves still gets the point across:

A man's sexual arousal cycle can be compared to a gas stove—instantly on, ready for sex; instantly off, ready for sleep. A woman, on the other hand, is somewhat like an electric stove. The control is turned to high, and for a while it seems as if nothing is happening. But eventually the stove warms up and can get very hot. When the switch is turned off, the burner seems as hot as the moment before and it takes some time to cool down.

A man needs to spend the necessary time so that his wife can become totally sexually aroused. He should not expect that when he hops into bed, she will be ready to have intercourse. Hours before, he needs to start the process of touching, complimenting, flirting, giving her those special little pats and touches that indicate she is special. When they go to bed, she will be partly warmed and ready.

Remember: Twenty minutes of begging is not considered foreplay. Masters and Johnson, in their book on sex and human loving, call attention to the importance of hours and days of "nonsexual closeness." They remind us that "without shared moments of nonsexual affection, it is hard to create a sense of intimacy the instant you're ready for lovemaking."[11]

In bed the husband needs to spend time holding his wife and massaging her body in a way that gives her pleasure. He should gradually move to the more sexually sensitive parts of her body. All of this touching and talking is not simply with the idea that he's trying to turn her on just so he can be gratified. His focus is to give her pleasure. As he desires to make her feel loved, contented, and pleasured, she will respond so that he also will experience pleasure.

The wife can increase her own sexual satisfaction by helping make moments of nonsexual closeness. She should respond to her husband's overtures, and she should initiate advances for a sexual encounter. She may not feel in the mood at first, but her feelings of sexiness may change rapidly if she gives herself permission. She should also be sure she is clearly communicating her sexual feelings and needs to her husband, so he doesn't have to guess—and maybe guess wrong.

Some women do not experience an orgasm because their clitoris is not adequately stimulated during sexual intercourse. Trying different positions as we have suggested may be helpful. If her husband stimulates her clitoris directly with his hand during intercourse, they may discover a terrific sexual experience.

Hysterectomy or Menopause

Early mid-life women wonder what will happen to them sexually after they have experienced menopause or if they have a complete hysterectomy, which includes removal of both ovaries and would, of course, bring on a surgically induced menopause. Menopause, by the way, is not a range of time, as the word is sometimes inaccurately used, but is the moment in history when the last menstrual period occurs. The climacteric is the period of time just before and after menopause.

Estrogen production begins to gradually decline sometime before menopause. It is dramatically reduced if both ovaries are surgically removed before menopause has occurred. This hormone reduction may affect a woman's sexual interest and fulfillment, but hormone replacement therapy can be used to help. Other glands in the body continue to produce hormones that affect the sex drive. In fact, sexual desire seems to be linked more to the testosterone hormone, which is produced by a woman's adrenal glands, than to estrogen.[12]

Hormones are not the only controlling factors of sexual interest and satisfaction. A woman's emotional and relational situations are probably the strongest factors. Her sense of wellbeing even affects the production of hormones in her body.

It's also important to be reminded that sexual stimulation is primarily related to the clitoris. Menopause is related to the function of the uterus and ovaries, not the clitoris, so sexual arousal does not need to be hampered.

After menopause there will probably be less natural vaginal lubrication, but using a suitable lubricating jell, such as K–Y Jelly, is an easy solution. A dry vagina makes intercourse painful for both partners. If the husband applies the jelly to his wife and massages her clitoris at the same time, they may find a new and fun way to solve a problem. The jelly can also be applied to the husband's penis with delightful results.

Benefits to a woman's sexual life because of menopause include not having to worry about an unexpected baby or continuing to use various contraceptives. Best of all, the postmenopausal wife is instantly available for sexual activity with a new and greater sense of freedom.

Physical Handicap, Heart Attack, Stroke

Sometimes people feel their physical disability will eliminate the possibility of sexual involvement. In many cases a sexual relationship can be continued, although some positions or methods may have to be altered. Your physician probably can help you.

Some people who have had a stroke or heart attack are afraid that the increased pulse rate during intercourse may bring on another heart attack. Dr. Earnest Friedman and Dr. Herman Hellerstein of Case Western Reserve University report that the pulse rate does not rise more during intercourse than it does during many other routine activities. The period of maximum acceleration usually lasts only about fifteen seconds. They conclude that "over eighty percent of men (and presumably women) who have had coronaries can fulfill the demand of sexual activity without evidence of significant strain."[13]

The problem may not be physical so much as a psychological fear. If you do have a physical limitation, talk to a specialist who understands your unique problem and who can give you specific help.

Male Impotence

Many men label sexual problems as impotence when, in reality, they only take longer to have an erection or an ejaculation. This slowing down is not considered to be impotence. In many ways, the slower pace is an asset. The process of intercourse is lengthened; therefore, the wife is likely to be more fully aroused and satisfied.

Until recently a general attitude about impotence was that the problem was "from the shoulders on up," meaning that impotence was only emotional not physical. But sometimes there are truly physical, chemical, or hormonal reasons for impotence. If a man does not experience an erection or ejaculation at all after trying some common sense solutions such as more rest, better diet, and longer foreplay, it would be helpful to see a medical doctor or professional counselor.

Hormone therapy, which is available now, can restore normal sexual functioning in many men. If the problem is due to stress or some other outside cause, an objective person such as a doctor or counselor may be able to help the man discover the changes he needs to make in his lifestyle.

A man can lose sexual interest because of mental or physical fatigue, use of drugs or overindulgence in food or alcohol. Or he may be preoccupied with his career or even afraid he may lose his job. These fears are enough to cause his sexual interest to sharply diminish or to disappear for a time.

Sometimes a cycle is established. A man may be experiencing stress or fatigue for some reason, and then if he is unable to have an erection or ejaculation in two or three attempts, he may become frightened that he won't ever again be able to perform sexually. This new fear of potential sexual failure becomes strong enough to truly reduce his sexual capacity.

An interesting study was conducted by Dr. Thomas Jakobovits in which he treated one hundred men for impotence. Most were in their seventies and eighties. Half were given oral hormone tablets and half were given placebos (imitation pills). After a month of treatment, 78 percent who were treated with medication were responding sexually.

Interestingly, 40 percent of the men who had been given placebos were also performing sexually. The conclusion of the study was that sexual performance is not only a result of hormonal stimulation but also because of psychological anticipation. Sexual confidence tends to improve sexual capacity.[14]

STEPS TOWARD SEXUAL INTIMACY

Masters and Johnson have been pacesetters in the field of sexual therapy, helping couples to re-establish or to improve their sexual relationship. They suggest the following six steps for rekindling sexual excitement in marriage:

1. Agree that things aren't what they should be and that you are going to make an effort to rebuild.
2. Make an effort to be attractive, interesting, and charming.
3. Agree that you are seeking to rekindle and revivify your sex life, but that temporarily you will postpone actual intercourse until *both* of you want it very much.
4. Do things that will enhance the mood; that is, an evening out, touching and massaging each other's body,

and talking to each other about what gives sexual pleasure.
5. Touch and manipulate each other genitally, but do not
have intercourse.
6. Have intercourse only after you both feel so impatient
that you can wait no longer.[15]

Additional Help

If you continue to have sexual problems, look for help.
Begin by reading books such as *Intended for Pleasure* by Dr. Ed
and Gaye Wheat.[16] Tapes by the same title are also available so
that you and your mate can listen together. If further help is
needed, consult your doctor or go to a qualified sex-therapy center associated with a university or hospital.

Don't expect a quick cure and avoid therapists who offer
one. Also avoid therapists whose treatment includes sex with
anyone other than your mate. Deal only with therapists who
have received supervised postgraduate training and who openly
reveal their education, plans for treatment, and costs.

The sexual problems that couples have shared with us
frequently can be answered through improved **attitudes** and
actions. As the emotional love improves, the sexual experience is
enhanced.

Bertrand Russell wrote in his autobiography: "I have
sought love, first, because it brings ecstasy—ecstasy so great
that I would often have sacrificed all the rest of life for a few
hours of this joy. I have sought it, next, because it relieves
loneliness—that terrible loneliness in which one shivering con-
sciousness looks over the rim of the world into the cold unfath-
omable lifeless abyss. I have sought it, finally, because in the
union of love I have seen, a mystic miniature, the prefiguring
vision of the heaven that saints and poets have imagined. This is
what I sought, and though it might seem too good for human
life, this is what—at last—I have found."[17]

Many of the mid-life couples whom we have interviewed
have watched their relationship grow to become, as Russell
said, something almost "too good for human life."

Key #7
Fun, Leisure,
and Humor

In the mid-life marriage, boredom, like arthritis, can develop. Movement is gradually restricted. Pain increases and the simplest tasks may become impossible undertakings.

Boredom is a creeping disease, which is both subtle and obvious. The husband and wife may live together, but they are never stimulated by each other. They eat together, sleep together, watch TV together, go to movies together, play golf together, attend church together, entertain friends together, and play bridge together. But the truth is that they could do all of those same activities with any of a thousand different people and find it a thousand percent more stimulating.

Problem: A Boring Marriage

It isn't that the bored mid-life couple hate each other. It isn't that they don't love each other. They're just apathetic. They have no interest in each other. Nothing is new in their relationship. They are trapped in the roles of marriage by obligations.

Living in a boring marriage is like being prisoners who are unable to escape from a prison camp. They have given up hope. They watch each other slowly age and grey, knowing that

156

they will die in this trapped existence. The more boring the marriage, the greater the vacuum. Sooner or later something will rush in and fill that vacuum. That something—or someone— may cause the marriage to break.

A boring marriage is like putting on extra weight. It happens gradually, but at some point you say, "Hey, I'm fat!" A dull marriage may exist quietly for many years, but at some point, quite often at mid-life, one of the partners will finally say, "Our marriage stinks."

In a boring marriage each partner increasingly turns away from his or her mate. They value each other less and less, and their commitment level drops year by year. After a while they have little commitment to the marriage or to each other, only a commitment to the children, to the church, or to other relatives.

Time for Fun and Games

Playing and laughing give vibrancy to marriage. All of life is more palatable if work and seriousness are mixed with fun. Tim Hansel in his liberating book, *When I Relax I Feel Guilty,* says: "Is it possible that your days are hurrying by so fast that you don't fully taste them anymore? Are *play* and *rest* foreign words in your living vocabulary? When was the last time you flew a kite, went for a bike ride, or made something with your hands? When was the last time you caught yourself enjoying life so deeply that you couldn't quite get the smile off your face? Chances are, it's been too long."[1]

Successful mid-life couples in our study have learned the secret of including fun, leisure, and humor in their marriage relationship. They don't think play is a waste of time or has to be expensive. Nor do they put off play for some distant day. They don't carry puritanical guilt that drives them to all work and no play with "the haunting fear that someone, somewhere, may be happy."[2]

Men, especially, seem to have difficulty with the use of leisure time. They know how to work and they know how to plop down in front of TV. With salted peanuts and a drink, they can watch hours of sports and movies over the weekend, but they have difficulty involving themselves in a leisure activity with their wife or family.

One man said to a reporter for the *Denver Post*, "That's just it—work is easier for me. It takes less effort for me to do a 'good day's work' than it does for me to do a 'good day's husband.'"[3]

WORK VERSUS LEISURE

The *American Couples* study reported, "People's jobs are commonly seen as competing with time and energy that could be spent on the relationship and so they are very often a source of conflict. Heterosexual women are the angriest with their partners about the intrusion of work on their private time together." The study went on to say that 50 percent of the married couples in their study fought over work and the amount of time that work took from them as a couple.[4]

When asked about this, one person said, "You know, it's been said that there are three life tasks—work, love, and friendship. And there's a tendency for a person to compensate in one if another isn't going well. So if you're having a hard time with your wife, you go to a bar for friendship or you stay at work. If your job isn't going well, you want more nurturing from your wife or family or your friends. Whatever isn't going well, you dump into the other two."[5]

Business and industry are not helping this problem. In the past, businesses frequently would interview a potential employee's wife to see if things were going well between the couple so the husband could do well at his job.

Now the approach is often the opposite. One company chairman said, "Find me someone who is as unhappily married as I am, so he'll really devote himself to the task at hand." Another executive complained to his company chairman that his marriage would break up if he took a promotion. The chairman replied, "Go ahead. I don't care—just raise our sales 30 percent." The marriage did break up.[6]

It used to be that men and women did their jobs around their personal and family life. Now with the hard-driving, success-motivated mentality, corporate advancement is seen as primary and everything else has to be set aside.

It's important to keep a wise perspective. We're not suggesting all play and no work. Rather, we're appealing for a balanced lifestyle. For example, it would be normal and expected that if one family member is under a special time crunch, the rest of the family members rally around and pitch in to pull the other person through until the deadline. After that, things should go back to normal.

Deadlines are choices. The point is, there shouldn't always be deadlines and work stress, always excuses and apologies, such as, "It's going to be different. We're going to get away. I'm going to change."

Perhaps work is the biggest competitor for leisure time. But as we look at the problem, it's really bigger than work. It's a **choice** to work and to be overextended rather than to spend leisure time with your mate.

We can hear you cry, "But you don't understand my problem." On the contrary, we do understand. We struggle with the same things you struggle with. We need to work more to pay bills. We need to work more to help other people. We need to work more to fulfill speaking obligations. In reality, we're the ones who've created the bills and have put ourselves in the position of obligation. We're also the ones who need to follow the Creator's wise guidelines and bring our lives and our marriage into balance.

SUCCESS ISN'T EVERYTHING

In our culture we've watched values change drastically over the past decades. The forties and fifties were heavily focused on the family and, at the same time, on success. The sixties and early seventies were focused on individual rights even if it meant splitting up families. By the midseventies some psychologists and sociologists were proclaiming that in years to come people would have serial-type marriages with a succession of mates—and their prophecy is tragically true for some.

By the mideighties we returned to a stronger sense of family, yet at the same time there seemed to be a strong drive for success. The yuppie (**Y**oung **U**rban **P**rofessional) movement became strongly focused on success, even at the expense of relationships.

Unfortunately, this strong drive toward material prosperity usually follows a pattern we have observed in previous generations: People who focus only on work, material possessions, and success lose touch with each other, and their marriage and families tend to fall apart. At the very time when Americans are crying out for more meaningful family relationships, a success-driven mentality subverts and tears marriages apart.

This success-oriented, materialistic, fast-paced life is typified by the yuppie woman described in a *Harper's* article: "She eats yogurt for breakfast in her car on the way to work, she lunches at the spa while she works out, and she pilots a small plane for her own pleasure. On the side she teaches at a woman's college and she leaves the kids with grandma. She leaves the kids with sitters. She leaves the kids period!" The author refers to this kind of person as "fast folk."[7]

Tragically, this type of fast-paced lifestyle seems to be very appealing. The money, the adventure, the position, the power are commodities and experiences many Americans seek. Leisure is, however, *crucial* to maintaining the important balance of work, marriage, and personal life.

WHY HAVE LEISURE?

The simple answer to this question is that leisure is good for you—physically, emotionally, and spiritually. It's also good for your relationships, including those in your marriage and family. Leisure keeps the other pieces of your life from falling apart.

We could ask why anyone should sleep or eat. The answer is that sleeping and eating enable the rest of your life to be effective. Inadequate sleep or improper diet will alter your outlook on everything else you do.

Life should be viewed as a whole, with many components in balance. We're not suggesting that life should be all leisure. Work and achievement are important components, but balance is the key.

Our survey couples reported leisure to be one of the major keys to keeping their marriage together and running smoothly.

A wife married to her second husband for thirty-five years said, "During my first marriage most of our leisure was separate (a factor in the divorce). Now most of our leisure is together—Praise the Lord."

A husband whose marriage had been on the verge of collapse because of his several affairs said, "Leisure is primary for us *now*." He went on to explain, "Earlier, leisure was difficult because we had so much conflict we didn't want to be together."

Perhaps the classic statement from the surveys regarding leisure is a catchy spin-off of an old saying by a wife married thirty-seven years: "All work and no play, makes you wonder: What for?"

Incorporating fun, leisure, and humor into your experience as a couple will strengthen your unity, whereas leisure activities apart from each other will weaken your marriage.

The major study in *American Couples* reported: "We find that those who spend a lot of time away from each other—take separate vacations, have separate friends, dine apart frequently—have a lower survival rate. This is true of married couples [not] only in the beginning years, but . . . for established relationships as well. Couples may lead separate lives because they value autonomy and reject accountability, and do not wish to operate as a couple all the time. For other couples the desire to be apart reflects incompatabilities which they may not consciously acknowledge. In either case, spending too much time apart is a hallmark of couples who do not stay together."[8]

Survival Isn't Enough

When I (Jim) was in college, I jokingly used a phrase that had a strong element of truth, "Well, I faked through another day." I was over my head in responsibility with classes that were very difficult for me, extracurricular sports and music, pastoring a small church, producing a film on a missionary's life, and keeping a courtship going with Sally. I was just doing what I had to do to get through day after day.

We keep thinking that next year is going to get better, the pressures are going to ease up. The reality is, unless we decide to do something now, next year is *not* going to get better. It will be the same old thing of just "faking through another day."

As Tim Hansel says, "Words like *wonder, joy, rest,* and

freedom have become faded replicas of what Christ taught. Time becomes a tyrant instead of a friend. Joy becomes something we will do later. Play becomes something for children. Creativity becomes the unattainable quality of artists and poets instead of the essence of our lives. Wonder is just the name of a bread, and imagination doesn't make enough money to be worthwhile."[9]

We have found that leisure is important for reducing stress in our lives. A walk around the park, a five-minute stroll to look at the flowers in our yard, or a half-day at the beach doing nothing but listening to the waves, watching the people, or reading the *Reader's Digest* can do wonders for reducing our overall stress level.

Ask yourself some questions about your life and your marriage. Do you frequently experience:

> ► a sense of urgency or hurry?
> ► an underlying tension resulting in angry words and misunderstandings?
> ► a deep desire to escape or be alone, to get in the car and drive away from the house?
> ► a constant frustration because there is more to be done than you can do?
> ► a feeling that time is passing too quickly, too much to do and too little time to do it?
> ► a craving for a simple life in some retreat, living off the land, being really kicked-back and relaxed?

These familiar symptoms are indicators that you need to incorporate more leisure time into your life so that stress can be drained off. Let's look at some hints about how to get more leisure time.

HOW TO CARVE OUT LEISURE TIME

1. It's not going to happen automatically. No one is going to assign you leisure time or pay you to do it. The two of you need to talk about a strategy to carve out the time.

One of our administrative assistants, Marilyn, and her husband have learned to take leisure time. Both of these mid-life people have heavy schedules. Dwight is a medical doctor and is director of his medical group. Marilyn works about half-time for us. In addition, they are very active in their church, teach classes for the deaf, and do other community and family-related activities.

Marilyn and Dwight (real names) have learned they can only relax if they get away from the house, so each Thursday is their day to go away with each other. It is an inviolable time. We know that we can't ask Marilyn to come into the office for extra help that day.

They have bought two collapsible five-speed bikes, and nearly every Thursday they load up the bikes and head for a new place to explore. It might be riding along a bike trail at the beach, in a forest preserve, or an old goldmining town. Besides getting some leisure time, this precommitted time to do new and stimulating things together has given an additional spark to their marriage.

2. *Think of short breaks.* I (Jim) have been working in my office all morning on this section of the book while Sally has been in her office working on other projects. I just took a little break. Sally rubbed some lotion on my shoulders that got sunburned yesterday. Wow! That felt good—her touch, the lotion, and the break. It took only a couple of minutes, but that short recess will help both of us to do our work better. If you think in terms of shorter, more casual times of leisure together, you'll be more apt to actually take breaks.

3. *Think of leisure as unorganized.* Try sitting on the patio in the cool evening breeze, going for a walk or a bike ride, or visiting spontaneously with neighbors. Try eating your dinner outside on the picnic table, in front of the fireplace, or around the livingroom coffee table while you lean against the couch. Spontaneous, unorganized changes of pace are keys to leisure.

4. *Split some of your vacation time into small segments.* For example, take one or two days of your vacation and tack them onto a national holiday that creates a three-day weekend. By adding two more days and driving home early the last morning, it will seem as if you've been gone a week. But you've really only used two days of your vacation time.

During the worst of Jim's mid-life crisis, he was experiencing heavy burnout each spring about March and could hardly make it until his summer vacation. His doctor advised him to take his vacation in small segments rather than using it all at one time and then waiting a full year for the next vacation. By breaking up the year with minivacations, the spring was not marked by those symptoms of heavy stress.

The problem is still basically one of choice. You *must* choose to spend some leisure time together. After you've made that decision, then figuring out how to get the time and what to do with it becomes part of the adventure.

5. Plan what *to do with time together.* You need to ask, "What is it that recharges our batteries?" Each of you should make a list of experiences, activities, places, and people that give you a sense of well-being. Compare your lists and find those items that are similar. Now you're in a position to decide what you're going to do.

It may be possible to use some of the activities that are dissimilar by combining them. For example, I (Jim) feel satisfied to sit in a sand chair on the beach and doze. Sally is nourished by reading. We both enjoy the ocean and walking along the beach. So we spend some time with Sally's reading and my dozing beside her and some time together, climbing on the rocks and walking along the beach. Sally doesn't force me to read, and I don't force her to doze or to climb endless miles over rocks. At the same time, we both get to experience a little of what restores us in a setting that provides a great deal of nourishment.

6. Develop a healthy play philosophy. We have had the privilege of doing some snorkeling in warm waters that are swarming with tropical fish. It's unbelievable! Sally has said, "It looks as if God gave crayons to first graders and told them, 'Color these fish any way you want to. Use as many colors as you want in any pattern.'"

When we look at the infinite variety of tropical fish, the giraffe, the flamingo, the rhinoceros, or the mole, we chuckle. Why are there so many kinds of animals, insects, flowers, trees, rock formations, and people? These things show God's creativity and his playful humor.

The creation account records that God rested on the seventh day. Was he so exhausted from his work that he had to rest? No, he set a pattern for us. He was saying, "It's O.K. to rest, to have leisure. It's O.K. to enjoy life." We must shake off the notion that leisure, fun, and humor are wrong. The workaholic, nonleisure person is violating the Creator's purposes.

7. *Plan inexpensive leisure.* Sometimes people complain that they can't have any recreation because it costs too much. Leisure is first an attitude. This attitude results in actions. Attitudes are free, and many activities you can plan are also free. Saying that you can't have any fun because it costs too much money is a cop-out for being too lazy to think creatively.

Why not do some of the following:
walk
visit a museum
hike in a park
bike
cross-country ski
garden together
visit a school for the blind
tour a food-processing factory
snorkel
fish
watch the sun rise or set
watch the moon rise or set
paint or pencil sketch
ride horseback
rent a canoe or a sailboat
dig for clams

Sometimes the best leisure is not organized. You don't have to be entertained. Create your own fun from simple things. The problem with TV sports is that you just watch. You aren't involved. That can also be the problem with Little League games, church picnics and luncheons, summer camps, or retreats. If everything is organized for you, you don't have to think or be creative. As a result, you get a small return on the leisure hours you spend.

When our three daughters were young teens, we took a trip to Florida, which graphically contrasted the real and the plastic. One night around midnight we walked the shore with flashlights, looking for giant green turtles that were coming in to shore to lay their eggs. It was fascinating to see these female turtles, about three feet in diameter, struggle up on the sand, turn around and face out to sea. They each carefully scooped out a deep hole with their rear feet and then laid soft white eggs, about half the size of ping pong balls, in the hole. Momma Turtle actually seemed to be crying as she dispensed the eggs; we could see a liquid seeping from her eyes. Then she carefully covered the hole, and returned to the sea. We felt we had been part of a very special secret.

On that same trip we rented a sixteen-foot Hobie Cat sailboat. We only used it an hour, because that's all we could afford. But the thrill of it lasts to this day.

Another night one of our relatives took the three girls scuba diving. The water was only about twenty-five feet deep over the reef, but the night world of multicolored fish and other sea life looked entirely different from what we had seen while snorkeling by day. This first scuba diving expedition was a treasured experience. We also spent many hours of that vacation sunning on the beach, playing in the waves, eating fresh fruits, and enjoying other delights that only midwesterners could fully appreciate.

On our way home we were told that we hadn't really lived unless we had seen Disney World. So we spent a day at Disney World, which cost us more than a hundred dollars (a lot of money for our family in the seventies). The sharp contrast impressed us all. We had just spent the last several days experiencing free real-life adventures. Now we were experiencing plastic make-believe, which was programmed by someone else and cost us a lot of money and waiting in long lines in the sun.

8. _Don't let your leisure become work._ We now own a sixteen-foot catamaran sailboat. Most of the time it's in our garage because we're so busy and it's inconvenient for us to put it in the ocean, even though we now live near the California coast.

Every now and then I drag Sally off to a boat show. We oooh and ahhh over the thirty-five- to fifty-foot sailboats with galleys, bedrooms, toilets, showers, microwave ovens, stereo music, and all the pleasures of home. We say to each other, "Wouldn't it be fun to have a sailboat in a nearby marina and all we'd have to do is drive down, jump on, and go sailing?"

The truth is, sailing for many people is not leisure; it's work. Go to a marine sometime to see how many people are repairing their boats, scraping off barnacles, and keeping up with the never-ending maintenance of owning a boat.

Or what about the vacation cottage? You know, the place where you spend the whole weekend repairing the pump, building a new pier, replacing a door, or cleaning squirrels out of the chimney. It sounds so glamorous, but sometimes our leisure projects become more "project" than "leisure."

And then there's driving for vacation. Rather than being fun, the trip becomes an endurance test. Instead of being physically and mentally restored, you get tense about covering a prescribed distance in a set time. You don't even enjoy the places you're seeing. If your trip is for a break in the routine and for recuperation, you need to be realistic in what you attempt. (We personally find we need to chop our original plans about 50 percent or we work ourselves to death **resting!**)

9. Don't put off leisure until "someday." Frequently the person who is uncomfortable with leisure puts it off but says, "I'm not opposed to leisure. In fact, I really enjoy it. Boy, some of the greatest times in my life have been when we've been able just to get away, kick back, and unwind. The problem is that right now I've got this project I really have to get done. But after I'm finished, boy, then we're really going to take off, have a good time, and catch up."

Recently we met a man who was a self-made multimillionaire by the time he was forty. The cost, however, was his continual absence from his family. His marriage started to fall apart. His wife gave clear warning signals, but he couldn't believe she would walk away. She really didn't walk away, she rode away in the lap of luxury. She literally took everything he had. He entered his forties financially broke, divorced, and disowned by his kids.

For about two years he was a defeated, depressed man. He said, "I thought I could have it all, but what I discovered was that I really traded my relationships for wealth. In the end I lost both—relationships and wealth. I thought my wealth and success would hold my family. Instead that's what separated me from my family."

He is remarried, but he is living a totally different lifestyle. His new focus is on his marriage and on people. He even changed his career from moneymaking to a public service job.

As I (Jim) tell this story, I realize I'm speaking to me as much as to you. I find it easy to delay leisure in order to stick in one more conference, one more book chapter, one more article, one more business meeting, or one more telephone call. Just now our middle daughter, Brenda, came to my office door and said, "Could you pull back the pool cover so we could go swimming?" "Just a minute," I said to her. "Let me finish this section." I'm still dictating while Brenda and her little boys are waiting for me to pull the pool cover back.

Let me assure you that I'm not going to keep my daughter and grandchildren waiting much longer, but I just want to make my point before I lose my train of thought.

There's no magic solution to my problem. I have a constant battle, and daily I have to remind myself to smell the roses, take those minibreaks, and not put off fun and leisure for sometime down the road. (O.K., O.K., I'm going!)

A half hour later, at three o'clock in the afternoon, I'm back to work at my desk. It's eighty-three degrees out and a beautiful summer, Friday afternoon. I have already worked over eighty hours this week. Brenda and the boys are swimming in the pool while Sally, Marc (Brenda's husband, who is counseling a mid-life woman by phone), and I continue to work. Now you understand what I said. Taking time to relax really is a problem for me, but we have agreed that in about an hour we're going to take a break and all go swimming.

HUMOR

As you include leisure into the flow of your life, try to think in terms of fun and humor—the small surprises—even the zany things. Humor and fun not only enrich leisure time; they also help your overall physical and emotional health.

Humor can heal. Norman Cousins in his book, *Anatomy of an Illness*, tells of having an incurable illness. With the help of a doctor, he set up a program of humor, enjoyment, and laughter. He read funny books, rented Charlie Chaplin films, and spent time with friends who liked to laugh. The result: He got well.[10]

Psychiatrist William Fry of Stanford University reports that, "Humor is a tremendous boon to physical health. Laughing steps up the pulse rate, activates muscles, enervates circulation of blood, and increases oxygen intake—all effects that match the beneficial aspects of physical exercise. But more important, laughter causes remarkable physical relaxation, reverse of stress, which can kill through hypertension and coronaries . . . . humor and fury cannot coexist."[11]

Humor smooths out rough spots. Humor can defuse some of the potentially difficult times in a marriage relationship. For years our family has used a couple of remarks that help redirect potential pouting times. We say to the one who may be struggling, "Watch out or the pigeons will land on your lip." Or, "Be careful not to be a pusi-cat." *Pusi-cat* is fabricated from a big word we learned in college: *pusillanimous,* which actually means lacking courage or resolution, being cowardly or timid. One of the remote meanings is that of withdrawal and a sense of self-pity. Over the years it has come to mean pouting in our family, and cautioning against being a "pusi-cat" is a lighter way of reminding someone not to slide into self-pity.

Humor makes lasting memories. Try some crazy stuff. It's O.K. to be a little off the wall. Surprise each other. The joy of an unusual surprise will last forever. A few months ago I wanted to give Sally a little treat as a minicelebration. Sally and I were both trying to lose weight, but I stopped by a special bakery and bought four big chocolate éclairs. I mean they were BIG, about six inches long and four inches across and stuffed with the most yummy light, delicate, and absolutely intoxicating Boston cream filling you can imagine. The roll was crispy and flaky, with a covering of thick, high-quality, mouth-tingling chocolate.

I sneaked the éclairs into the house and put them into the back of the refrigerator where Sally couldn't see them. After dinner, when we were sitting in the family room, I casually went to the kitchen and came marching into the family room with a scrumptious éclair for each of us. After we finished eating, and while we were thinking of the last bites, we commented on how great they were. Then I said, "Wouldn't it be fantastic to just pig out and eat another one?"

"That would be terrific," she agreed. "It would be sinful but wonderful!"

I sat on the couch for a few more minutes, innocently reading the paper. Then I went to the kitchen and came back with the other two éclairs on clean plates. She was just blown away with delight. We laughed together about how utterly crazy it was to be pigging out on these great-tasting éclairs when we were supposed to be losing weight. The fun we had together that night and the jokes we make every time we see éclairs are worth the extra calories.

An absolutely delightful man in our survey who was married forty-one years talked about leisure: "The benefits of leisure are in the expectation of doing it, the realization of experiencing it, and finally the memory of a good thing shared."

The two of us many times have shared leisure in all three dimensions, and we have been three times nourished.

CHAPTER

Key #8
Realistic
Expectations

Early married life is usually built on an unrealistic idealism. Many young couples start out with high expectations, but frequently these very expectations become major sore points, which may bring about marital collapse.

The adolescent years are often filled with fantasies and imaginations about the opposite sex and marriage. Each one dreams of this wonderful person he or she is going to meet. Songs like "Some Enchanted Evening" from *South Pacific* support that magical notion. Some enchanted evening you'll see a stranger across a crowded room. You'll be drawn to each other as magnets. It will be true love.

THE SET-UP

Popular music through the years has fed these unrealistic and romantic expectations. You are going to meet this wonderful person. Your relationship will be electrifying and exhilarating. Your sexual experiences will transport you to unbelievable heights of ecstasy. In short, you will live happily ever after.

Recently we've had contacts with several divorced young

adults. Each one has a sad story to tell, but a familiar line keeps coming through all of them, "It just didn't work out."

What does that mean? As we continue to listen and gently ask questions, we begin to hear comments such as:

—— ▼ ——

"I never thought it would be this way."

"She became a different person."

"We never really did the things I thought we would."

"Our marriage changed us as individuals. Maybe we never should have gotten married. Then our relationship wouldn't have changed."

—— ▲ ——

Young Adult Blindness

The young adult tends to see life in black and white boxes. Listen to the conversation of adolescents and see if you hear any middle ground or grey areas. Their language is marked by extremes symbolized by the catch words of the day: whether it's totally awesome, totally rad, or totally cool. The alternative to being terrific is totally disgusting, totally gross, or totally sickening.

It's easy to see how unrealistic expectations can be established when this black-and-white approach to life is incorporated into marriage. Anyone who is acceptable enough even to be considered as a marital partner is exceptionally wonderful. The others not in the running are exceptionally awful. Young people don't see that almost everyone would fit into a middle category.

When we finally choose a marriage partner, a part of us recognizes that the other person is imperfect, but we believe we can change him or her. Furthermore, we don't want to admit out loud that our partner is flawed (or even a normal human being) because that would indicate we were somehow flawed in choosing this person.

Denying the facts—who our mate really is and how little we're going to change him or her—causes us to be disappointed with our powerlessness. We react with anger or grief when we finally discover that we're not going to be able to correct our mate's imperfections.

One husband said, "Our sex life has always been *very un-satisfying* for me. My wife never saw her parents express affection and never learned how to be loving herself. For years I was jealous of other men whose wives were warm and sexy. I was tempted to be unfaithful just to get even with my wife, but my moral values wouldn't let me. Even though our sex relations are still a problem, I've decided to focus on the other parts of our marriage that are good."

Mid-Life Revelations

One of our survey wives said, "In the early years I was very unrealistic. Recognizing and accepting myself and my spouse 'as is' gave me freedom to grow and develop the relationship." Her husband said on his questionnaire, "Being realistic has been difficult but it has helped me cope."

This couple is highly educated and from a conservative church. They had been married twenty-four years. At some time in the marriage the husband had an affair, but they were back to working together to improve their marriage.

In another section of the questionnaire the wife wrote, "When I became aware of my 'fantasies' and unreal expectations and was willing to make realistic and constructive changes, our marriage became more satisfying."

As we come into the mid-life years, several forces are at play that help us to have more realistic expectations.

Ambiguity. The first is that we've had years of life experience with partial success and partial failure. We've faced questions without answers. We've struggled with human tragedy, disappointment, and conflict so that we now see the vast grey areas of life along with its black and white extremes. We know firsthand about uncertainty and ambiguity. A question may have four answers, which are all good, or four answers, none of which is good. This capacity to see the greys in life helps us as mid-life people to view our marriage more realistically.

Mid-life crisis. By their late thirties or early forties many people will have experienced a mid-life crisis. At the beginning of mid-life crisis, which may last from three to five years, people are usually driven by strong idealism and a desperate desire to recapture the past. They want to go back to their young adult days. They may attempt to relive those days by lifestyle changes, wearing different clothes, working out at the gym or spa, taking up new sports, hanging around with younger people, or driving a car that portrays a youthful image.

This is a last grasp at trying to recapture youth. It's a denial of reality, which reverts back to the thinking style of the adolescent, the world of dreams and fantasies. We attempt to make all of life be Camelot, the ideal kingdom where everything and everyone is perfect. At the same time, we are faced with some unavoidable realities that make these fantasies impossible.

Drooping body, empty nest. Flying in the face of all the fantasy, however, is the stark reality of mid-life: looking in the mirror and seeing the wrinkles, the receding hairline, the greying hair, the sagging muscles and breasts, the ballooning stomach, the bulging buttocks, and the varicose veins. Reality means that your kids are moving out of your home, and the good old days with your little kids gathering around the Christmas tree or jumping into your arms from the picnic table are gone.

Career consternation. Reality also sets in at your work. You've gone about as far as you're going to go. You always thought it would be different by now. You thought you'd be more financially secure by this time in life. You thought you'd be enjoying your job instead of hating it. You thought you'd be looking forward to retirement, but now retirement makes you angry. You've watched your company push other people into early retirement and you know you're next.

Discrimination. Reality hits you as people begin to treat you differently. When you were in your twenties, you could hardly wait to be thirty—"Then I'll finally get some respect." Now it's like the John Denver song, "When I was young, people asked me how things are. When I'm old, they'll ask me how things were. And all the pretty girls will call me sir."

The death specter. Reality sinks in as we begin to face death more frequently. Our parents will likely die during our mid-life years. They have always been there to protect us, for us to fall back on, as if they were a fence erected along the edge of a cliff. We could play freely anywhere near the edge, because the fence was always there.

When our parents die, it's like a part of the hill has fallen away and carried the fence crashing down the mountain side. No other fence is between us and the edge. Instead we are now the fence. We are put in place to protect and help the younger generation, to be their hope and security.

The truth of death's inevitability and our position in the line of death causes a great deal of evaluation. Mid-life people are forced to make adjustments to this reality.

ACCEPTING AND ENJOYING

The successful mid-life couples in our survey revealed that they had become more realistic about life in general and their marriage in particular. This growing perception of reality had brought them to a settled sense of acceptance.

Their acceptance didn't mean they pretended everything was terrific or no weaknesses and flaws existed. Accepting reality wasn't the ostrich-head-in-the-sand approach of denying truth. Rather, these couples had faced themselves, their mate, their marriage relationship, their career, their extended family, and God in such a way that they were able to say, "No, my life isn't perfect in all areas, but I can live with it. I can accept things as they are right now. I'll keep on growing and hoping for changes, but I can live with life as it is now."

These mid-life couples weren't following an all-or-nothing attitude about life—that is, "If it can't be perfect, then I don't want to be involved in it. If I can't have it my way, then I'll be angry." The realism and acceptance in these successful marriages was focused in several ways.

*1. **They have given up the desire to change their partner.*** They have come to see differences as strengthening, broadening, and stimulating rather than abrasive. Some of these couples are able to laugh at their own idiosyncrasies and unique ways of facing life.

They are also able to accept a situation that may not be exactly as they desire. A man married thirty-eight years said in our survey, "One of our biggest problems is my wife's sexual coolness following menopause. It is a problem still not solved, but I am accepting the 'condition.'"

A wife married twenty-seven years said, "I finally accepted the unchangeable about him and am grateful for what he is compared to what he might be."

2. They have come to accept their own and their mate's limitations and have focused on their strengths. One man said, "No, she doesn't have the greatest body in the world, but she is fun to be with. She accepts me with all of my weaknesses, and that's worth more than a great body."

A mid-life woman said, "In some ways I wish my husband had accomplished more in his career, but that doesn't seem to be important to him. His more easy-going approach to life has helped to level me out, and at this age in life I'm glad he saved me from being such a hard driver."

3. They are realistic about other people's attractiveness. They enjoy members of the opposite sex and their mates have friends of the opposite sex, but they keep their balance in their relationships with others.

Some couples shared with us that in their early married years other friends were part of their fantasy life. They wondered how he would be as a husband or how she would be as a wife. Now that they have come to better understand people and realize no one is perfect, they know that just switching partners would not solve their problems.

In an article entitled "The War Within; An Anatomy of Lust," the author shares some practical insights from his personal experience. He had been trapped in sordid fantasies about other women to the point of unhealthy obsession. He finally was able to break free and become realistic about other women's sexual qualities.

"I have not mentioned the effect of lust on my marriage. It did not destroy my marriage, did not push me out to find more sexual excitation in an adulterous affair, or with prostitutes, did not even impel me to place unrealistic demands on my wife's sexual performance. The effect was far more subtle. Mainly, I think, it cumulatively caused me to devalue my wife as a sexual being. The great lie promulgated by *Playboy*, television commercials, and racy movies is that the physical ideal of beauty is attainable and oh, so close. I stare at a *Playboy* centerfold. Miss October has such a warm, inviting smile. She is with me alone, in my living room. She removes her clothes, just for me, and lets me see all of her. She tells me about her favorite books and what she likes in a man. Cheryl Tiegs, in the famous *Sports Illustrated* swimsuit issue, sweetly walks toward the camera, letting the coral blush of her breasts shine out boldly from underneath a net bikini. She lets me see them—she has no inhibitions, no prudency.

"The truth is, of course, if I sat next to either Cheryl Tiegs or Miss October on an airplane, she would not give me the time of day, let alone take off her clothes for me. If I tried to strike up a conversation, she would brush me off. And yet, because I have stared at Cheryl's breasts and gone over every inch of Miss October as well as a throng of beauties that Madison Avenue and Hollywood recruit to tantalize the masses, I start to view my own wife in that light. I expect her to have Farrah's smile, Cheryl's voluptuousness, Angie's legs, Miss October's flaming red hair and sparkling eyes. Envy and greed join hands with lust. I begin to focus on my wife's minor flaws. I lose sight of the fact that she is a charming, warm, attractive woman and that I am fortunate to have found her."[1]

Mid-life couples have a broader life perspective that enables them to see other people and their mate in a wholistic way so that, without any phoniness, they can say, "I would rather be married to you than to Cheryl Tiegs or Robert Redford."

4. They believe divorce is never a choice for them. This came through clearly in our study as well as in other studies.[2] As we mentioned earlier, 94 percent of our survey couples strongly agreed or agreed that a commitment to stay married was important in helping hold their marriage together.

A man married twenty-eight years wrote, "We only had each other and we both wanted our married life to be permanent. It wasn't until years later that we realized our commitment was never really discussed but just *done.*"

A medical doctor who had been married twenty-nine years put it this way, "I always wanted to be married only once for all my life."

A wife said, "When we got married, we just assumed it was for life."

Even when divorce could have been for moral reasons, many of our survey respondents wouldn't consider it. A wife said, "Although my husband has committed adultery and my friends tell me I should divorce him because I have legal grounds to do so, I would never think of divorce."

We have found that couples who never mention divorce as a possibility for themselves avoid the heartache experienced by couples who toy with the divorce idea. Once divorce begins to be a consideration, an erosion starts that is very hard to reverse.

5. They have more to gain than to lose by staying together. In some ways, our mid-life couples seemed to be coldly objective as they evaluated their marriage. Some of them had chosen to stay together because they'd made a careful assessment of their partner, their extended family, and their history together. Then they asked themselves, *What is the possibility of scrapping this marriage and establishing a second one that would be better?*

Their conclusion was that the pain of divorce for them personally and for their family, friends, work colleagues, and community would be too great. This, coupled with the realization of the remoteness of establishing a better second marriage, had caused them to redirect their energies toward improving their present marriages.

Such blunt, cold realism was startling to me (Jim) at first, because I wanted our research to show that couples stayed together during the mid-years because of "chemistry," true love, or the magic of their relationship. Instead, we discovered that a realistic evaluation had caused them to make strong choices and had reinforced deep commitments.

One husband who had had an affair said, "When I look at my children, I am reminded of my commitment to my marriage. I would not want to lose their respect so I stay in the marriage."

A wife said, "I looked at what I'd gain and what I'd lose if I left him. I decided that I had more with him than without him. Even though there were still problems, as soon as I decided to stay and work at the marriage, I knew I had made the right decision."

6. Their realism and acceptance also touched their spiritual lives. During mid-life crisis some people say to themselves or aloud, "I don't think God understands my particular situation. Or, at least, he can't expect me to stay in this marriage any longer. Perhaps that old view of marriage as a permanent relationship is a cultural idea that is outmoded and should be ignored." In essence, they are questioning God's plan for a couple to stay together all of their lives.

Being forced to evaluate many areas of life as they work through mid-life crisis causes people to rethink their spiritual foundations. Some may become angry or indifferent toward God, but many men and women in our survey acknowledged new spiritual growth and a more vital relationship with God.

One couple had been through many stresses, including the husband's mid-life crisis, a teenage daughter's pregnancy, and the death of both fathers. The husband said, "In the last four years I have gotten my life on track with God and that is making all the difference in how I handle problems now. While I was dealing with all that was happening to me and my family, I began to think about God seriously for the first time in my adult life."

A wife wisely observed, "I finally realized I had to let my husband be who he is and let God guide me in my responses to him. God has to be the one in control."

The successful mid-life couples had come to the point of affirming, or reaffirming, that God's plan for lifelong marriage was right. They believed their energies ought to be directed toward spiritual and emotional growth rather than toward fantasies of someone better out there somewhere.

7. *They had learned to forgive.* Realism and acceptance resulted in a new level of tough love that included forgiveness. Sometimes an idea promoted is that tough love means we should get firm with people, tell them off, and kick them out. "Shape up or ship out."

A time **may** come when you have to face a hard decision that a relationship is finished, but first you need to consider carefully what forgiveness is all about. We agree with Ed and Gaye Wheat that your job is to do all you can to love your mate and meet his or her needs.[3] More marriages are saved by forgiveness than by delivering ultimatums.

Shirley said to us, "I've been able to forgive Bruce because I love him. He has sometimes hurt me deeply and we still have some unresolved problems, but I keep forgiving him anyway. I remember that 'love covers a multitude of sins,' so I just put my love and forgiveness in the place of his wrongs toward me. Each time I do that, it's like a fresh start on a clean sheet of paper."

Forgiveness is a multifaceted gem that involves:
- ▶ Confession to God and asking his forgiveness
- ▶ Confession to your mate and asking his or her forgiveness
- ▶ Accepting God's forgiveness
- ▶ Accepting your mate's forgiveness
- ▶ Granting forgiveness to your mate
- ▶ Restoring your mate through positive affirmation

Forgiveness is easier when we believe *any* temptation that *any* other person has experienced is possible in our own lives. Forgiveness is also easier to grant when we realize that we often need to be forgiven ourselves.

Practicing forgiveness is easier when we realize that bitterness, hate, and grudges really have more effect on us than on our mate. The very act of withholding forgiveness keeps the bitter green juices flowing. We develop ulcers in our stomachs and lines on our faces. Forgiveness has a wonderful releasing power, not only for the other person but also for ourselves.

Sylvia has been hurt over and over by her husband's attention to other women. She watches Jerry appreciate and praise certain women for things they do, how they look, and qualities they possess, but he never acknowledges those things in her. Friends who see what goes on between Sylvia and Jerry are amazed at Sylvia's graciousness. She does not seem angry or bitter.

We asked her how she could live with Jerry's flattery of other women—and obvious sexual attraction to many of them—while he rejects her. She replied, "Of course, it hurts. I can't help but notice how nice he is to other women. I get tired of never hearing a kind word from him. But no matter what he thinks of me, I know who I really am. And when I acknowledge his 'humanness,' I feel free from personal hurt. I just choose to forgive him and go on."

One husband, who had separated from his wife for a time and then reunited with her, said about her, "She has always been ready to pick up the pieces and reassemble our lives after every shattering event. She doesn't look back, always ahead—with enthusiasm."

Forgiveness comes easier when we trust God to do the

changing in another person's life. Sometimes we unconsciously say, "If I don't punish her, she may do the same dumb thing over again. I'm going to help her out by withholding forgiveness and teaching her a lesson." Forgiveness means that we relinquish judgment to God and trust our mate into God's hand to let him work it out.

A final word about forgiveness. Frequently God has forgiven, the mate has forgiven, and perhaps the community has forgiven, but we don't forgive ourselves. God has provided forgiveness for us and wants us to feel good about ourselves.[4]

It's like swimming in salt water. After you come out, your body is sticky and you feel yuckie. But a freshwater shower washes away all that stickiness and you feel much better. Accepting God's forgiveness is like taking a good shower.

8. *They know good marriages are a process.* Realistic expectations have helped these couples not to expect overnight cures; instead they see their marriage as a journey and their personal growth as part of that process. Disappointments or scares may have come along the way, but those have been incorporated so that they became part of the strength of the fabric, not an acid to destroy it.

Many people whose marriages have been threatened by a divorce action, an affair, or another serious break are moved to work on building a solid, satisfying relationship. As one woman, whose husband had filed for divorce, wrote on her questionnaire, "It made both of us look inward for the cause." This couple and others like them have turned an event that nearly ended their marriage into a tool for building a good marriage.

9. *They realize that future failures won't be fatal.* Successful mid-life couples have not only dealt with past failures in positive ways, but they feel that if something happens down the road, they can handle it. After all, by now they have developed a history of endurance. They know they're tough. They've learned some ways to cope with problems. They're survivors. They believe God will be there to help if a future stress time comes.

10. *Successful mid-life couples march to a different drumbeat.* They focus on relationships, not on the material, the physical, or the strong push toward success. They see the big picture rather than just the immediate, small parts. They hear other sounds. They're pulled by other meanings in life—their relationships and especially their marriage.

Tim Hansel uses an illustration that applies well to the focus of strong mid-life marriages:

"An Indian was in downtown New York, walking along with his friend, who lived in New York City. Suddenly he said, 'I hear a cricket.'

" 'Oh, you're crazy,' his friend replied.

" 'No, I hear a cricket. I do! I'm sure of it.'

" 'It's the noon hour. You know there are people bustling around, cars honking, taxis squealing, noises from the city. I'm sure you can't hear it.'

"Finally on the other corner he found a shrub in a large cement planter. He dug beneath the leaf and found a cricket.

"His friend was duly astounded. But the Indian said, 'No. My ears are no different from yours. It simply depends on what you are listening to. Here, let me show you.'

"He reached into his pocket and pulled out a handful of change—a few quarters, some dimes, nickels, and pennies. And he dropped it on the concrete.

"Every head within a block turned.

" 'You see what I mean?' the Indian said as he began picking up the coins. 'It all depends on what you are listening for.' "[5]

Key #9
Serving Each
Other

We recently visited our dear friends Tim and Anne (real names) who are in their early mid-life years and are a splendid example of a couple who serve each other. Tim is a busy pastor, and Anne ably fills her role as a pastor's wife and mother to their young son, Luke. She also works in her profession as a nurse and is studying for a graduate degree.

Tim and Anne's home is a comfortable place to visit. It isn't just the charming country interior of the house or the woodsy, bird-inhabited setting. Neither is it the delicious meals served in relaxed elegance, nor the toasty warmth from the roaring fire in their huge fireplace. Those elements are all part of the enjoyment, but it's the loving atmosphere in their home that invites us to relax.

You don't have to be there long before you see that Tim and Anne spontaneously love and respect each other. There is a mutuality in their relationship. They quietly and unassumingly serve each other even though they probably don't even know they do it.

We all know that no woman can be housewife, mother, pastor's wife, nurse, and student—and keep her sanity— without some help. And no man can be an effective husband, father, and busy pastor without the support of his wife. Tim and Anne have a beautiful blend of carrying out their separate roles while helping each other.

The day we were there, we saw Tim and Anne share in caring for Luke after school, transporting him to and from a friend's house, helping with homework, and carrying out his bedtime ritual. They worked together in serving us a gourmet dinner. Then we enjoyed hours of stimulating conversation in front of their fireplace.

Anne needed to be at work very early the next morning and left before the rest of us were awake. Tim fed Luke his breakfast and got him off to school. Then he served us a tasty breakfast. Tim had to be at an important meeting before we left the house.

Jim and I packed our car and closed their front door. As we drove away, we knew we had been in a special place. Tim and Anne had been a spiritual refreshment to us at a time when we needed a rest during a heavy speaking tour. But, most of all, they had shown us that an invigorating, but tender, graciousness permeates a home where husband and wife serve each other. They are busy people, but the gears of their complex life run smoothly because of the oil of love, courtesy, and mutuality they share.

Reflecting on Our Love

As we continued down the road away from their house, I mused about all the ways Jim has shown his servant attitude toward me through the years: helping with the housework when he could, sharing the parenting of our three daughters, encouraging my going back to school to finish my bachelor's degree and then obtain a master's degree, and putting up with simple meals and skimpy housekeeping so that I could manage all of it!

Jim's serving attitude has made it possible for me to have a career in teaching, writing, and conference speaking now that our daughters are grown and gone. He does as much of the meal preparation and cleanup as I do. He insists that I have someone to help clean the house, and he helps me with the parts we do ourselves. He shares in shopping for groceries. (He even offers to help with the laundry, but that's one job I'm hanging onto for myself. After all, I might start feeling guilty that I don't help him more with the yardwork!)

Most humbling of all are the many times when he puts my wants and wishes ahead of his. I know him well enough that I can tell when something is not his first preference, but he often graciously does it to meet my needs. Do you know what that does to me? It makes me want to look for ways to serve him!

A MUTUAL MARRIAGE

When a couple serve and care for each other, as do our friends Tim and Anne, a mutual marriage results. Some essential ingredients to develop that kind of relationship are discussed in the next pages.

A mutual valuing. If we really believe that all are created equal and that God has given each of us gifts to be used to strengthen other people, then we must believe that God also has given valuable abilities to our mate.[1] The Creator values our mate as much as he does us. He has entrusted gifts and abilities to him or her, even though they may be different from ours.

In the Genesis account of the creation of mankind, we see that Adam was created incomplete and Eve was a counterpart to complete him. Eve was also incomplete and needed Adam. We humans are not born as whole entities. We cannot live as isolated islands in the sea or as hermits in the desert. We are, rather, created by God to be in relationships, each contributing to another's life.

Happily married couples appreciate what they each bring to the relationship. Their union is more than just the process of addition. One plus one now equals a deep sense of valuing and being valued.

Mutual responsibility for growth. We are not just rooming house boarders who live separate lives. We are people accountable to each other. The growth of our mate is correlated to our investment of concern, time, and energy in helping him or her grow.

Sometimes in life one person is up and the other down; one is weak and the other strong. Then, because of changing circumstances or inner resources, the strong and the weak may reverse. A mutual marriage means that the stronger one assumes the responsibility to encourage and support the one who is temporarily down. They take turns going the second mile when necessary so that each one can survive and grow.

Mutual submission. In a mutual marriage, one isn't the boss (generally the husband) and the other a servant (often the wife). Instead two servants offer to each other their gifts and abilities, each honoring, respecting, and loving the other. Jerry and Barbara Cook, authors of *Choosing to Love,* have aptly defined this servanthood type of submission:

"True submission does not deny my own value or negate our differences. It *offers* my ideas, opinions, and strengths to you with the motive of adding something to you that only I can give; but this is an *offer,* not a command; a sharing, not a takeover; a giving of myself, not a power play.

"In submitting to you I do not give up my true self; rather I give *out of myself,* not denying who I am but offering who I am as an act of love and trust. True submission cannot take place if I deny my true self because I then have nothing of substance to offer to you—not a real person, only an empty shell."[2]

THE GREATEST OF ALL

During the final hours that Jesus was with his disciples, he carried out a shocking act of servitude. He was their leader, teacher, and model. He was God right there in the flesh. Yet he took a basin of water and, person by person, washed their feet, including those of Judas who would betray him.

Footwashing was supposed to be done by a servant, but this was a private meeting because of the political and religious animosity toward Jesus. Therefore, no servants were present to do the menial task of washing feet. None of the disciples moved to do it, but Jesus the Creator and Sustainer of the universe did.

Christ's act of serving not only shocked the disciples, but also grabbed their attention so he could explain his purpose. He performed this lowly task to teach us that we all are to serve each other.[3] The truly great person is not the one who is served as the boss, the head, the president, or the hot dog. A great person is the one who serves.

Modeling the Greatest

The servant attitude runs counter to our culture in general and also is frequently missing in the Christian subculture. Why is it that Christian males skip over Christ's teachings and pattern of servanthood, demanding "bosshood" in their homes? Many men, including students of theology, are blind at this very point. They assume that their wives are not their equals and, therefore, should fill lesser roles in marriage, church, and society.

Frequently these men are insecure about their lives in general or their maleness in particular. We like the bumper sticker that reads, **Men of quality are not threatened by women seeking equality.** The truth is that men of quality will **help** women have equality.

Some men have adapted to our contemporary cultural changes for women, but many still try to run their marriages "the way Dad did." Christians sometimes use the concept of headship from Ephesians 5 as a basis for male dominance. If headship is interpreted as meaning privilege, authority, and dominance, we violate the meaning of that section of Scripture and of Christ's teaching and modeling. *Headship* more accurately means "source," as in source of life and nourishment. (See the analogy of man with Christ in Ephesians 1:22; 4:15; 5:23 and Colossians 1:18; 2:18–19.)[4]

Unfortunately, in many marriages headship indicates male privilege, which is then interpreted as "I get to do the things I want to do." "Family decisions are primarily for my benefit." "Money is spent to promote my ambitions." The wife is supposed to be contented with whatever is left over.

The two of us find that we serve each other mutually both by actions and by attitudes. Actions of servanthood can be anything from special surprises to the nitty-gritty of daily life, including running to the auto parts store for your husband while he works on the car; hanging the drapery rods late at night, when you'd rather be resting, so your wife can get her new curtains up before her mother arrives the next day; or cleaning up after the other one has been sick on the bathroom floor.

Attitudes include knowing that each other's ideas and feelings are important. You respect each other's decisions. You put the other one first and realize he or she needs tenderness from you. The two of us have a goal of "outdoing each other with love." With that as an attitude, actions follow naturally.

SERVING—HOW TO DO IT

In our survey of lasting mid-life marriages, we discovered that the successful marriages were practicing mutuality or moving toward it. They had grown beyond maneuvering over who would be boss and were submitting to and building up each other in their daily interaction. Serving each other includes some of the following common, everyday ingredients.

1. Give Affirmation

We need each other. We were born dependent upon others for our survival. As we mature, we are better able to provide for ourselves, but we will always need others if we are to flourish emotionally.

To be nourished by others doesn't mean we have to be in a big crowd, but we do need to be in affirming relationships with people. We need someone who will complement us, someone to "complete" us. Notice that complement is spelled with an *e*. Compliments (spelled with an *i* and meaning "expressions of praise and admiration") are necessary, too, but someone to complement us is essential to our wholeness.[5]

Since we need others in our life and they need us, we should let them know we're glad they're in our world. We certainly like to know they enjoy having us on earth. We appreciate their affirmation of our being, talents, and efforts, and we need to reciprocate.

An interesting study by David Mace, a family researcher, provides a clue to the strengths possessed by strong families: "The members of these families liked each other, and kept on telling each other that they liked each other. They affirmed each other, gave each other a sense of personal worth, and took every reasonable opportunity to speak and act affectionately. The result, very naturally, was that they enjoyed being together and reinforced each other in ways that made their relationships very satisfying."[6]

Affirming your mate with your words is one way of serving him or her. If this is hard for you, try a little project. Plan to give your mate one compliment a day for the first week. The second week try for two compliments a day. The next week, go for three, and so on. By the time you have practiced several weeks, you should develop a normal pattern of expressing admiration and praise frequently. Your affirmation will have a very positive effect on your mate and on your relationship.

Affirmation takes place as you say positive things to a person about his or her qualities and accomplishments. This can be as small as these examples:

"Thanks for being an understanding person."

"Thanks for marrying me."

"I'm glad you're financially frugal. That makes it easier for me."

"Thanks for the emotional and spiritual input you have in our children's lives."

Another way to affirm people is with your body. A twinkle in your eye says, "You're special to me." A flirty smile says, "You really turn me on." You affirm your mate with a touch as you pass in the kitchen. A gentle hug that enfolds him in your arms gives him a sense of security and belonging in the midst of a world of loneliness.

You give affirmation with a kiss that is long and slow from lips that are relaxed and soft. Another form of affirmation is your sexual relationship, in which you give pleasure to your mate and communicate how much pleasure you're receiving. Our bodies do have a language and we should use them, as well as our words, for messages of affirmation to our mates.

2. Recognize Equality

Serving each other can be demonstrated by the respect that we give to each other. If a husband and wife look down on each other, treat each other with contempt, or even use the Bible as a club to beat the other one down, they have lost the sense of serving each other.

Some modern writers and speakers who tell women how to get along with their husbands make subtle—and sometimes not so subtle—suggestions that men are fools. "You just have to know how to get around them in order to get your own way. Give them the position and power they want, but use your feminine and sexual wiles to get what *you* want," they say. That's actually a put-down to men, and it is certainly not equality.

Sometimes husbands do the same to their wives. Men laugh and say, "Oh, my wife wouldn't know anything about that. She only understands women's things around the house. The only other thing she can do is shop 'til she drops."

Sometimes a woman plays the little-girl/helpless-dumb-blonde routine, so that it is difficult for her husband to think of her as a mature woman who is responsible enough to care for herself and other people. Etta was this way; but when her husband, Casey, had a serious heart attack and was unable to work or make family decisions for a time, she took over very responsibly. She enjoyed caring for the finances and seeing that the business details of the family ran smoothly. Casey was surprised when these hidden abilities were revealed and was pleased to let her share in managing the finances even after his recovery.

Sometimes men deliberately resist sharing their feelings. They think if they don't, they'll automatically be excused from participating fully in all that family relationships demand. After all, supposedly males aren't ever as sensitive as females. Actually, many men play the game of being tough and macho, even when they really are tender inside. By staying aloof, they are robbing their wife and children of a valuable part of themselves. They also cause their wife to carry an unfair share of the psychological responsibility of the marriage and family life.

Equality is a two-way street. It's a way of thinking of your mate, and it's also a way of thinking of yourself in relationship to your mate. It means that you value your mate and yourself as equals and as peers. It also means that both mates commit themselves to helping the other grow. Family time and money are used for the growth of both husband and wife.

I (Jim) remember when it first hit me that we had been using family resources for *my* education and *my* development and very little for Sally's. I had earned two master's degrees, attended several pastor's conferences, added many volumes to my library, and was planning to start doctoral studies. Sally had quit undergraduate studies when we got married and had worked to put me through my graduate studies.

The inequity suddenly struck me. As a result, I encouraged her to go back to school to finish her degree. My conscience also kept after me so that I later helped her decide to get a master's degree.

3. Promote a Positive Self-image

Serving also means doing all you can to help your mate feel good about himself or herself. Insecure people generally find it difficult to serve other people. If they do serve, they serve with the hope that they'll be rewarded for the service—"If I do good things for you, then you will love me." Their service really becomes a working for love rather than serving to enrich the other person. Secure people, on the other hand, are able to give themselves in service to other people, without thinking of a return.

After each of us was born, many other people had positive and negative impacts on our lives over the years. As we grew up, we developed an emotional bank account. When people gave affirmation or encouraged us, we stored this as "love dollars" in our emotional bank. As people cut us down and belittled us, it was as if we were losing love dollars.

If you or your mate has only a few love dollars in your bank, you will find it very hard to serve each other. In one sense, the best way to strengthen your marriage is to concentrate first on growing as a person. As you feel more worthwhile, you will build more love dollars into your account, which will then provide a reserve to draw on for serving your mate.

You can accumulate more love dollars by listening carefully to people as they affirm and appreciate you. When they congratulate you for something you've done or how you look, don't brush that compliment aside, as is the tendency of a person with a low self-image. Instead, listen carefully, look them in the face, and say, "Thank you very much. That really felt good," or, "I needed that," or, "I'm glad that you're such an affirming person."

You can also build love dollars into your life by listening more carefully to what God is saying about you and how he values you as a person. God will affirm your self-esteem as you read the first two chapters of Ephesians (preferably from *The Living Bible*). Also see Psalm 139 and Romans 5:1–11.

Many of the women and some of the men in our survey talked about how an increase in their self-esteem had improved their marriage. Very often the other mate had been the one helping the self-image to become more healthy.

Emily referred several times to the low view she had held of herself as a young wife. She was insecure and highly critical of others. She had an unhappy childhood and expected that marriage to Wayne would bring happiness. When she learned Wayne was having an affair, she fell to pieces.

At the same time, a severe problem with a child forced Emily and Wayne to get counseling. A perceptive counselor helped Emily see that many of their marital and parenting problems stemmed from her poor self-image. Wayne wisely realized his need to help Emily and ended his affair. Along with Emily's own efforts, he started to build and affirm her.

As Emily grew, Wayne found her much more desirable than any other woman. When she felt secure with him, her self-esteem grew even more. Their child's problem also improved because their home was now more stable and loving. For more than sixteen years they have had a satisfying marriage and Emily is confident about herself as a person.

Chapters 13 and 14 of this book include some more help on how to build a more positive self-image, and you can be helped from such books as Josh McDowell's *Building Your Self-Image* and David Seamands' *Healing for Damaged Emotions*.[7]

4. Encourage Your Mate's Unique Gifts

Theodore Roosevelt said, "Far better is it to dare mighty things, to win glorious triumphs, even though checkered by failure, than to rank with those poor spirits who neither enjoy much nor suffer much, because they live in the grey twilight that knows not victory or defeat."[8]

You serve your mate by helping him or her not to "live in the grey twilight" and by encouraging the discovery and development of his or her unique gifts and abilities.

Helping may mean arranging your schedule to care for the kids while she attends classes, or living on less income while he changes jobs, or other hands-on involvement from you. When you say, "Go for it!" you must include all the physical and emotional support you can give.

By helping your mate use his or her gifts, you are building your mate's positive self-image and reinforcing the fact that you value him or her. In addition, the world is enriched because of the talents you have helped to unleash.

Elaine was about thirty-eight when we met her. She was restless as she realized her husband, Scott, had his successful career; her children were needing her less; and she didn't know what she would do after they no longer needed her. She and Scott began to spend hours talking about what she could do to feel more fulfilled. They carefully evaluated what she had been doing all those years as a mother, wife, and volunteer in the church. Out of all the many kinds of jobs she had performed, she most enjoyed talking with people and helping them with their problems. She felt she would like to get more training to be able to counsel effectively.

Scott encouraged her to start graduate studies while their two youngest sons were in high school. He enlisted their help with household chores and took more of his own time to drive their youngest to his soccer practice. Today Elaine has a master's degree and is contentedly counseling several hours a week in a well-established marriage and family clinic. Scott's encouragement has enabled Elaine to be fulfilled at the same time she is making a needed contribution to the world.

5. Focus on Commitment

Dr. Urie Bronfenbrenner says that the family is "a group which possesses and implements an irrational commitment to the well-being of its members."[9] Sometimes you best serve your mate by having an "irrational commitment" to him or her and your marriage.

You can serve your mate by thinking of your marriage commitment as a tree that you have planted. Expect that tree to be there through every season of life. Marriage should not be thought of as a coat that you put on and take off depending on the weather. You are committed "come hell or high water."

Commitment provides a stability that frees the two of you within your marriage to grow and to develop all of your potential. You're not wasting your energies looking over your shoulder, wondering if the rug is going to be pulled out from underneath you because you're afraid your mate is going to leave.

Do you remember how Emily (with the poor self-image)

and Wayne's marriage improved as he committed himself to building Emily's self-esteem and by being faithful to her? His commitment to her freed her to blossom as an individual and as an enjoyable marriage partner.

6. Meet Your Mate's Needs

Our recent work with mid-life couples confirms what had been our growing observation over the years: **People stay together in marriage because their needs are being met.**

At first glance, that idea appears to very self-centered. But we've discovered that couples whose marriages are tenuous can experience a deepening sense of commitment, a desire to stay together, and an ability to express affection as they understand each other's needs and specifically focus on meeting those needs.

Sometimes at marriage conferences we give time for couples to go for a walk together and talk about their most important needs. We've first asked each of them to write down four of their own needs and then what they think are their mate's four most important needs.

We encourage them to compare their lists to see how closely they understand each other. Beyond that, they are to explain the meaning of each of these needs by talking about the feelings associated with those needs. Then they are to talk about practical ways they could more adequately meet each one's major needs.

For example, while Gene and Sandy were on their walk, Gene said, "I don't feel my life is important." Sandy listened to Gene as he wrestled with the question of whether life—especially his—had meaning. Gene also questioned how much time and energy he had left to make a mark in the world. He asked Sandy, "Will the world be any different because I've been in it?"

Sandy gently helped him focus his concern and begin to count the ways he was important: to his family, in his work, with present friends, with old friends and colleagues, and to her specifically. Together they remembered his successes and counted his positive personality traits.

After the marriage conference, Sandy looked for times to reinforce Gene's importance. She prompted herself to be sure she listened when he had an idea or was making a decision. She respected his opinions. She didn't manipulate, patronize, or repress her own opinions, but she genuinely respected Gene and his ideas. She couldn't do much about how things were going at work or in other parts of Gene's life, but from her part as his wife, she could meet Gene's need to feel important.

Another example is Debbie who wrote on her list of needs "to do some things just for myself." As she and her husband, Don, walked and talked, he asked her exactly what she would like to do and offered to help create the time and finances to make it possible. She suggested three things she'd like to do. One was to take an art class. Don said they could take money for the tuition and supplies, and he would babysit the kids that evening each week.

Then she said she'd like to just get out and go shopping occasionally. He agreed with her about how much they could afford and told her to make plans to go. Debbie's third request was to do something to lose weight. Don encouraged her to get a membership in a fitness class and said he'd cheerfully join her in eating smaller meals.

Couples frequently have told us that this exercise of chatting with each other about their needs was the most significant part of the conference, because it opened up a door for continuing discussion and changes for years to come.

Understanding the needs of your mate and trying to meet those needs becomes very powerful, not only for serving your mate, but also for strengthening your marriage relationship. One man in our survey said, "When I learned how to be tender to Linda and to meet her needs, our deteriorating marriage turned around."

7. Respect Your Mate

Isn't it strange that a husband will open the car door for a woman guest who is riding with the couple, but he won't normally open the door for his wife? It's sad that we withhold common courtesy and respect from each other. We interrupt, badger, put down, ignore, or condemn our mates, when we would never think of doing that to another person.

Respect means that you not only value your mate, but you let your mate teach you. If your mate has important God-given abilities that you don't have, his or her contribution to your life is essential.

Respect also includes the other dimensions we've noted about serving each other: affirming your mate and treating him or her as an equal, helping your mate to develop a positive self-image, encouraging your mate's personal growth, meeting needs, and being committed to the marriage relationship.

I (Jim) have found that the more I respect Sally and her abilities, the more I am able to trust her. The more I trust her, the more she is free to exercise her gifts, which, in turn, gains my respect.

Recently we were speaking at a couples' retreat at Forest Home Conference Center in California. We had shared equally in all of the sessions until the Sunday morning when I was supposed to do the last session alone.

I told Sally that I thought we ought to share the session even though this was a Sunday worship service. Sally had heard me speak several times from the Scripture passage I was going to use, and she agreed to join me.

I was delighted as she contributed new and important ideas to our message. The overall impact of the message was heightened and so was my respect for her. The side benefit was that the retreat couples were able to see a couple modeling a couple relationship, not just hearing one of us talk about it.

Respect acted upon will generally increase your esteem for your mate and free him or her to be more creative.

Serving your mate is like going on a special surprise date. You personally have the fun of planning and experiencing the evening. You also have the elation of watching your mate's eyes sparkle as he or she experiences your thoughtful, loving plans. When you serve each other, something wonderful happens to both of you.

Key #10
Personal
Growth

When Dana and Sharon came to us for marital counseling, we asked them a question we often ask, "What attracted you to each other?" If we learn this, we often know how to help revitalize a struggling marriage.

Sharon and Dana had met one Sunday while Sharon was still in college. When we asked them what drew them to each other, Dana remarked, "Sharon had an infectious smile and a mischievous twinkle in her eyes."

Dana was a guest teacher in Sharon's church class. Dana reflected on that class by saying, "I made several funny remarks as I taught the lesson, and when I looked at Sharon she winked at me. I knew then that she was a special person with a great sense of humor."

They spoke of several incidents of doing crazy things together before they were married, such as when Sharon dropped Dana off at the airport. He wanted to passionately kiss her good-bye, but there was no quiet place. So he took her to a service elevator. When they got inside, he didn't push any buttons but kissed her again and again until finally someone else wanted to use the elevator.

Sparkle Lost

After they were married, however, there was a sharp change in their lives. The spontaneity and sparkle seemed to get lost in the raising of kids, paying off mortgages, and fulfilling of responsibilities with PTA, the church, and Dana's job. As they came into their mid-life years with their children in their late teens and early young adulthood, they were deeply frustrated with their personal lives and their marriage.

When we began to talk about their personal needs, we discovered that both of them had a strong need for independence and felt stifled by their marriage relationship. They each felt their creativity and uniqueness were being reduced.

Although Sharon had graduated from college, she had wanted to go on for a master's degree and perhaps even a doctorate. The responsibilities of children, the home, and Dana's expanding career had caused her to put off some of the other things she had really wanted to do.

Dana also felt trapped. He freely admitted that it wasn't all Sharon's fault. He had easily bought into the materialistic, money-focused success his organization pushed. But, in addition, he was disappointed that the sparkle had gone out of their relationship. He needed more of the unusual and unpredictable. He wanted more of the crazy elevator experiences or the fun little notes that she used to leave for him.

This couple is classic. They were attracted to each other because their unique needs were met by the other. Their courtship allowed them to grow and flourish as people. When they got married, however, they changed their way of relating to each other and then felt they had fallen out of love with each other.

Sharon indicated this when she said, "I need to be stimulated by something outside the home so that I have something fresh to bring to the marriage. I feel that when we got married, I stopped growing."

Sparkle Found

In our counseling with Dana and Sharon, we focused on helping them understand each other's needs and get started in some personal development. As we talked about how each one could grow and how they could reintroduce the sparkle and excitement into their marriage relationship, they realized they needed to redefine their values as well as their activities.

One of the outcomes was that Sharon enrolled in a local university to begin her work on the long-delayed master's program. Dana also made some changes in his career, which reduced pressure and slowed him down in his climbing of the corporate ladder.

They decided to redirect their lifestyle to provide the money they needed for Sharon's education and to have time for travel and the sparkle they wanted in their life. As a result, they sold their large five-bedroom house and moved into a nice two-bedroom condo, which enabled them to reduce their mortgage and reduce the time needed for house and yard maintenance. Now they had more time and money to focus on each other's needs and their relationship.

It may sound like a fairy tale, but we had the fun of watching this couple experience a rebirth of their relationship. They reported that the thrill and sparkle had come back. They each felt freer, with a new zest for living and learning. Their time away from each other in business and education enriched them as people so that they had something fresh to offer to each other when they were together.

Successful mid-life couples reported that their individual growth helped their marriages to be fresh. They spontaneously wanted to be together. These couples were future-focused individuals who may have had some severe marital difficulties in the past but had worked through those problems. They were now concentrating on how they could grow as individuals and as a couple to make their personal lives and marriage effective.

Marriages grow stale when the people in them aren't growing. Marriages that are in trouble usually can be helped if both husband and wife are willing to grow and change.

LIFE FORCES US TO GROW

Growth is a sign of life and vitality. It often appears to be spontaneous, but growth of any organism occurs because the conditions are right. In human beings, a condition for growth is often created by a need to change something about one's life situation. When something—such as an affair, a health problem, a move, or any change—throws off the equilibrium of our normal routine, we are more open to learning.

Sometimes we're forced into changing without any deliberate choice on our part. Other times we are sensitive to a need to grow and do something before it hits us smack in the face. I (Sally) enjoy growing more if I can plan for it ahead of time. But even with the best of forethought, I'm still often unaware of all the changes I'm going to have to make.

For example, I knew all along that one day Jim and I would have an "empty nest." I even agreed with our friend Ruth, who says that the nest isn't really empty when the kids leave because Mom and Dad are still there.

I was looking forward to the fun and freedom Jim and I would have as a couple with none of the daily responsibilities of parenting. I had many active outside interests and for years I had been waiting for extra time to leisurely catch up on some projects, such as photo albums, scrapbooks, and a family history. We were happy with what our three girls were doing in their lives, so I had no sadness about the reason for their absence.

I had done some casual reading and formal research about the empty nest. I had listened to other women's stories of their experiences—both good and bad—when their children left home. I determined that this was going to be a well-adjusted stage of my personal life. And our marriage was going to be vibrant with just the two of us!

You've already guessed what I'm going to say next. In spite of my good attempts to be prepared, nothing prepared me for what the empty nest is really like.

No one could have described ahead of time how it would feel to sit in the Sunday evening church service alone while my husband preached. The truth is, our girls hadn't sat with me in church for years. As they became teenagers they sat with their friends, and they often went to some other activity afterward, so Jim and I went home without them. *But* they were going to be coming into the house later!

Now we went home without them and went to bed without the expectation that we'd see or hear them sometime. No one told me that I'd want to bawl like a cow who's been separated from her calf.

No one told me what a buffer children are between husband and wife irritations. If Jim didn't feel like communicating, I could talk with one of the girls about something. If I was disappointed about something I felt he wasn't doing right, I could concern myself about some matter for one of our daughters.

Now our raw edges just stuck out there, waiting for the other to rub on them. Of course, that forced us to get to work on the raw edges and to be more sensitive to each other's needs. We had to learn to negotiate our differences and not hide behind the business of running a family.

We've both found we needed to grow in ways we'd never dreamed before. We **are** enjoying being a couple again and it's great to be able to pursue more outside interests. (I still don't have the photo album, scrapbook, or family history projects finished.)

WHERE DO I NEED TO GROW?

Obviously, the final answer of where you need to grow must come from you, based on the particular circumstances of your personal life and marriage, but we can point you to some general areas to consider.

1. Physical Growth

We hope that at mid-life you aren't literally growing physically (getting fat) but that you're thinking about your physical needs. Typically, a mid-life person's weight shifts to the middle. Metabolism changes so that one gains weight more easily and muscle tone decreases.

You're probably having difficulty with your sight. Have you noticed how much smaller they are printing the telephone directory these days? You may also be having trouble with your hearing, and probably you've noticed a slower overall response in rebounding from loss of sleep or too much stress.

Now is the time to focus on several things to make your body the best it can be:

> ▸ A balanced diet, which is high in fiber, fresh vegetables and fruits, chicken and fish, and low in salt, sugar, caffeine, and red meat

- ▸ A vitamin supplement, which includes B–complex and minerals
- ▸ Eight hours of sleep a night
- ▸ An exercise program of twenty minutes three times a week with your heart rate at about 120
- ▸ Thirty-two ounces of water each day

It's worth the effort to get yourself in physical shape. If you're in good physical condition, you're better able to handle stress. You'll like yourself better and your marriage is likely to be stronger.

A study entitled "Physical Attractiveness and Marital Adjustment in Older American Couples" discovered that if people perceived themselves and their mate as attractive, they viewed their marital adjustment as good. The positive association was most strongly linked with the husband's good feeling about the marital relationship.[1] It seems to be especially important for a man to feel good about himself and to feel good about his wife's physical body.

2. Psychological Growth

If there is a single major factor that we would identify as the most fertile seedbed for mid-life marriage stress, it is the person's image of himself or herself.

Each of us carries within us a view of ourselves. We think of ourselves as talented or klutzy, friendly or shy, confident or insecure. We believe that we are attractive or ordinary, smart or dumb. We see ourselves as successful or stumbling along through life. Whatever we believe about ourselves affects everything we do. We choose jobs, friends, the places we live, even vacations and the ways we spend money, according to our view of ourselves.

Choosing a marriage partner is the most important choice in human relationships, if we have decided to get married. We choose that person on the basis of who we think we are. The tragedy is that sometimes there is a mismatch. Family and friends ask, "Why did he or she choose *that* person? They don't seem to be suited for each other." The book entitled *Mate Selection* accurately predicts that we will marry a person who meets our needs even if those needs happen to be immature.[2]

Dave was typical of many young men. He was trying to

find himself. Making decisions was hard for him because he had a very dominant mother who thought for him. He was making his own decisions at work, but he had an unconscious longing for a place of security. Marriage seemed the obvious answer.

As one might guess, Dave married someone who would fill the leadership gap in his life. Coincidentally, Carla had been looking for someone who needed her, a person on whom she could use the training she had unconsciously received from her strong-willed father. She had always wanted to be just like him.

The two of them got married, thinking that Dave was in charge and would make the major life decisions for the family while Carla ran the home. Because Dave didn't know how to make decisions, Carla jumped in "just to help him out." Later she came to realize that he actually was inept, and she despised him for his lack of ability. He in turn despised her for her dominance, manipulation, and intrusion into his life.

It's not difficult to imagine what happened in a marriage like this. As the pressure continued to build, each one ignored the other, while children and relatives took sides. The problems of the early years, which were then obvious only to a trained observer, became obvious to everyone as both of them got involved in affairs and the marriage broke up.

Many times one or both partners have a dismally low view of themselves, which then results in all kinds of actions, reactions, and counteractions that are negative for the marriage relationship.

We frequently see some of the following actions and attitudes, which are a direct result of a low self-image, in troubled marriages:

- ▶ **Unconscious role reversal:** Review the earlier illustration of Dave and Carla.
- ▶ **Extramarital affair:** "I feel insecure and unfulfilled in my marriage. I must show myself and other people that I'm worthwhile."
- ▶ **Passivity:** "I don't feel good enough about myself as a person so I won't participate. Then no one will know that I feel inadequate, or else maybe they will reach out and give me love."
- ▶ **Desperate for approval from other people:** "I continually change to gain the approval of people around me, so I'm not ever sure who I really am."

▸ **Materialism:** "I use possessions to impress people. If they like my car, my house, my clothes, or my free use of money, then I feel good about myself even if my marriage is rotten."

▸ **Perfectionism:** "If only I can be more perfect, then I can gain the approval of people important to me, and I will like myself better. I also want my mate to be more perfect so that it will reflect well on me and people will like me better."

▸ **Criticism:** "Because I'm a perfectionist, I have no tolerance for people who don't come up to my standards. It's easy for me to criticize the weaknesses in other people, especially my mate."

▸ **Depression:** "It's easy to get down because I realize how seldom I am perfect. I often criticize myself. Probably other people criticize me as well. In fact, I'm not sure that I ever do anything worthwhile or that life is even worth living."

▸ **Constant apology:** "Because I feel inferior, I frequently acknowledge to other people that I am failing. If they realize that I recognize my own weakness, they might be more tolerant of me. I continually say, 'Oh, I'm sorry,' 'I don't know,' 'Well, that's just like me,' 'I did the same dumb thing again.'"

▸ **Ego-centered:** "I continually talk about myself and my achievements; otherwise, how will people know that I'm really worthwhile? If I impress them, then they'll love me and not know that I feel insecure."

▸ **Inability to trust God:** "In reality, how could a perfect God love me, a person who fails so frequently? God must think I'm awful, just as other people do. It's impossible to impress him. Ultimately everybody looks out for himself, and you'd better not trust anybody, even God."

People who don't know or appreciate themselves find it difficult to believe that anyone else appreciates who they are. A low self-image is a constant problem, which we've observed through various ages of the life span. Mid-life is the time to really blossom as a person and to enjoy all that makes you unique, not to continue to be stifled and stunted by a low self-image.

Elizabeth shared, "I remember an evening eleven years ago, my first date with a man I would later live with but who was still a remote and elegant stranger whose approval, I had convinced myself, was necessary to my very survival. We were at the movies, and I was panicking. What would I say about the movie when it was over?

"The problem here, you understand, was not ascertaining my opinion of the film; the problem was divining what *he* thought of it so that I could agree with him and be found worthy of his continued attentions. It would not have occurred to me at that time that I could gain approval simply by being myself or that, if I were comfortable being myself, it would matter considerably less whether I had his or anyone's approval.

"And so, as the movie neared an end, my apprehension increased. Peripheral vision told me only that he was neither bored or enthralled. But at the movie's climactic moment, he shifted in his seat, shook his head, and made a thumbs down signal—at which point I knew, to my vast relief, that I did not like this film at all. Later, over ample portions of Chinese food, his favorite cuisine, which I despise, I held forth on the film's insufficiencies with some conviction and style. He beamed at me. It did not bother me that I had gained his approval at the cost of mine."[3]

Does Elizabeth's story sound familiar? We see this pattern again and again, in marriages and other personal relationships. We want the other person to like us, so we deny who we really are in order to be liked by the other person.

I Am Who I Am. Growing psychologically means that you are willing, perhaps for the first time in your life, to say, "This is who I am. God made me this way. I'm a worthwhile person. I will be myself."

You don't have to be obnoxious, but in gracious ways confirm that you are a special person with a unique contribution for the world.

A Personal Inventory. Frequently we are asked, "How do I find out who I am? How am I supposed to appreciate myself if I don't know who I am or what my special abilities are?"

a. Start by focusing on the unique way that God has created you and the unique interests, abilities, and experiences he has given you. We suggest that you make some lists.

List music styles, song titles, and musicians that you like, along with the kinds of books and magazines you like to read. Be sure that you don't start to list the most popular songs or books on the bestseller lists. You may think, "Well, I ought to like those artists or that magazine." If you think that way, you are becoming a conformist and you'll not discover who you are as a unique person. For this exercise you have to set aside what everybody else likes and ask, "What do *I* like, even if I'm the only one in the world who likes it?"

Do the same with clothing styles. List the recreational activities you enjoy. List the friends you really like to be with and identify the characteristics about them that you find attractive and their qualities that nourish you. Think in terms of nourishment, not obligation. Not, "I ought to like that person because he is my second cousin," but rather, "I like this guy because he emotionally charges my batteries when I'm with him."

Make lists about everything in your life: work, neighborhood, art, movies, food. By now you've gotten the idea. Temporarily, you're not going to allow other people's opinions to influence what you like. You are looking within yourself to understand your uniqueness.

b. Now make a list of all the things that you like to *do*, whether serious or frivolous and whether or not your friends would think they are good or bad.

c. Follow that list with another one that includes all the things you want to do before you die. Listen to your inner self. Let yourself "dream the impossible dream."

d. Sit back with all of your lists and, in a sense, detach yourself and say, "Who is this person? How would I describe him or her? What kinds of things does he or she like? What does he or she really value in life?"

e. Knowing who you are is one part of the process of developing a good self-esteem. The next is to affirm who you are. Say to yourself, *That's good.*

f. Now live out the things that are on your list. Begin to become in reality the person that you have just defined in all of your lists. The more accurately you live as the person God has created you to be, the more confident and effective you will be.

3. Intellectual Growth

Many of the mid-life couples we surveyed mentioned types of intellectual stimulation that were important for enriching their marriages. They referred to special classes on couple communication or marriage enrichment. Others mentioned that getting more education or moving into a more stimulating work situation had improved their marriage.

Still others referred to skills and insights provided by counselors. Lois told us that her counselor had been her greatest resource for change. In fact, she credited him with helping her grow as a person so that her husband no longer wanted to divorce her.

Lois was one of those people who believed that her husband should love her and feel committed to their marriage no matter what she did or didn't do. Unfortunately, Lois had become very overweight and hadn't thought a new thought in the last twenty years. She had caught her man and didn't feel any obligation to keep winning him each day.

Her husband's affair shocked Lois as much as if she'd touched bare electrical wires. She called her counselor, crying and pleading for help. For several months she was coached so that she became a stimulating, and slimmer, person who again was attractive to her husband.

Some women, in our survey, said that reentering or continuing to participate in a career outside the home had contributed to their growth. Eleanor, who is now a sprightly senior citizen and would be considered a conservative in many areas of life, had a profession of her own when she married her husband nearly sixty years ago. When asked about the part her career had played in their marriage, she said, "It made me a more interesting person. I had more to contribute as a wife."

4. Social Growth

Psychologist Bernard Rimland from the Institute of Child Behavior Research in San Diego, California, gave 216 college students a simple test. They were to make a list of the ten people they liked best and who were the most attractive to them. Next to each name they were to mark an *H* if the person was generally happy or an *N* if they were generally not happy. Then they were to go through the list adding a second letter—*S* if they were selfish people or *U* if they were unselfish.

These college students rated almost 2,000 of their friends. Of these 2,000, 827 (42 percent) were judged as happy (H) and unselfish (U). Of the four possible combinations (HU,

HS, NU, NS), the lowest ranking of their best-liked friends (4 percent) was for the people who were rated as happy (H) but selfish (S).[4]

How would your friends rate you? Are you seen by them as a grumpy, easily irritated, unhappy person? Or are you sought out as a happy person who sees the best in people and life? Do your friends think of you as selfish or giving?

Growing socially for you may mean beginning to develop so that you are happy with yourself. You may need to come to grips with some of your problems, such as a low self-image, so that your internal problems don't keep eating holes in you. You also should think of ways to serve and care for others so that your life will have meaning.

Another dimension for your social growth can be that of facilitating other people's growth. Identify one or two of your friends who seem to feel insecure or who are not living up to their potential. Start a deliberate plan to understand your friends by listening to them and trying to see life through their eyes. Become their encourager by affirming the strengths you see in them. Tell them about positive traits you see that are just beginning to grow. Encourage them as they take small steps of risk. Stand with them if they slip and fall on their way toward growth and success.

As you help someone else grow, two wonderful miracles take place. You have the joy of deeper friendships, and you mature because your own life is sharpened and affirmed by your friends.

5. Spiritual Growth

This is a difficult area to measure. Unfortunately, sometimes we judge our spiritual life by how many times we attend church, how many committees we serve on, or how many Bible verses we memorize. Spiritual growth should probably be evaluated by asking if our friendship with God is growing and if we are becoming more like him as we respond to people and the world around us.

A number of people who have studied moral and spiritual development point out that the earlier stages tend to be marked by concreteness. A person in the early stages tends to view life in literal, concrete, black-and-white terms. That person likes to have his spiritual life, as well as other aspects of life, very explicit and firm, with clearly defined boundaries of right and wrong, do's and don'ts.[5]

Later stages of moral and spiritual development tend to become more porous, flexible, and complex. The person is prepared to live with ambiguity, mystery, and apparent irrationalities. The person in the later stages of moral development tends to be more vulnerable, with a readiness to take risk. There is an openness in this person that could lead to his or her modifying of values and rethinking of life. Now this person is better able to see the positions and viewpoints of other people.

According to Fowler and Keen, the most advanced stage of moral development "requires that one knows suffering and loss, responsibility and failure, and the grief that is inevitably part of having made irrevocable commitments of life and energy."[6] Age thirty is the minimal age for this growth level, if it comes at all. This stage is often associated with a mid-life crisis, when all of life is reassessed.

Obvious Differences. We have noticed that at mid-life people tend to divide into two groups in their moral and spiritual development. They either become troubled by the complexity of life and retreat to the more comfortable, structured patterns of do's and don'ts, or are challenged by life's ambiguities and the world's complexity and try to understand these complexities from God's point of view. These people are willing to live with the inconsistencies of life.

The spiritually growing person may question why a prayer was apparently not answered or why there are troubles in the world. Their questions don't mean they are abandoning their faith; rather, they are trying to understand life and God in a richer, more complete way.

We have some friends whose major concerns in their spiritual life center around studying the exact time of Christ's return to earth, using the "correct" Bible translation, and following the proper style of worship service.

However, they are not moved by the plight of the poor and homeless in our cities who have no hope and may not have a personal relationship with God. These friends think that those who help divorced families, or young, unmarried, pregnant women, or drug-addicted teens are wasting their energy and are misguided. Our friends are more secure if they focus on concrete issues rather than on people issues with no easy answers.

As you look through the pages of the Bible, you get a clear picture that God's major concern is the plight of people in the world. The timetables for his activities or our order of church worship are only incidental to the great work he is doing with people. If you wrestle with the concerns of people, you will be closer to the heart of God.

Putting It All Together. You now stand at the crossroads of life. You have experienced enough of life to provide a springboard for your continued spiritual development. You should try specifically to push away from the complacent and comfortable and toward the confrontation of some of the paradoxes in your world.

To start the procedure, develop a growing and expanding friendship with God. You can do this by telling God that you want to be his friend and you want to think as he does, even though this may be scary.

Then begin reading sections from the Bible daily. As you do, ask yourself some questions such as, "How would a person who is not a believer interpret and relate to this section of Scripture? How would an atheist react? Or a hungry family in Africa?" Remember, you're trying to sensitize yourself so that you can take the content of Scripture and your relationship with God and relate them to the real world.

Don't dodge the current issues, but think about them. Try to avoid saying to yourself, "Well, Dr. So-and-So says that we should believe such-and-such; therefore, the issue is closed." Rather, be an independent thinker. Ask yourself some hard questions. "Why do we do things the way we do and how did we get started with these certain patterns?" For example, wrestle with the following issues:

▶ Why do we go to church on Sunday mornings? Why not earlier? Why not in the afternoon?

▶ Why do we sit in rows looking only at the back of each other's heads? Why isn't the church constructed in a circle so we can look at each other instead of just the preacher and the choir?

▶ Why is Sunday school on Sunday morning when millions of "latchkey" children need to be cared for after school on weekday afternoons?

▸ Why do we encourage a woman missionary to go to a foreign country to win men and women, disciple them, and teach them how to be elders in a church, but in the United States women are often only allowed to teach women and children, bake cookies for church socials, sing in the choir, or wash the communion glasses?

▸ Why was the "swing and sway" music of the forties considered evil by the church and now the same big band, easy listening music is acceptable? Why is a rock-and-roll style not acceptable?

▸ Why is the current dress and style of hair always unchristian, but in ten years it will probably be adopted by Christians?

▸ Why do we have so many privileges and so much material wealth when half the world goes to bed without enough to eat, if they can find a bed?

▸ What is it that causes non-Christians to be turned off by Christians, while at the same time they desperately want a solution to their loneliness, guilt, and questions about life after death?

The list is endless. You can wrestle with questions such as genetic engineering, world hunger, apartheid, euthanasia, abortion, surrogate motherhood, biblical inspiration, and women's roles in the church. Remember that the purpose of the wrestling is for you to grow personally and spiritually. It isn't even necessary that you come up with answers, but it is important for your growth that you wrestle with the questions.

You may end up coming humbly before God and saying, "God, I don't know. There doesn't seem to be an answer. It is too complex. But I love you, and I trust you with my life and with these very difficult questions. Help me to think as you think. Help me to be concerned for the world as you are concerned."

The Good Results of Growth

The marriages that stay together over the long haul are composed of two people who are growing in all areas of their lives. Growing becomes part of the glue that holds them together. They are not the same old people with the same old problems. They are continuing to improve and mature, and this growth gives both of them **hope.**

Remember Dana and Sharon. You, too, can have sparkle in your marriage as you continue to change and grow.

PART THREE

▼

Blueprint
for Strengthening
and Rebuilding
Marriage

Making a Good Marriage Better

"**I**t was a dark night as the captain cautiously piloted his warship through the fog-shrouded waters. With straining eyes he scanned the hazy darkness searching for dangers lurking just out of sight. His worst fears were realized when a bright light loomed up at him through the mist.

"To avert disaster he flashed out a warning for the oncoming ship to turn ten degrees south.

"To his amazement the foggy image did not move. Instead the image audaciously ordered the captain to alter his course ten degrees north.

"Appalled by this intransigence, the captain ordered the apparition to change course ten degrees south.

"A second time the ship refused and repeated its instructions for the captain to turn ten degrees north.

"Angered and frightened, the captain desperately flashed out, 'Turn ten degrees south, I am a battleship!'

"The response was chilling, 'Turn ten degrees north, I am a light house!' "[1]

When difficulties and disagreements loom up in a marriage, at least one of you must make a move to change your course. You cannot both stubbornly stand your ground and insist on your way.

All marriages experience some degree of discord at one time or another. After reading this far, you've probably come to realize that problems in marriage are quite normal. Even the most successful marriages have periods of breakdown, doubt, disillusionment, and conflict, but a breakdown in your relationship need not cause the ultimate collapse of your marriage.

Many partners do wonder if their marriage can continue. We hear repeated themes:

—— ▼ ——

"It isn't working out the way I thought."

"He or she has changed so much."

"I've changed; he or she hasn't. The gap between us is too great."

"I want something different in life from what my mate wants."

—— ▲ ——

The problem, as you see it, is *always* with your mate. You want your spouse to be different. The words from *My Fair Lady* bring into focus much of our conflict in marriage. Professor Higgins asks the question of Colonel Pickering, "Why can't a woman take after a man?" He then says that men are pleasant, easy to please, easy to be around; they don't care if you don't talk or take a drink or two and aren't upset if you don't send flowers. Higgins sums up his frustration by saying to Pickering, "Why can't a woman—be like you?"[2]

In other words, men want women to be like men and women want men to be like women. The difficulty in understanding the opposite sex may always be there, yet a mutual marriage where we appreciate our differences is within reach.

TAKING RESPONSIBILITY TO ENRICH YOUR MARRIAGE

You may have a good marriage and want to strengthen it, or have a marriage with some moderate problems and dissatisfactions, or have a marriage with major problems, such as an affair, separation, or divorce. Several suggestions follow that can be used by anyone who wants to enrich his or her marriage.

Refocus on Your Marriage Partner

When you dated, you focused massive attention on each other to get acquainted and to build a history together. You were analyzing whether you could live your whole life together. It was a very pleasurable and nourishing process.

In that magnetic relationship, you craved to know the other person better, how he or she thought, and what his or her goals and values were. You were continually drawn together during courtship, engagement, wedding, honeymoon, the setting up of housekeeping, and the coming of your first child.

But after you got established as a couple, forces began to pull you away from each other: careers, community and church activities, the children's needs, and the humdrum familiarity with each other. As these pushed you apart, you began to think your marriage was boring and you had nothing in common. Both of you may have been totally unaware that you were changing and your needs in the relationship were also changing.

Mid-life men usually are rethinking their career, becoming more feeling oriented, and trying to re-establish family contacts. Women are often more assertive and more career and goal oriented. Therefore, to assume your mate is the same person as when you first married is totally wrong.

The life of a young married couple can be compared to leaves caught in a whirlpool, with the suction drawing them closer and closer together. But mid-life couples are like kids on a playground merry-go-round, in danger of being spun away from each other as it goes faster and faster. The outward pull of the mid-life marriage makes it necessary for the couple to hang on by refocusing on each other.

If you're going to renew your marriage, you must invest more of your time and energies on your mate. As you do, your relationship will grow and will provide some of the fun you want in life.

Refocusing on your mate means that you did have a focus at one time. You were concerned for your spouse's good. Somehow that focus got lost. Now you need to redirect your energies toward your mate with the expectation that your marriage will be enriched because of your new lifestyle and changed thinking.

Nourish Your Mate

Mother Teresa, who cares for Calcutta's poor, was awarded the 1979 Nobel Peace Prize. During her tour of the United States, she said, "Loneliness—the hunger for human love—is the world's worst ill." The seventy-one-year-old nun spoke of the terrible pain of being unwanted: "People today all over the world are suffering more from loneliness than from poverty."[3]

Burned-out marriages are made up of two very lonely people, who feel misunderstood, unappreciated, exploited, and dead inside. Your mate is as malnourished emotionally as you are.

John Powell, in his book, *The Secret of Staying in Love*, says "My love must empower you to love yourself. We should judge our success in loving not by those that admire us for our accomplishments, but by the number of those that attribute their wholeness to our loving them, by the number of those that have seen their beauty in our eyes, heard their goodness acknowledged in the warmth of our voices."[4]

In Ephesians 5, husbands are encouraged to "nourish" and to "cherish" their wives in the same way that Christ does the church. The idea of the word *nourish* is to emotionally feed, to encourage, to bring about, as John Powell says, "their wholeness." The word *cherish* means to warm. It's an emotional word that means to help the other person feel special and secure.

Nourishing and cherishing—how to do it. Paul came to me (Jim) in desperation. His wife, Linda, was involved with another man whom she had met while they worked together in the community theater. I asked Paul what the other man was like. What drew Linda to him so much that she was willing to risk a scandal in their small town just to be with this other man?

Paul said, "I was gone on business so much. She was always alone. That's why she started with the theater group. Even when we were together, we never talked. Maybe she was just bored with our eighteen-year-old marriage. She once told me, 'At least, he knows I'm alive—he pays attention to me.'"

I encouraged Paul to think about the areas that the other

man was meeting in Linda's life and try to meet her needs himself. Then she wouldn't have to look to someone else.

"Remember," I told Paul, "Linda must have felt very neglected by you or she wouldn't have risked it all for a stranger."

I asked Paul if he still loved Linda and was willing to pay the price to win her back. He assured me that he was. So I told him that true love exists "when the satisfaction, security and development of another person becomes as significant to you as your own satisfaction."[5]

"Let's put those ideas into action," I challenged Paul. "What will give Linda satisfaction? What will give her security? What will help her to develop or grow?"

Together we talked about several ideas and settled on one simple action to be repeated several times a day. Paul was to verbally express appreciation and gratefulness to Linda about who she was, how she looked, and what she could do.

Paul assured me, "I'll give it my best, but it will never work. It's just too simple."

We met each week, working on Paul's growth as a caring person. About the fifth week Paul reported that Linda had asked him, "Why are you giving me all of these compliments about everything?"

Paul's response to her turned the corner for their marriage. He said, "Because I didn't realize, until you almost left, how beautiful, caring, talented, and sensitive you are. I love you very much and want the best for you, even if that 'best for you' means that our marriage breaks up."

It wasn't a magical healing, but they were now started on the right road, which resulted in a far better marriage than they had before.

Nourishing your mate causes a fascinating thing to take place. As you nourish, you will also be nourished by your enriched mate and by your giving. Linda returned Paul's love, which cemented their growth toward having a healthy marriage.

Develop Common Interests Yet Allow Individual Space

Successful mid-life marriages are those where the couple enjoy each other as persons and enjoy common pursuits. Your shared activities and experiences can be part of your new commonality in life that is so crucial for marriage renewal.

The two of us enjoy walking together, looking at a rose in our garden, spotting an interesting bird, sitting on the seashore, and hiking in the mountains. We also spend hours reading books aloud together. The opposite side of the coin is that we are *not* one person. We are two distinctly different individuals who enjoy things the other doesn't and who need private space.

The author of *How to Keep Love Alive* has wisely said, "No doubt you have shared close moments when the boundaries between you seem to have melted, but that is not going to be a day to day reality. Only if you can accept your distinct uniqueness will you be able to clarify, and communicate, your expectations. This means accepting the fact that the two of you are not one. This is the lovers' paradox: the more you can accept each other as being *autonomous* the better your *mutuality* will be."[6]

Larry and Judy fought so often that they thought their marriage was hopeless. We discovered that they never were apart. They worked side by side in their photography business. During one of Larry's explosions, he said, "I feel like a caged bird! I need some time alone! I don't know who I am anymore! Do I even exist without you?"

Larry's outburst shocked Judy, who at first felt attacked. She thought Larry was saying he didn't love her.

As soon as Judy was able to give Larry more emotional space, the relationship improved. They agreed that Larry would spend more time with the guys from church and that they would separate their work on certain projects so that they could develop more personal identity as photographers.

M. Scott Peck says, "[Some] couples . . . are too much married, too closely coupled . . . They need to establish some psychological distance from each other before they can even begin to work constructively on their problems." He suggests to some of his clients that they take occasional vacations *from* their spouses as well as *with* their spouses.[7]

Couples find a stronger marriage as they learn that differences of opinion and a need for being alone don't necessarily mean that their marriage is poor. Healthy individuality allows them to enjoy sharing their common interests.

Revive the Chase

Don't be embarrassed to be romantic and to renew "the chase." As you reconstruct your marriage, remember your courtship attentiveness and spontaneity. Think of creative ways to keep sentimentality alive and thereby let your partner know he or she is still a desired and needed person.

We have found that an unexpected rubbing of the shoulders, a kiss on the neck, or a flirty glance is part of the chase for us. Recently, after the secretaries had left for lunch, Sally called me over the intercom between our offices and said in a sexy voice, "I *need* you." I liked that unexpected invitation.

The chase demands time to think up and carry out special little gestures. Our study, as well as others', confirms the fact that couples in strong marriages plan time together, time where they focus on each other in "the chase."

The idea is said very well by a man of sixty who wrote "Dear Abby," telling her he had a beautiful wife and family but needed more excitement. He went on to confess that he had renewed an acquaintance with a woman with whom he had had a very romantic relationship years ago. The same magic happened again for both of them. He then said, "You see, the woman I renewed the acquaintance with was my wife."[8]

Take Personal Responsibility for Your Marriage Renewal

Renewing your marriage is going to require that you make changes in your living and thinking. You can't expect only your mate to change.

Recently Sally and I were talking about some revisions she suggested for this chapter. You need to know that when I have written something, I am very sensitive when anyone wants to cut it out or alter it.

Sally said, "I think we need to drop this part."

I resisted. I was a teensy bit obnoxious.

She said bluntly, "You're just as stubborn as your dad!"

Soon words were flying between us, and we were really at it. When we cooled down a bit, Sally said, "I'm sorry," and waited for me to respond.

Unfortunately, I thought *she* had *caused me* to get angry, so why should I apologize? Some time later I was willing to own my emotions and say that I was sorry for being touchy and angry.

Taking personal responsibility for marriage renewal is going to be difficult but you must face it. Your marriage burnout and failure is not your mate's responsibility. It's yours. It isn't that your spouse or someone else makes you angry or jealous or causes you to lust. These are your problems.

Yes, we know what you think. Your mate *caused* you to react. In reality, however, it was you who reacted. Until you own it, you'll continue to blame your mate for something that is your fault.

Marriages that have burned out are characterized by each person's blaming the other and neither one taking the responsibility for what's happening. It's amazing that as soon as the partners begin to own their responsibility for marital stresses, healing begins. If you're serious about your marriage renewal, you must start by repeating these four words, **"I am at fault."**

List the areas in which you are at fault. Practice owning a larger segment of the fault than you normally do. For example, try taking the entire blame in some given area. That process will free your mate so that he or she no longer has to be defensive. Then your mate can take an objective look and will very likely accept the portion of the blame that truly is his or hers.

Your new lifestyle for marriage renewal must include that personal growth we talked about earlier. If you don't change, your marriage will revert to its same former sick state. You personally are responsible for the change and growth that is your individual contribution. Your mate's change is not your obligation, but *your* change *is* your obligation.

Betty Coble, author of *Woman: Aware and Choosing*, has a pointed illustration from two people playing tennis. She reminds us that we each have a responsibility to play in our own court and to hit the ball back into our mate's court. It's wrong for one to hop over the net to hit the ball back. That's the other player's responsibility. We are to stay on our side of the net and tend to our court while our mate stays on the other side to tend to his or her court.[9]

You must concentrate on your own personal growth and change and leave your mate's growth and change up to your mate and God. **Remember, the troubled mid-life marriage doesn't need you to switch to a new partner; it needs you to switch to being a new person.**

Have Confidence in Yourself, Your Mate, and God

Marriage renewal will require you to forget the past— your failings and your mate's failings—and to hope again. You will need a renewed confidence in yourself and in your mate.

It might help to take a cold, hard look at the alternatives to working on your marriage. One option is to live with your same dead relationship for years to come. Or you could be legally separated or get a divorce. All of those options are costly, financially and emotionally.

Also, think about shopping around for another mate. When you've found one, *you* would still be the same person. Then you would have to learn to live with another person. At least, you've got your present mate partly figured out.

Think about all the cost of the divorce or separation: the financial expense of separate living quarters, the emotional conflicts with kids and relatives, explanations to friends, and the damage to your self-worth.

Don't forget that several studies show that people who get divorced usually ask themselves, "What if I had worked harder? Could I have made it work?" Other studies show that second marriages are less happy and more divorce-prone than first marriages.

What is the alternative? There is no middle ground. You pick up and go on with life, realizing that no marriage is perfect; neither are you perfect. Every marriage, no matter how good, needs to be revitalized and strengthened. So take another cold, calloused look at what you would gain and what you would lose.

One man in our survey said, "When it came right down to it, I was only comparing one woman against another. Then I realized I needed to include all of the other pieces—my kids, my folks, friends, our whole married life. When I included all the pieces, my wife won."

Also take a good look at God. Let him touch your life so that there is genuine confidence in yourself and in your mate—a supernatural confidence, an ability to love and to trust against all human odds. Let God give you the ability to hope when all your past experiences would teach you to doubt. God can give you confidence so that you can pick up, go on with life, and make your life and marriage something outstanding.

One of the key inspirations for hope and persistence in our lives is found in the verse, "Forgetting the past and looking forward to what lies ahead."[10]

WHERE TO GO FROM HERE?

As you near the end of this book, you need to spend a few minutes reflecting on the information that you have read and the counsel you've received from the couples in this survey. In addition, reflect on your own feelings and thoughts as you've progressed through the book. Which areas made you laugh or cry? What were the sections that caused you to feel successful or say to yourself, "This is an area I want to change"?

To help you in this process we're going to list again the ten keys on the following **Mid-Life Marriage Health Evaluation Chart**. Rate how well your marriage is functioning in each area. Then jot down additional reflections for each key.

Remember, no marriage is perfect. All of us are continually growing and changing. So as you rate your marriage, don't let it cause you to be depressed.

Be happy about the areas that show any degree of success. They indicate strength in your marriage. We also hope, as you look back over the ten keys, you'll be able to identify the weaker areas and then go back to reread those chapters and commit yourself to special growth in those areas.

MID-LIFE MARRIAGE HEALTH EVALUATION CHART

KEY 1: **Commitment to Marriage**
High   5   4   3   2   1   0   Low
Write your reflections _____

_____

KEY 2: **Good Communication**
High   5   4   3   2   1   0   Low

Write your reflections _____

_____

KEY 3: **A Vital Spiritual Life**
High   5   4   3   2   1   0   Low
Write your reflections _____

_____

KEY 4: **Effective Conflict Resolution**
High   5   4   3   2   1   0   Low
Write your reflections _____

_____

KEY 5: **Impact from Other People**
High   5   4   3   2   1   0   Low
Write your reflections _____

_____

KEY 6: **Sexual Intimacy**
High   5   4   3   2   1   0   Low
Write your reflections _____

_____

KEY 7: **Time for Fun, Leisure, and Humor**
High   5   4   3   2   1   0   Low
Write your reflections _____

_____

KEY 8: **Realistic Expectations**
High   5   4   3   2   1   0   Low
Write your reflections _____

_____

KEY 9: **Serving Each Other**
High   5   4   3   2   1   0   Low
Write your reflections _____

_____

KEY 10: Personal Growth
High   5   4   3   2   1   0   Low
Write your reflections _____

_____

Any of the areas where you circled a number higher than zero indicates that this is already functioning as a real or potential strength in your marriage. Thank God for what's already working. Keep that part going as you focus on the areas that you want to improve.

No Marriage Is Flawless or Hopeless

Most couples go through some stressful times during their marriage. The couples in our survey all had marital problems to one degree or another. Some problems were traumatic—abuse, affairs, separations, and divorce—but these couples had learned that with hard work they could have a successful marriage.

Chuck and Evelyn have been married over twenty years. A few years ago, however, it looked as if their marriage was finished. According to them, their relationship had become a battleground of proving who was "right." They had spent years in building resentments.

Evelyn resented having to carry the responsibility of keeping their financial budget balanced; she looked at sex as a duty; and, as she said, "I was constantly disappointed in my husband because he seldom lived up to my expectations."

Chuck admitted that for most of their marriage he held unrealistic ideas about all that his wife should be and that, until recently, he had a hard time being emotionally open. "We just 'stuffed' our resentments and carried them around with us," he told us.

When Chuck got involved in an affair, both Chuck and Evelyn knew they had to do something dramatic if they were to save their marriage. They were separated for a time, but through professional counseling and their determination to change, they each began to grow and develop into the kind of people that made the relationship satisfying for both of them.

They are now able to discuss conflicts and work them out instead of repressing them. Chuck is able to be more open about his feelings and is enjoying being tender toward Evelyn. He works at meeting her needs. Evelyn told us she decided to be "the sexiest lover he could have" and has found that she likes sex immensely. She now has a part-time career and, even though she still considers homemaking her priority, she and Chuck feel she's a more interesting person because of her outside work.

They are **enjoying** being married to each other. They both say that their relationship with each other is now the top priority of their lives, and they are more relaxed about their differences. They told us that their marriage was saved because their counselor helped them grow as individuals.

Chuck was coached about how to take more responsibility for family leadership and especially the finances. He also learned to understand Evelyn's need to be a person in her own right.

Evelyn lost weight, returned to school, and updated her wardrobe. She began to like herself better and was able to be more sexually open.

During the counseling sessions they had some heated arguments, but with the counselor as a referee they were able to discuss some long-buried feelings and finally to understand each other. This understanding gave them the basis for meeting each other's needs—**and a new marriage.**

We have repeatedly found that marriages can be healed. Our survey, our conferences, and our mail verify this. Just today we received this letter:

▼

Thank you for helping me when Glen left me two years ago. We have been back together for eight months now and have a better marriage than ever. We both have had to do a lot of changing, but it has been worth it.

I'm grateful for the things you suggested that I do and that you kept encouraging me not to give up . . .

May God bless you as you continue in this much-needed work of helping people with their marriages. Tell them to be patient and to work at it. God is on their side.

▲

Go for it! Try for a change of course before you abandon ship. Expect restoration through patience, prayer, and practical modifications. Trust God to change you and work a miracle in your relationship.

CHAPTER

Rebuilding
a Crumbling
Marriage

The newspaper article was headlined **"Computer Sets Up Couple for Rematch."** The article went on to say: "Maybe computers know best. A man who divorced his wife after a bitter six-year court battle and turned to a computer service to find himself the ideal mate was surprised when—from 2,000 prospective brides—the machine selected his former wife.

" 'I did not know that my ex-wife had been the ideal counterpart for a marriage. I decided to give a try by being more tolerant toward her.'

"The couple, whose first marriage lasted 21 years, divorced nine months ago due to 'severe disharmony' after living apart for six years.

"Each one, without the other knowing, turned to the same municipal computer matching service to find a new partner."[1]

The good news is that there's hope! Your marriage can be restored once you decide that's what you want. You may have lived with open conflict for years and you can't take it any longer. Some of you have a marriage that's in serious trouble—it's breaking or seems totally broken. **You *can* rebuild your mar-**

riage. We'll talk about how, but first let's review what has caused your marriage to deteriorate.

COMMON STEPS OF MARITAL COLLAPSE

Marital collapse seems to follow predictable steps toward the ultimate destruction of the marriage. This is verified in a study on marital burnout that lists these stages:

1. Unrealistic Expectations: "characterized by partners who hold high expectations of what the relationship should be and how the spouse should fulfill their needs."

2. Manipulation: "an attempt to make the other spouse conform to his or her expectations. This phase is usually volatile and intense as each spouse continues to believe that the partner can and must be changed."

3. Hostility: anger marked by "detachment and a gnawing sense of futility."

4. Hopelessness: resisting "suggestions to improve . . . In despair, they either experience emotional divorce and feel trapped while staying together, or conclude that actual divorce would be less painful."[2]

In more than thirty years of counseling experience we have seen a consistent pattern of people not looking for help in the early stages of marital trouble but waiting until things are desperate. If they seek help in the **hostility** stage, they come with much disillusionment but still with a glimmer of hope.

If they don't seek help until the **hopelessness** stage, they usually are in total despair. In fact, they may be using the counselor as an authority figure to verify that their marriage is a failure and to justify getting a divorce.

This is what Jack revealed as he slouched down in my (Jim's) office chair. His legs were stretched in front of him, his arms folded defiantly, and he grumbled, "We've been to marriage enrichment weekends, we've read marriage books and articles, and we've been to three different counselors. You're the last counselor we're going to see. I don't have any feelings for her anymore. I want out!"

These words exploded out of this man who had experienced long periods of hopelessness in his marriage. He was in mid-life crisis and was making a desperate grasp for some kind of new life. He wanted to taste some things he felt were missing. He really believed it was impossible to change his marriage and wanted a divorce.

As I listened to Jack talk, I thought with tongue in cheek, *Wow! This is a terrific way to start a counseling session. This guy is so open to change!* I felt as if I were pushing a giant boulder up a hill, but the boulder kept rolling back down over me. Jack was just using me to prove his marriage was hopeless.

DEMOLITION MAY OCCUR BEFORE REBUILDING

Your marriage doesn't need to collapse. We hope you'll be more open to change than Jack was. Practical steps can be taken to stop the downhill slide; however, things may get worse before they get better. Your marriage may experience some of the following hard things, but they also can be part of the healing.

Recognition

The problems may have become so great that you're now forced to pay attention to each other and to your marriage. One of you may finally say, "I want a divorce." Or, "I've never loved you." Or, "I hate you." Or, "I'm in love with someone else." Or, "I feel . . . ."

Physical abuse may be taking place, or a dreadful separateness, silence, or alienation that finally brings your relationship to the breaking point. Perhaps it's alcohol, drugs, an affair, or a temporary separation that brings the awareness. The first step usually is not something you actively choose to do, but "recognition" is forced upon you by the accumulation of problems and disillusionment.

Explosion

You may confront each other with intense anger. One of you may shout, "I hate you and our marriage!"

Most of this second step involves blaming and faultfinding. "It's all your fault." "How could you do that to me?" "You never . . ." "You always . . ." Each one batters the other as the pent-up disillusionment, frustration, and anger are finally vented.

This ventilating process is frequently very vicious and dehumanizing and may seem as if it's going to kill the marriage. A lot of the repressed hostility is finally pouring out. In reality, this is an important step, because now the two of you are finally communicating with each other—with truth.

Cooling Off

After a heavy confrontation, you need time to cool off and get away from each other. Go to a different part of the house or for a walk, a drive in the car, or a bike ride. Get away and think about what's happening. Think about what the other person is saying. This isn't the time to be developing your arguments to defeat your mate in the next round. Instead, consider the things that were spoken in anger. These feelings never would have come out in the old marital status quo.

Now you can see your mate objectively for perhaps the first time. As you stand off and take another look, you are able to answer the question, Is there enough in this relationship to keep us together?

This objective, new look at your mate enables you to ask some hard questions:

Do I really like and respect this person?
Do we have common interests and values?
Is there sexual attraction?
Is there a compatibility in temperament?
Is there an enthusiasm to help the other one grow?
Do we have a shared spiritual commitment?

It may be that you don't match your mate in some of these areas, but you also may find that some of the conflict areas are growth opportunities for your personality and your marriage. This objective evaluation should be used to enable you and your mate to take corrective measures to make your relationship successful.

Death

Realize that your former marriage is dead. Maybe it's the best thing that ever happened. Your old way of living and relating is gone forever. You're going to have a new openness, a new way of relating to each other, new expectations, and a new degree of authenticity. You're looking at each other through different eyes. Of course, risk is involved in this process, but it's worth it. Your old relationship has withered. Your marriage can come back to life but—happily—in a new form.

INGREDIENTS FOR RESTORING YOUR MARRIAGE

Sometimes after a major marital problem, the mountains seem impossible to climb. All kinds of questions terrorize and torment:

> What if my mate gets restless again?
> How can I keep from reverting to my old patterns?
> How do we build trust?
> What if "she" or "he" calls?
> Can I really forgive?
> What if I can't perform sexually?
> What if I find indications the affair really isn't over?
> What about re-entry with our friends or our church?

We have summarized answers to typical problem areas as you think about rebuilding your marriage.

1. Don't Consider Your Relationship Hopeless Even If There Has Been Serious Conflict, an Affair, Separation, or Divorce

Many times these acts are cries for help. They indicate that a problem desperately needs to be worked on. Don't give up in the face of a problem; rather, focus on the **cause** of the problem.

What is the pain that forces a mate to leave? Is there a lack of understanding or a failure to meet needs? Concentrate on the **reasons**, not the separation. Remember, an affair is not the problem; your failing relationship is the problem.

2. People Change Slowly, but They Do Change

Growth is not a straight upward line. It's a jagged up and down line that is gradually making upward progress. Be tolerant of yourself and your mate. You may fall into old patterns for a short period of time or you may get restless again, but that doesn't mean you're going back to your old ways of living. Don't say to your mate, "You'll never change." That will only discourage change. Instead, verbally appreciate any small improvement.

3. Bad Patterns of Living or Mistrust Can Be Unlearned

Patterns of thinking are like cassette tapes that you plug into your brain. You need to take the old cassette out and plug in the new one. The message on the new cassette will become automatic only after you have played it dozens of times.

Trust doesn't happen because another person says, "I want you to trust me." It happens as you have a series of trusting experiences. Trust can happen more quickly if you consciously reinforce it. Talk to yourself and appreciate your mate after a new trust experience. Now store it away in your computer bank and let it build the unconscious level of trust within you.

4. Let Your Mate Handle His or Her Past

If there is some surprise connection with your mate's recent past—a telephone call, a chance meeting, a movie stub—let your mate care for it. Handle your own past. Trust each other with those responsibilities. Don't act as parents to each other regarding these sensitive areas of the painful past.

5. The Sexual Relationship Will Grow as You Confidently Begin the Courting Process Again

Remember, when you first met, you didn't agree to get married during the first ten minutes. You got to know each other over many months. You shared a growing understanding and a deepening sense of commitment. Later you talked of marriage and a date was set. The engagement was official. Then came the wedding day. All of those events and experiences moved you to deeper levels of commitment so that your married sexual relationship was a natural flow from your emotional relationship.

Now you are starting over. You aren't impotent or frigid just because you feel uncomfortable with sex at this time. Start by just holding each other and rubbing each other's back. Gradually expand your touching as both of you feel comfortable. Make the commitment that you will not have sex until both of you deeply want it, until both of you will not be satisfied without intercourse.

Many of our survey couples mentioned that their sexual relationship had greatly improved after a traumatic time. One wife said, "It took twenty-three years and my husband's affair for me to wake up sexually. I finally went for help. Now I can say I truly enjoy having sex—we both do!"

6. Give Authentic Expressions of Your Current Expectations and Desires

Your new lifestyle change is built on the reality that your old ways of relating are dead. Your old marriage didn't satisfy you. It only produced stress and low satisfaction. Now you are moving toward being more real as you talk about your current expectations and desires.

Yes, you take a risk. Yes, there is the potential of conflict. You are creating a new relationship that *must* deal with the truth of who you are at this age and stage in your life.

Many of our survey couples indicated that when they finally got honest with each other, their marriage began to improve. One man said, "We now talk constantly. Some differences are not resolvable, but we have agreed to love each other in spite of differences."

One woman talked about the risk of revealing her true self to her mate: "It's scary, especially if, as a child, you weren't given love for being yourself. And your partner *may* get upset. You are not four years old, and that person is not your parent. He's just a person, and he's scared that the changes in your life and self may exclude him, or change his life without his consent."[3]

If you are compassionate about your mate's apprehensions, you may be able to win his or her support. But even if the changes you are making to be your real self cause some temporary problems between you, it is not necessarily the end. Temporary distance is often a part of the process of growing and making the marriage satisfying enough for both of you. Genuine, healthy talking will move you toward each other in a stronger, more mature way.

The more authentic you can be with yourself and your mate, the better you will feel about yourself. You'll also be more attractive to your mate. By mid-life, you are tired of game playing. You want reality. You don't want to live with the status quo of a dead relationship. Talking about your current expectations and desires will lead to an authentic peer friendship, which will become a strong base for your new marriage relationship.

For many years Henry and Mary had conflict with regard to money. They attended one of our couples' retreats and came to us for help with their problem. As we talked, we encouraged them not to run from conflict, but to keep in mind several guidelines:

a. Avoid blaming your partner for all of the problems. (We encouraged them to each tell how they had contributed to the problem.)

b. Look for common grounds of agreement, not polarization. (They talked about what money meant to each of them so that they began to see that in several areas they were strongly united. In the past, they had focused only on the few areas of disagreement.)

c. Be clear on priorities so that not everything must go one person's way. (Together they decided to work only on one major area, a budget. They were to bring us a tentative draft of their budget before they left the conference. We warned them about the next guideline while they worked on the budget together.)

d. Don't attack the other one's judgment or question his or her motives. (In addition, we wanted them to risk talking in other areas of their lives, so we gave them the next guideline.)

e. Set regular times to discuss who you are and who your partner is.

Some months later they wrote, telling us how our brief

times with them at the retreat had helped their marriage relationship to open up so that they were not afraid to *really* talk to each other.

7. Forgive and Release the Past

David Augsburger, in his book *Caring Enough to Forgive*, says, "Forgiveness is letting what was, be gone; what will be, come; what is now, be.

"In forgiving, I finish my demands on past predicaments, problems, failures and say good-bye to them with finality. I cancel my predictions, suspicions, premonitions of future failure and welcome the next moment with openness to discover what will be . . . .

"Resentment dissipates as one gently lets go of resenting. Suspicion fades as one stops pursuing the fantasies of the other's plotting, hating or betraying. The secret is in letting go."[4]

So the question is not, Can I forgive? Can I let go? Rather it is that you *must* forgive! You *must* let go of the past! There is no middle ground. You cannot forgive verbally and yet emotionally say, "I'll never forget." You cannot pass it off as "nothing," then later use your mate's past failures as a club to pummel him or her.

You won't immediately have a complete mental erasure of past events. In fact, you may find the memories and imaginations flashing back frequently at first. But if you deliberately say to yourself each time, *I forgive again,* the flashbacks will eventually cease. They will lose their sting. If something does bring a painful event to mind, you'll be able to look at it objectively and mentally acknowledge that it did happen, but it will no longer emotionally gnaw at you.

You'll also find that it helps to deliberately program positive thoughts in place of the bad memories. If you keep telling yourself, *I will forgive my mate for such and such,* and continue to carefully rehearse the details, it will stay with you longer. If, instead, you count all your mate's recent positive gestures and actions and focus on his or her strengths, complete forgiveness will come more quickly.

Forgiveness isn't one of our natural tendencies. When we're hurt, we tend to react with anger, bitterness, revenge, or self-pity. Yet, if marital healing is to take place, we *must* forgive.

True forgiveness can happen when we realize how much we've been forgiven—by others and by God. In fact, because God has forgiven us, we have an inner power that enables us to forgive our mate. From Scripture we are advised: "Be kind to one another, tenderhearted, forgiving each other, just as God in Christ also has forgiven you."[5]

You might find further help with forgiveness from *Forgive & Forget: Healing the Hurts We Don't Deserve* by Lewis Smedes.[6]

Don't be discouraged if you lapse back into ventilating pent-up anger and resentment from past years. That may happen again and again in the talking stage, but you will discover that your relationship is strong enough to handle more truth and honesty.

8. Enlist Outside Help

You reached for outside help when you picked up this book. Read other books that we have suggested along the way. Talk to couples who are working through mid-life concerns. Consider going to a marriage counselor, a marriage enrichment weekend, or a special class in your church or local community that focuses on marriage renewal.

Don't look back. Your old marriage will never be the same. You're growing and changing; so is your marriage. Look ahead to the totally new lifestyle in your relationship.

For additional help in all of the above areas, see our other books, *Men in Mid-life Crisis, You and Your Husband's Mid-life Crisis,* and *Women in Mid-life Crisis.*[7]

IT'S ALWAYS TOO EARLY TO QUIT

We've known Hal and Edie for many years. In fact, they were one of the first couples that I (Jim) married as a young pastor. Like all young couples, they were full of hope and optimism. The future seemed bright and they were wildly in love with each other.

Hal pursued his career in dentistry and Edie filled the role of wife and mother in a growing family while she followed a casual interest in photography.

Life seemed to be progressing with more blessings than pain. Five children were born to the family, and even though money was a little tight, they were able to have a nice house in a good neighborhood.

The first big jolt came with the death of Hal's father, who was also a dentist and had helped Hal get started. The death was shocking enough, but there was a clear suggestion from the police that he had taken his own life by deliberately driving into a tree.

The untimely death of Hal's father produced a host of problems. His mother was a very dependent woman. What would they do with her? Hal now became responsible for the entire dental practice so that he was overworked. He was also executor of the estate, which put him in the position of being mistrusted by his own mother. At the same time, Edie's parents began to exert more pressure on their lives. They didn't approve of some of Hal and Edie's child-raising practices or the way they spent money.

Each time a child was born, Edie seemed unable to shed the extra pounds she had picked up through pregnancy. Because of all of the stresses descending on the couple, she found it easy to overeat. Food became a sort of gratification, an island of escape in the sea of problems around her.

A growing distance developed between Hal and Edie, and it turned into an unspoken suspicion on Edie's part. During these years a young dental assistant, Ginger, had become more than an employee to Hal. Hal found her to be a breath of fresh air to look at, to be with, and to talk to. These times weren't too frequent, but Ginger filled an emotional need in Hal's life, so he had a growing emotional dependency on her at the same time that there was a distancing from Edie.

By the time Edie reached her late thirties, the kids were starting to leave the nest, going off into their own careers and marriages. Now Edie made some sudden changes. She decided to pursue more actively a career in photography and attended a number of classes and seminars in their local community as well as in Chicago, three hours away.

It was exhilarating to Edie as she realized she had a real knack for portrait photography. She moved into a new world where she was viewed as an equal. She enjoyed the adulation that was coming to her, not because of her husband's work or her kids' performances, but because of her own abilities.

At the same time, she started a weight loss program. Within a year she had lost eighty pounds and was able to get into her wedding dress. She had surgery to make her nose smaller and straighter. The plastic surgery, her weight loss, and a new wardrobe caused her to look like a new woman, and her new looks were not unnoticed by the men around her.

Soon there were many more seminars to attend, business conferences, and exhibitions for her to display her work. Her life was a whirlwind of praise and admiration, other men, parties, hotels, business trips, and then a series of affairs.

Edie seemed to be two people—one that was desperately thriving on the excitement of her new life, another that was desolate. Yes, the parties were fun. The attention was great. And romance with Hal had never been this good. But there was an emptiness inside, a loneliness.

Hal was experiencing the same desolation. He knew he had lost his wife. What now?

The two of us were involved in many counseling sessions and long phone calls with Hal. Should he just abandon Edie? After all, Ginger was waiting in the wings. They had always hit it off so well.

Edie filed for divorce. "I want out," she said. "I need my freedom. At last, I've found someone who really cares for me."

We encouraged Hal to delay the process as long as possible, but Edie would not be stopped. The divorce was finalized. Hal was further devastated.

More counseling and long phone calls. We encouraged Hal to look at the reasons for their marital failure. We urged him to make necessary corrections in his life so that when Edie got tired of running and looked at him again, she would see the potential for re-establishing their relationship.

Hal started to make some changes, such as getting his own weight down, complimenting Edie instead of criticizing her when they talked, and learning to take time from work to have fun occasionally. At the same time, Edie was struck with a large case of the "guilts." They attempted a reconciliation, but neither of them had changed enough to make remarriage a real possibility.

New blowups over the kids and property threw them into a number of court battles. Each legal hassle pushed them farther apart and caused another round of desolation in Hal, resulting in more counseling. Edie responded by running faster in the other direction with her new friends.

Then the youngest daughter, the pride of the family, became pregnant. A quick church wedding took place with grandeur, complete with bridesmaids, Hal walking the bride down the aisle, and Edie standing proudly in the front row, as if a one-day truce had been declared in the middle of a war.

After Peggy's marriage, the animosity between Edie and Hal returned. A baby boy was born, but Peggy and her husband started to have trouble in their own marriage. Soon Peggy was following the pattern of her mother: running with a wild crowd, abandoning her family, and filing for divorce. Peggy's divorce was barely final before it was discovered that she was pregnant again. There was a second quick wedding and another temporary parental truce.

For the next eighteen months the family seemed to be locked in a holding pattern. All of the kids were now married, living their own lives, trying to avoid being caught in the conflict between their parents. Hal and Edie had come to accept the fact of their divorce, but their animosity toward each other was lessening. They were still talking to us, and neither of them had married anyone else.

A number of gradual changes turned the corner for this couple and their family. Edie had an increasing sense of hopelessness. Even though she was receiving temporary kicks from her fast life, it didn't satisfy her personally. She wanted something more. She wanted her family again.

There was a growing gentleness in Hal. He acknowledged his failures and his emotional dependency on Ginger, and he began to recognize Edie's worth and her gift in photography.

A new minister came to their local community. He seemed less pious and pretentious than the other pastors. He extended himself in friendship to both Hal and Edie, and soon they started attending church. Slowly they both began to feel God was drawing them together. It was time to work on their relationship, and God would help them.

They began to talk to each other, to go out to dinner, to

reminisce about the early years when the children were growing up. Life together, they realized, had been good as well as painful. Before long they were seeing a lot of each other. Without any announcements or fanfare, Edie moved her things back into the house.

For the next few months, they lived as husband and wife without remarrying. Then after church one Sunday, Edie said to Hal, "I think we ought to get married."

The wedding was a simple service in their new church, with just the family members attending. Both Hal and Edie now felt a new settledness and contentment, along with a fresh sense of optimism about their future together.

Everything didn't change immediately, but their marriage relationship and their family interaction has become increasingly positive. The bonds between Hal and Edie are now stronger than they ever were. They both are working to meet the other's needs. They do more things together. Hal even helps Edie with her photographic work at times. They are growing spiritually and have a mature response to difficulties that come along with their children, their aging parents, and their careers. It is a joy to watch their lives flower.

They are experiencing the fulfillment of a promise from God: "And I will give you a new heart—I will give you new and right desires—and put a new spirit within you. I will . . . give you new hearts of love" (Ezekiel 36:26 *The Living Bible*).

Jim and Sally Conway
Co-directors of
MID-LIFE DIMENSIONS
a ministry to
the mid-life generation
through

conferences
books
radio and TV
tapes
articles
and counseling

For information write to:

MID-LIFE DIMENSIONS
P.O. Box 3790
Fullerton, CA 92634

Notes

CHAPTER 1

1. David and Vera Mace, *We Can Have Better Marriages If We Really Want Them* (Nashville: Abingdon Press, 1974), 150.
2. Jim Conway, *Men in Mid-Life Crisis* (Elgin, IL: David C. Cook Publishing Co., 1978).

Jim and Sally Conway, *Women in Mid-Life Crisis* (Wheaton, IL: Tyndale House Publishers, 1983).

Sally Conway, *You and Your Husband's Mid-Life Crisis* (Elgin, IL: David C. Cook Publishing Co., 1980).

CHAPTER 2

1. Mel Roman and Patricia E. Raley, *The Indelible Family* (New York: Rawson, Wade Publishers, 1980).
2. Gary Smalley and John Trent, *The Blessing* (Nashville: Thomas Nelson Publishers, 1986).

Paul A. Mickey with William Proctor, *Tough Marriage* (New York: William Morrow & Co., Inc., 1986), 52–70.
3. Philip Blumstein and Pepper Schwartz, *American Couples* (New York: William Morrow & Co., Inc., 1983), 34.
4. Philippians 4:11.
5. Eda J. LeShan, *The Wonderful Crisis of Middle Age* (New York: David McKay, 1973), 161.
6. Floyd and Harriett Thatcher, *Long-Term Marriage* (Waco, TX: Word Books, 1980), 21.
7. William J. Lederer and Don D. Jackson, M.D., *The Mirages of Marriage* (New York: W.W. Norton and Co., 1968), 27.
8. U. S. National Center for Health Statistics, *Monthly Vital Statistics Report*, Vol. 31, No. 12 (March 14, 1983).
9. Hugh Carter and Paul C. Glick, *Marriage and Divorce: A Social and Economic Study*, rev. ed. (Cambridge, MA: Harvard University Press, 1976).

Arthur J. Norton, "Family Life Cycle: 1980," *Journal of Marriage and the Family*, Vol. 45, No. 2 (May 1983), 267–275.
10. James A. Peterson, *Married Love in the Middle Years* (New York: Association Press, 1968), 20.
11. Thatcher, 20.

12. Richard L. Strauss, *Marriage is for Love* (Wheaton, IL: Tyndale House Publishers, Inc., 1973), 9–10.

13. Carl W. Wilson, *Our Dance Has Turned to Death: But We Can Renew the Family and Nation* (Wheaton, IL: Tyndale House Publishers, Inc./Renewal Publishing Company, 1981).

14. "Most men would remarry wives, survey finds," July 13, 1986, *The Orange County Register*, A25.

15. "Love and Marriage in America," *Reader's Digest*, 55.

16. Strauss, 9–10.

17. Additional results from our study of lasting mid-life marriages are as follows:

• Children were seen as both positive and negative for strengthening marriages.

• Marital stress was increased by problems with relatives, lack of money, and job or career pressures.

• Marriages where an affair had occurred generally had sexual problems.

• Traumatic events for all the couples were death of parent, money problems, illnesses, and parenting.

• The most stressful event for the least stable marriages was a potential or real affair.

• Money management, sexual problems, and parenting were the biggest continuing problems in all marriages.

• Problems with in-laws, communication, and work were also near the top for all marriages.

Resources

We asked our couples to tell us what they used to help themselves when their marriages were in trouble. We gave nineteen suggestions and asked them to check the most helpful. We also provided space for them to tell us what other resources had been helpful. Our suggestions were:

Discussions with a relative
Discussions with a friend
Being alone to think
Seminars
Professional or pastoral counseling
Prayer
Listening to music
Small groups
Sermons
Reading the Bible
Reading other books or magazines
Radio or TV programs

Movies
Adult education classes at high school
Continuing education classes at college
Weekend retreats
Sunday school
Tapes
Hobbies
Other (please specify)

Our survey couples picked the following items out of the resource list as the most helpful:

- Prayer
- Reading the Bible
- Reading other books or magazines
- Being alone to think
- Attending seminars
- Friends or Counselors

The Threatened Couples were less likely to attend seminars and use books and magazines for resources. They were more likely to have discussions with friends and to seek professional or pastoral counseling.

In another section of the questionnaire we asked if the couples strongly agreed, agreed, disagreed, or strongly disagreed that certain suggested factors were important in helping their marriages survive. The factors were:

Commitment to stay in the marriage
Our children
Friends
Willingness to change (flexibility)
Keeping marriage as a priority
Realistic expectations about my partner
Ability to cope with stress
The way finances were managed
Involvement with our extended family or relatives
Our leisure time
Our sexual relationship
Communication between my partner and me
Ability to resolve differences
Our leadership style
Our spiritual life
Effects of my getting older
My career or job

After every category there was space to make more comments. Most people added many helpful insights in these spaces. In some cases, we asked for more specific information, such as:

Our *leadership style* primarily is:

Husband as main leader

Wife as main leader

Shared leadership

Most couples said that a commitment to stay together, keeping marriage as a priority, a strong spiritual life, and good communication were consistently important factors through the years.

Younger couples reported three other important factors: their sexual relationship, children, and leisure time. All three of these were of equal or greater significance to people by mid-life, but were found to be less important in the later marriage years, age 55 through 70.

Couples reported that flexibility was another important ingredient that helped their marriage to survive, especially at mid-life. The ability to handle stress was listed by the mid-life couples as very significant. This need may have been greater in mid-life marriages because of the overwhelming number of stress-producing events that occur at that time of life. Almost all factors listed on the survey tended to grow in importance as the couple reached the middle years.

18. Over the years there have been many different studies of marriages. Some of those studies specifically look at mid-life marriages. One done in the early sixties of 437 people in middle age found that most of these marriages were filled with conflict and apathy and very few were really satisfying. Over and over again the researchers pointed out that there was no vitality in these marriages, that they were "passive" and "dull."

They divided the results of their study into five different types of marriages.

1. Conflict-habituated relationships. There was a great deal of incompatibility and conflict was always present.

2. Devitalized relationships. There was not any serious tension nor was there any meaning. The marriage was "essentially empty."

3. The passive-congenial relationship. This marriage was characterized as having "little vitality" and "passively content."

4. Vital relationships. These marriages were characterized as having vibrant and exciting sharing of some important aspects of life.

5. Total relationships. "All important aspects of life are mutually shared and enthusiastically participated in." [John Cuber and Peggy Harroff, "The More Total View: Relationships among Men and Women of the Upper Middle Class," *Marriage and Family Living*, Vol. 25 (May 1963), 140–145.]

The book *American Couples*, released in 1983, is a study of approximately 6,000 married respondents. The authors divided their couples into four groups: (1) married couples, (2) cohabiting couples but not legally married, (3) lesbian couples, and (4) gay male couples. Their study focused primarily on three aspects in each of the couples' relationships: (1) money, (2) work, and (3) sex. [Philip Blumstein and Pepper Schwartz, *American Couples* (New York: William Morrow, 1983).]

McCall's, January 1980, published a study of more than 20,000 women responding to a questionnaire titled "How satisfying is your life together?" Twenty-six percent of their sample were women age 35 through 49.

CHAPTER 3

1. Barbara R. Fried, *The Middle-Age Crisis* (New York: Harper & Row, 1967), 6.

2. Kahlil Gibran, *The Prophet* (New York: Knopf, 1963), 15.

3. Eda LeShan, *The Wonderful Crisis of Middle Age* (New York: David McKay, 1973), 100.

4. Robert O. Blood, Jr., and Donald M. Wolfe, *Husbands and Wives* (New York: Free Press, 1960) 241.

John Scanzoni, *Opportunity and the Family* (New York: Free Press, 1970).

F. Ivan Nye, et al., *Role Structure and Analysis of the Family* (Beverly Hills, CA: Sage Publications, 1976), 82–83.

"Marriage: What Women Expect and What They Get," *McCall's* Jan. 1980, 151.

5. Nye, 82–83.

Philip Blumstein and Pepper Schwartz, *American Couples* (New York: William Morrow & Co., 1983), 52.

Erica Abeel, "When Wives Work . . . Must Husbands Hurt?" *Ladies' Home Journal*, Jan. 1981.

6. *McCall's*, 151.

7. Nye, 82–83.

Blumstein and Schwartz, 52.

8. Blumstein and Schwartz, 105.

9. Women's Bureau of the Federal Department of Labor quoted in *Christian Women at Work* by Patricia Ward and Martha Stout (Grand Rapids: Zondervan Publishing House, 1981), 11.

Bureau of Labor Statistics, quoted in *The Two-Paycheck Marriage* by Caroline Bird (New York: Pocket Book, 1979), 4–6.

Information Please Atlas and Year Book, 36th edition (New York: Simon and Schuster, 1981), 54.

10. Blumstein and Schwartz, 136.

11. Smiley Blanton, *Now or Never* (Englewood Cliffs, NJ: Prentice Hall, 1959), 85.

12. James A. Peterson, *Married Love in the Middle Years* (New York: Association Press, 1968), 87.

13. Marilyn Elias, "Affairs: Women Look for Intimacy," *USA Today*, Nov. 6, 1984.

14. Anne Kristin Carroll, *From the Brink of Divorce* (Garden City, NY: Doubleday-Galilee, 1978), 139–140.

15. Jim and Sally Conway, *Women in Mid-Life Crisis* (Wheaton, IL: Tyndale House Publishers, 1983), 262–283.

CHAPTER 4

1. Dr. Joyce Brothers, quoted by Kathy Lowry, "Marriage Makes a Comeback," *Family Weekly*, Dec. 31, 1978.

2. Alfred C. Kinsey, Wardell B. Pomeroy, and Clyde E. Martin, *Sexual Behavior in the Human Male* (Philadelphia: W. B. Sanders Co., 1948), 544.

3. Philip Blumstein and Pepper Schwartz, *American Couples* (New York: William Morrow & Co., Inc., 1983).

4. Donald M. Joy, *Bonding: Relationships in the Image of God* (Waco, TX: Word Books, 1985).

Donald M. Joy, *Re-Bonding: Preventing and Restoring Damaged Relationships* (Waco, TX: Word Books, 1986).

5. Joy, *Re-bonding: Preventing and Restoring Damaged Relationships*, 5.

6. William H. Masters and Virginia E. Johnson in association with Robert J. Levin, *The Pleasure Bond* (Boston: Little, Brown & Co., 1974), 251, 252.

7. David A. Seamands, *Healing for Damaged Emotions* (Wheaton, IL: Victor Books, 1981).

David A. Seamands, *Healing of Memories* (Wheaton, IL: Victor Books, 1985).

Lewis B. Smedes, *Forgive & Forget* (San Francisco: Harper & Row, 1984).

8. Nick Stinnett, et al., eds., *Family Strengths: Positive Models for Family Life* (Lincoln, NE: University of Nebraska Press, 1980).

9. Viktor Frankl, *Man's Search for Meaning* (Boston: Beacon Press, 1962), 65.

CHAPTER 5

1. Adapted from Howard L. Philip, *A Psychologist Looks at Sex* (London: Hutchinson, 1945), 75.

2. Roy Rhodes quoted by Jeanne Sara Dorin, "Cheating," *Dallas Morning News*, May 28, 1978.

3. David R. Mace, "Strictly Personal," *Marriage and Family Living*, Sept. 1980.

4. Dolores Curran, *Traits of a Healthy Family* (Minneapolis, MN: Winston Press, 1983).

5. John Powell, *The Secret of Staying in Love* (Niles, IL: Argus Communications, 1974), 123–127.

6. Natalie Gittelson, "Women Who Feel Trapped in Lonely Marriages," *McCall's*, March 1981.

7. Powell, 131.

8. Paul Tournier, *To Understand Each Other* (Atlanta: John Knox Press, 1967), 8.

9. Ephesians 4:15.

10. Ephesians 4:32.

11. A. Mehrabian, *Silent Messages* (Belmont, CA: Wadsworth, 1971), 43.

12. Howard L. Barnes, Walter R. Schumm, Anthony P. Jurich, and Stephan R. Bollman, "Marital Satisfaction: Positive Regard Versus Effective Communications as Explanatory Variables," *Journal of Social Psychology*, Vol. 123, 1984, 71–78.

13. 1 Corinthians 13:1 *(The Living Bible)*.

14. Luke 12:34.

CHAPTER 6

1. Dolores Curran, *Traits of a Healthy Family* (Minneapolis: Winston Press, 1983).

2. Nick Stinnett, et. al., eds., *Building Family Strengths* (Lincoln, NE: University of Nebraska Press, 1979).

Nick Stinnett, et. al., eds., *Family Strengths: Positive Models for Family Life* (Lincoln, NE: University of Nebraska Press, 1980).

3. George Gallup, Jr., "Emerging Trends Newsletter," Princeton, Vol. 1, Nov. 4, 1979.

4. Lewis B. Smedes, *How Can It Be All Right When Everything Is All Wrong?* (San Francisco: Harper & Row, 1982), 109–117.

CHAPTER 7

1. Sheldon Vanauken, *A Severe Mercy* (New York: Harper & Row, 1977), 37.

2. Ed Wheat, M.D., *How to Save Your Marriage Alone* (Grand Rapids, MI: Zondervan, 1983).

3. Philip Blumstein and Pepper Schwartz, *American Couples* (New York: William Morrow & Co., 1983), 98.

4. M. Scott Peck, *People of the Lie* (New York: Simon and Schuster).

M. Scott Peck, *The Road Less Traveled* (New York: Simon and Schuster, 1978).

5. Nick Stinnett, et al., *Building Family Strength* (Lincoln, NE: University of Nebraska Press, 1979).

6. Carol Krucoff, "Need 'Space'? Don't Wed, Have Kids," *Denver Post*, May 29, 1981.

CHAPTER 8

1. Romans 5:8
2. 1 Corinthians 13:4–7 *(The Living Bible)*

CHAPTER 9

1. Michael Novak, "Frequent, Even Daily, Communion," in *A Catholic Case for Contraception*, Daniel Callahan, ed. (London: McMillan and Co., 1969), 98.
2. Robert Lee and Marjorie Casebier, *The Spouse Gap* (Nashville: Abingdon, 1971), 112.
3. Philip Blumstein and Pepper Schwartz, *American Couples* (New York: William Morrow & Co., Inc., 1983), 222.
4. Stephan Prasinos and Bennett Tittler, "The Existential Context of Lovestyles: An Empirical Study," *Journal of Humanistic Psychology*, Vol. 24, No. 1, Winter 1984, 95–112; 105.

The six lovestyles were:

a. *Agape*—altruistic love, love without expectation, gentle, caring, and guided by reason more than emotion.

b. *Ludus*—playful or game love, pluralistic, promiscuous, and relatively short-lived.

c. *Eros*—the pursuit of the lover's physical type.

d. *Storge*—slowly developing affection and companionship, a gradual disclosure of self.

e. *Pragma*—focusing on the "vital statistics" of the beloved: education, vocation, religion, age.

f. *Mania*—obsessive, jealous, needing repeated reassurance of being loved.

In healthy love relationships all of these lovestyles are present, but the agapic is the most beneficial. When the lovestyles were ranked from most affirming to least affirming, the result was: agapic, ludic, erotic, storgic, pragmatic, and manic.

5. Philip Blumstein and Pepper Schwartz, 312.
6. Anne Kristin Carroll, *From the Brink of Divorce* (Garden City, NY: Doubleday, 1978), 225.
7. See 1 Corinthians 7:2–5 in *The Living Bible*.
8. Saul Pett, "Hubert Humphrey: The Old Warrior Faces Up to Another Crisis," *Dallas Morning News*, Jan. 23, 1977.
9. Ed and Gaye Wheat, *Intended for Pleasure* (Old Tappan, NJ: Fleming H. Revell Co., 1977), 73–82.
10. Anthony Campolo, Jr., *The Power Delusion* (Wheaton, IL: Victor Books, 1983), 17–18.
11. William H. Masters, Virginia E. Johnson, and Robert C. Kolodny, *Masters and Johnson Sex and Human Loving* (New York: Little Brown & Co., 1986).

12. Dianne Hales and Robert E. Hales, M.D., "The Bonding Hormone," *Orange County Register,* Jan. 24, 1983, C1, C5.

Penny Wise Budoff, M.D., *No More Hot Flashes and Other Good News* (New York: Warner Books, 1983), 3–9, 129–154.

13. Berniece and Morton Hunt, *Prime Time* (New York: Stein and Day, 1975), 79.

14. Thomas Jakobovits, "The Treatment of Impotence with Methyltestosterone Thyroid," *Fertility and Sterility* (Jan. 1970), 32–35.

15. As quoted in Hunt, 88–90.

16. Ed and Gaye Wheat.

17. *The Autobiography of Bertrand Russell* as quoted by Robert Lee and Marjorie Casebier in *The Spouse Gap* (Nashville: Abingdon Press, 1971), 126.

CHAPTER 10

1. Tim Hansel, *When I Relax I Feel Guilty* (Elgin, IL: David C. Cook, 1979), 11–12.

2. H. L. Mencken as quoted by Dolores Curran, *Traits of a Healthy Marriage* (Minneapolis: Winston Press, 1983), 129.

3. Lyn Balster Liontos and Demetri Liontos, "Couple Life," *Denver Post*, Jan. 18, 1981.

4. Philip Blumstein and Pepper Schwarz, *American Couples* (New York: William Morrow, 1983), 174.

5. Liontos and Liontos.

6. Roger Ricklefs, "Single Mindedness: Firms become willing—or eager—to hire divorced executives," *The Wall Street Journal*, May 18, 1978.

7. Lewis T. Grant in *Harpers*, Oct. 1979.

8. Blumstein and Schwarz, 312.

9. Hansel, 12.

10. Norman Cousins, *Anatomy of an Illness* (New York: Norton, 1979).

11. Marilyn Elia, "The Human Angle," Crown Syndicate Inc., 1980, as quoted by Curran, 132.

CHAPTER 11

1. Anonymous, "The War Within: An Anatomy of Lust," *Leadership*, Fall 1982, Vol. III, No. 4, 38.

2. J. Allan Peterson, *Myth of the Greener Grass* (Wheaton, IL: Tyndale House, 1983).

Dolores Curran, *Traits of a Healthy Family* (Minneapolis: Winston Press, 1973).

Jeanette Lauer and Robert Lauer, "Why Marriages Succeed," *Orange County Register*, June 19, 1985.

3. Ed and Gaye Wheat, *How To Save Your Marriage Alone* (Grand Rapids: Zondervan Publishing House, 1983).

4. Psalm 103:11,12; Ephesians 1:7.
5. Tim Hansel, *When I Relax I Feel Guilty* (Elgin, IL: David C. Cook Publishers, 1979), 146, 147.

CHAPTER 12

1. 1 Corinthians 12:4–28.
2. Jerry and Barbara Cook, *Choosing to Love* (Ventura, CA: Regal Books, 1982), 57.
3. John 13:1–17; Matthew 23:11,12.
4. For more understanding of the meaning of "headship," see Gilbert Bilezikian, *Beyond Sex Roles* (Grand Rapids: Baker Book House, 1985), 157–162.
5. After God had created the first man, he said, in essence, "I will make another human who will complement Adam, fill in the gaps in his life, change his sense of aloneness" (Genesis 2:18).
6. David Mace, "Strictly Personal: Expressing Affection in Families," *Marriage and Family Living*, Nov. 1980.
7. Josh McDowell, *Building Your Self-Image* (Wheaton, IL: Tyndale House Publishers, 1986).
    David Seamands, *Healing for Damaged Emotions* (Wheaton, IL: Victor Books, 1981).
8. Floyd and Harriett Thatcher, *Long Term Marriages* (Waco, TX: Word Books, 1980), 43.
9. From "The American Family" tape; The Harvard Seminar series (Cambridge: Harvard University Press, 1981).

CHAPTER 13

1. John L. Peterson and Constance Miller, "Physical Attractiveness and Marital Adjustment in Older American Couples," *The Journal of Psychology*, Vol. 105, 1980, 247–252.
2. Robert F. Winch, *Mate Selection* (New York: Harper & Row, 1958).
3. Elizabeth Kaye, "Self-esteem: Can You Get It If You Don't Already Have It?" *McCall's*, April 1984, 94.
4. Bernard Rimland, *Psychology Today*, Dec. 1982.
5. Bonnedell Clouse, *Moral Development* (Grand Rapids: Baker Book House, 1985).
    James W. Fowler, *Becoming Adult, Becoming Christian* (San Francisco: Harper & Row, 1984).
    Lawrence Kohlberg, *The Psychology of Moral Development* (San Francisco: Harper & Row, 1984).
6. Jim Fowler and Sam Keen, *Life Maps: Conversations on the Journey of Faith* (Waco, TX: Word Books, 1978), 81.

CHAPTER 14

1. Quoted by Chuck Workman, Bravo Ministries, San Diego, CA.
2. "A Hymn to Him," *My Fair Lady,* as quoted by Pierre Mornell in *Passive Men and Wild Women* (New York: Ballantine Books, 1979), 4.
3. Mother Teresa quoted in *The Register*, Santa Ana, CA, June 5, 1982, A6.
4. John Powell, *The Secret of Staying in Love* (Niles, IL: Argus Communications, 1974), 55.
5. Harry Stack Sullivan, *Conceptions of Modern Psychiatry*, as quoted in *The Secret of Staying in Love*, 44.
6. Ari Kiev, *How to Keep Love Alive* (New York: Harper & Row, 1982), 58.
7. M. Scott Peck, *The Road Less Traveled* (New York: Simon & Schuster, 1978), 93.
8. *Orange County Register*, Santa Ana, CA.
9. Betty J. Coble, *Woman—Aware and Choosing* (Nashville: Broadman Press, 1975), 22–23.
10. Philippians 3:13, *(The Living Bible)*.

CHAPTER 15

1. *Orange County Register*, Nov. 15, 1986, A2.
2. David R. Leaman, "Needs Assessment: A Technique to Reverse Marital Burnout," *Journal of Psychology and Christianity*, Vol. 2, No. 2, Summer 1983.
3. Annie Gottlieb, "Staying Together," *McCall's*, April 1984, 16.
4. David Augsburger, *Caring Enough to Forgive* (Ventura, CA: Regal Books, 1981), 52–57.
5. Ephesians 4:32 (NASB).
6. Lewis B. Smedes, *Forgive & Forget: Healing the Hurts We Don't Deserve* (San Francisco: Harper & Row, 1984).
7. Jim Conway, *Men in Mid-Life Crisis* (Elgin, IL: David C. Cook Publishing Co., 1978).

   Jim and Sally Conway, *Women in Mid-Life Crisis* (Wheaton, IL: Tyndale House Publishers, 1983).

   Sally Conway, *You and Your Husband's Mid-Life Crisis* (Elgin, IL: David C. Cook Publishing Co., 1980).